T0098062

Wildbranch

Wildbranch

*An Anthology of Nature, Environmental,
and Place-based Writing*

EDITED BY FLORENCE CAPLOW
AND SUSAN A. COHEN

FOREWORD BY H. EMERSON BLAKE

THE UNIVERSITY OF UTAH PRESS
Salt Lake City

Copyright © 2010 by The University of Utah Press
All rights reserved

The Defiance House Man colophon is a registered trademark of the
University of Utah Press. It is based upon a four-foot-fall, Ancient
Puebloan pictograph (late PIII) near Glen Canyon, Utah.

14 13 12 11 10   1 2 3 4 5

LIBRARY OF CONGRESS CATALOGING-IN-PUBLICATION DATA
Wildbranch : an anthology of nature, environmental, and place-based
writing / edited by Florence Caplow and Susan Cohen.
     p. cm.
A collection of essays and poetry.
     ISBN 978-1-60781-124-4 (pbk. : alk. paper)
     1. Nature—Literary collections. 2. Ecology—Literary collections.
     3. Environmental protection—Literary collections. I. Caplow,
     Florence. II. Cohen, Susan, 1956-
PS509.N3W56 2010
810.8'036—dc22

                                        2010035085

Lines excerpted from "Eagle Poem" by Joy Harjo from *In Mad Love
and War*, copyright © 1990 by Joy Harjo. Reprinted with permission
of Wesleyan University Press. www.wesleyan.edu/wespress

Lines excerpted from "Grandfather in the Garden" by Robert Minhinnick from *Selected Poems*, copyright © 1999 by Robert Minhinnick.
Reprinted with permission of Carcanet Press Ltd.

Cover painting by Thomas Aquinas Daly, *The Bend to Bluestone*
(detail). Watercolor, 12" x 18". Used by permission of the artist.

I am drawn to the workshop, initially, because of its name—
Wildbranch. I know nothing of its origin or meaning but
I have a particular affinity to it; even the word on the page
is enticing. Capital W, top-heavy but standing firmly, an-
nounces authority. In the middle of the word d and b stand
back to back like two duelers facing outward: an opposing
symmetry. Lastly, c and h, ch, concludes in a soft whisper.
Wildbranch: respect, balance, tenderness.

After I arrive in Vermont I learn Wild Branch is a tributary, a rivulet that flows into a larger body of water, the
Lamoille River. Like many rivulets, sections of Wild Branch's
banks, filled with sediment, slide into the river and become
muddled with a mixture of soil and water. As writers, we too
join the cycle of creation and erosion but in a different manner: we create our own free flowing narratives by placing letters side by side, the only means we know in the telling of our
stories. With the help of instructors at Wildbranch, we tap
into fluid sentiments, assemble our river sentences, and then
send them downstream.

—Eve Quesnel, Wildbranch participant 2008

Contents

x CONTENTS

Foreword

For many years, the first evening at the Wildbranch Writers Workshop has been spent with a gathering of the workshop's participants—students, faculty, and organizers—in the large common room in Kane Hall at Sterling College. People take turns introducing themselves and describing why they chose to take a week away from their families, friends, and jobs to devote to a writing workshop. It's always an exciting, somewhat nervous evening, as people—from all over the country and all walks of life—begin to transition from their workaday lives to a week of intense reflection on how to write about nature.

On one such evening when he was describing why he was at Wildbranch, faculty member Scott Russell Sanders said, "I write in order to understand our mysterious existence more deeply, to bear witness to the beauty and loss and promise I find in the world, and to speak on behalf of the voiceless, including the land and all its creatures." Scott's statement cuts to the heart of the matter and summarizes what Wildbranch is about. As a culture, we are past the stage where we need to keep saying that we have mistreated the planet. Too far past it. Scientific data and information that supports what we have done to the world is critically important and will always be necessary, but what is really needed now is the resolve to change the way we live. The writers who come to Wildbranch, regardless of where they are in their careers, come because they care deeply about the planet and because they are striving to connect other people to the natural world through their writing.

It's not easy. Writing effectively and compellingly about nature requires many tools. It asks the writer to have an uncanny openness to the world. It expects the writer to grapple with extremely complex and disparate issues. It demands complete accuracy and a solid familiarity with science—even if the writer has no real scientific background. It needs to project urgency and resolve, but not so much that the writing becomes shrill or pious. It must deal with loss, but not to the point that the writing overwhelms the reader. And, above all, it requires good writing and good storytelling. In short, the writer has to bring the world, its creatures, its places, its processes, and its mysteries alive. It is no small task. But these are the skills that the writers who have attended Wildbranch have worked toward, year after year.

Has the writing that grows out of Wildbranch made any difference? We could point to the Wildbranch attendees who have gone on to successful writing careers; many students have had their work appear in major magazines and any number have published books. At least a few "alumni" have gone on to genuine accolades—Janisse Ray's book *Ecology of a Cracker Childhood* was selected in 1999 as "the book that all Georgians should read," and Jeff Lockwood's essay "Voices from the Past"—which he worked on at Wildbranch—was selected by the John Burroughs Association as the best natural history essay of 2002. But just as important as the students who have published books and articles—and maybe more important—are the dozens of educators, communication directors, community organizers, administrators, grassroots activists, technical writers, scientists, engineers, farmers, fundraisers, policy experts, and others who have attended Wildbranch, and whose ability to communicate on behalf of what they care about (as Scott Sanders would say) was sharpened by their experience at Wildbranch. Those developed voices, I am sure, have made a difference in the workplaces, communities, bioregions, neighborhoods, and homes of those participants.

Wildbranch: An Anthology of Nature, Environmental, and Place-based Writing gives readers a sense of the writing that emerges out of the workshop. It cannot, however, capture that feature that is most extraordinary about Wildbranch: the closeness of this community of people and the spirit of giving that takes place there. "It's an astonishing gesture of generosity," wrote one student at the end of the week, "in a world obsessed with scarcity." That feeling, maybe, is what stays with the faculty and students more than anything else, perhaps because that sense of community is so important to writers who are trying to tackle the most difficult issues of our time.

We at *Orion* are grateful for our long association with Wildbranch, and for the opportunity to come together once a year with faculty and students who are at work on the same core questions that *Orion* has been addressing for almost thirty years. The magazine has built many important relationships there over the years, and hearing what is on the minds of the people who participate in the workshop shapes the way we approach our work. Many thanks to all who have attended Wildbranch, and to all who will come in the future. We invite you to join us.

H. EMERSON BLAKE

Preface

There is a long American tradition of writing about the natural world, from the careful observations of early naturalists like William Bartram and John James Audubon to the impassioned advocacy of Rachel Carson and Edward Abbey, but in the last few decades this tradition has evolved into a rich and variegated literary culture. The works in *Wildbranch* are expressions of this contemporary culture, gathered from students and faculty of a unique writing workshop held each summer at Sterling College in the hills of northern Vermont, in the watershed of a creek called "Wild Branch."

The Wildbranch Writing Workshop has encouraged thoughtful natural history, outdoor, and environmental writing for more than twenty years. Wildbranch founder E. Annie Proulx and director David Brown organized the first weeklong summer workshop in 1988. *Orion* magazine has been involved with the workshop since 1994 and became a workshop cosponsor in 2006.

The exceptional Wildbranch faculty has included its founder E. Annie Proulx; the essayists Edward Hoagland, Scott Russell Sanders, and John Elder; poets Alison Hawthorne Deming and Sydney Lea; environmental journalists and activists Bill McKibben, Michael Frome, and Sandra Steingraber; ecophilosopher David Abram; novelist and science writer Sue Halpern, and many other notable authors. A number of Wildbranch students, including some whose work is collected in this anthology, have already made significant literary contributions of their own.

From the inception of Wildbranch, both students and faculty have been drawn from a wide geographic area and from many backgrounds. The poetry and essays in this anthology offer the reader glimpses into places as diverse as the forests of West Africa, the tallgrass prairies of the Midwest, the canyons of the Sonoran desert mountains, and the fields of New England, and they reflect the perspectives of field biologists, hunters, farmers, environmental educators, wilderness guides, academics, and artists.

Wildbranch: An Anthology of Nature, Environmental, and Place-based Writing includes an extensive range of writing styles and themes, from what could be considered more traditional, observational nature writing to what is sometimes called "the new nature writing," —writing that responds to global environmental crises and is more experimental in style and structure. In the spirit of traditional writing about the natural world, some of the pieces in the anthology are reflections on places less traveled and less damaged; places closer to something our collective memory recalls as wilderness. Other pieces recognize the rapidly changing nature of our world. Sometimes elegiac and sometimes hopeful, they document lost and damaged landscapes, personal displacement, global inter-connectivity, and the search for greater sustainability.

Regardless of style or theme, many of the authors in the anthology join close observations with a personal, relational connection between the human and natural world. In some cases this intimacy is with a beloved, imperiled place, as in Linda Maree's "Hiking the Fakahatchee Strand"; in others it is a closeness with a wild animal, as in Jennifer Barton's elegiac "To Liv," or in the lyric poems of Alison Townsend, where the boundaries between personal and natural blur and dissolve.

We have grouped the essays and poems in the anthology into five thematic sections. They are, in order, Intimacy, Speaking of Place, What Comes from the Land, On Perceiving and Knowing, and For the Children/For the Future.

We define intimacy as relationship in its many forms, from Paul Grindrod's "Des Ta Te: A Love Story," which explores the complex relationship between the author and a rescued bald eagle, to an essay like Jim Collins's "Fishing with George," a reflection on a friendship that developed over years of fishing the streams of New England together.

The poetry and essays in Speaking of Place focus on personal connections and responses to particular geographies, which may be as small as a nearly forgotten Appalachian mountain spring or as large as an entire region. In What Comes from the Land, the writers, several of whom are hunters or farmers, explore their direct, embodied relationship with the food, water and wood that the land provides. The pieces in On Knowing and Perceiving focus on careful attention and observation of the natural world, and in some cases on the nature of perception itself, as in Edward Hoagland's essay "Earth's Eye," or the poems of Sydney Lea and Mira Bartók.

The title of the final section of the anthology is taken from our concluding essay, Scott Russell Sanders's "For the Children," which is in turn based on a line in a poem by Gary Snyder. Each writer in this section addresses a different vision of the future, from Aleria Jensen speaking directly to her unborn child in "Peepers," to April Newlin's essay, "Hatch," where we are allowed to join the author as she patiently watches over a nest of endangered sea turtle eggs.

The writers of Wildbranch remind us that we all, wherever we may live and however much or little we know of the natural world, have the possibility of waking up to crickets and beans and prairie grasses, the deer outside our window and the whisper of owl's wings on a winter's night. The awe expressed in these writings can be our own, if we stop to see the light on the hills, or to hear the first birds of morning.

It has been a joyful process to create this anthology, and to have the opportunity to bring forward the beautiful voices of fifty-six established and emerging nature writers.

Acknowledgments

We would like to thank Dave Brown, Thomas Aquinas Daly, the staff at Sterling College, *Orion*, Chip Blake, Anne Arundel Community College, the staff at the University of Utah Press, and Wildbranch founder E. Annie Proulx. Our particular thanks to Glenda Cotter for her support and hard work, and to all of the Wildbranch students and faculty who submitted their writing to this anthology.

Susan would also like to thank her wonderfully patient husband, Jeff Passe, and Florence would like to thank Skip Kimura for his good advice, encouragement, and deft literary instincts.

❦   SUSAN A. COHEN AND FLORENCE CAPLOW

A Brief History of Wildbranch

The earliest correspondence in my cardboard box archive of Wildbranch material is dated January 1986. The letter was written by Annie Proulx, a freelance writer living nearby in northern Vermont. A mutual friend had introduced us the previous fall, and we soon discovered a number of common interests including trout, ruffed grouse, apple cider, and wooden canoes. At that time I was on the faculty of Sterling College, a small (less than 100 students), nontraditional college with a program combining academic and hands-on work in the natural resource fields.

Annie felt a need for a program targeted at people such as foresters or wildlife biologists who knew much about the outdoor world but less about how to share that knowledge with a wider audience. In one of her early letters she wrote, "These people all know a tremendous lot about the outdoors, and most of them eat their livers out because they 'can't write.' Indeed, it would be a big job plus for many of them if they could handle the written word. . . . And I would rather teach people who already know the outdoor world than to get a bunch of soft-handed A+ English students who didn't know spruce root from goose gut, since a large part of good writing technique is keen observation with a fresh eye. And you have to know at what you are looking."

Lacking the facilities and support staff to offer such a program, Annie asked me if Sterling College would consider hosting such a workshop. At that point Sterling's facilities were only lightly used during the summers. Her inquiry received a favorable response, and I agreed to work with Annie to flesh out her idea.

Annie already had an extensive network of contacts in the publishing world, including book and magazine publishers, editors, photographers, and other writers. I began putting together a mailing list derived from the National Wildlife Federation's *Conservation Directory*. This annual directory included listings of all the federal, state, local, and private agencies involved with natural resources as well as all the colleges and universities with programs in forestry, wildlife management, agriculture, and so on. We agreed to start with a weeklong session and chose the last week of June in 1987.

On St. Patrick's Day in 1986, Annie and I drove down to Massachusetts to meet with Ed Gray at *Gray's Sporting Journal*. On the way down we were struggling to come up with a name for our new writing workshop. The Wild Branch, a local tributary of the Lamoille River, came to mind, and by changing this to one word we felt we had a promising name. Ed generously agreed to provide some advertising for the new writing workshop. Annie lined up a list of faculty for the inaugural session, wrote text for the brochure and poster, and asked her mother Lois to do a pen-and-ink sketch of an alder branch, which became the Wildbranch logo.

The results of our mailings were disappointing. As the dates of our first session approached, we realized we lacked enough participants to run the program. Reluctantly, we cancelled the 1987 workshop and agreed to get a much earlier start on the mailings for the next year.

Mailing results the following year were much improved, and we ran the first Wildbranch session in late June of 1988 with 28 participants and 9 faculty. The week was completely packed with presentations and talk of writing, but provided neither the time nor the framework for actual writing and feedback.

One of our initial interests in putting together the workshop was to strengthen connections between the fishing and hunting community and those with other interests in the outdoors. Many of the attendees in earlier years represented agencies such as the U.S. Forest Service, U.S. Fish & Wildlife Service, the Appalachian Mountain Club, Nature Conservancy, Ducks Unlimited, the Wilderness Society, state fish and wildlife departments, and others.

For the 1989 brochure cover I began using a painting by watercolor artist Thomas Aquinas Daly. This tradition continued through 2005 when we discontinued printing a brochure. One of my favorite tasks each fall was selecting a painting from a batch of transparencies of recent work Tom would send. It is very pleasing that Tom has agreed to provide the artwork for this book's cover.

By the third year we had arrived at a structure that struck a good balance between presenting information and providing time for serious writing and feedback. Faculty and participants also spend time enjoying the very special place that is Craftsbury in June. The format has endured to this day with only minor changes.

Annie remained actively involved with the planning and teaching through the 1990 session, after which she bowed out of the picture. This left me, with some trepidation, holding the reins. Shortly after this time, Annie's writing received a great deal of national and international attention, and she moved away from Vermont. With Annie's departure, I relied heavily on faculty members who in many cases found me, rather than the other way around, and who were extremely generous with suggestions and ideas.

Beginning in 1989 and continuing through 1995, the Orvis Company provided much-appreciated advertising and scholarship funding. From 1997 through 2006 the Outdoor Writers Association of America provided a scholarship for a member to attend each year. A Vermont-based magazine, *Northern Woodlands,* provided advertising for several recent years. We gratefully acknowledge the support of these organizations.

1994 marked the beginning of a long relationship with *Orion* magazine. A member of the magazine's editorial staff has presented during the workshop each year since then. In 2006, the Orion Society became a cosponsor and assumed much of the responsibility for promotion and faculty recruitment. This relationship has brought a huge increase in the number of applicants, and even during the current unsettled times it feels as though Wildbranch is on solid footing.

I feel incredibly grateful for all the random events that culminated in the publication of this anthology. The last twenty-two years have brought more than 450 participants from all over the world and almost fifty faculty members to Craftsbury and Sterling College. Many of these people have become dear friends, and my life has been immeasurably enriched by my involvement with Wildbranch, a result of that chance meeting with Annie many years ago.

Special thanks to Sterling College's administration and staff for their unflagging support through thick and thin; to Chip, Steve, Ted, Diana, Gale, Annie, Jennifer, and Joel, who returned on the faculty for many years and shared most generously; and to Susan, Florence, and Glenda for bringing this anthology to life.

   DAVE BROWN

Wildbranch

PART I

Intimacy

Our sense of community and compassionate intelligence must be extended to all life forms, plants, animals, rocks, rivers, and human beings. This is the story of our past and it will be the story of our future.

—Terry Tempest Williams,
   from *Red: Passion and Patience in the Desert*

Des Ta Te: A Love Story

✖ PAUL GRINDROD

We see you, see ourselves and know
That we must take the utmost care
And kindness in all things.

—Joy Harjo, from "Eagle Poem"

The eagle and I are surrounded. We are in the center of an open pavilion with dancers circling us, moving to the syncopated rhythm of a pair of drums. Many of the dancers wear elaborate plumed headdresses, and all have rattling shell anklets. One step involves the dancers leaping and bowing towards the center where we stand; when they do, the longest of their pheasant tail plumes brush against us.

The eagle fidgets. The lead dancer leans in, without missing a beat, and asks if the bird is nervous. "A little," I reply, "but I think she'll be okay." I close my eyes and concentrate for a second on the drums, trying to will myself invisible so that only the eagle is there. I feel her shift on my wrist and open my eyes to check on her, talking to her softly. The dance lasts for several more minutes and then the music ends. The dancers pause to catch their breath. As I take the eagle back to our corner, the group's leader acknowledges her once more. Back safely to her perch, she promptly hops into her water bowl and starts scooping mouthfuls.

In Mexico, where it originated, this dance would celebrate the golden eagle, the eagle with a snake dangling from its talons that adorns the Mexican flag. But we are at a powwow in Utah with a bald eagle, and the visiting dancers asked if she would join them in the arena for this dance. It is too interesting a cross-cultural, cross-species opportunity to pass up.

The eagle's name is Des Ta Te, a western Apache word for a feeling of ease, comfort, and contentment in place, what in Spanish is called *querencia*. The figurative translation of her name is "may the sun shine on your face and in your heart in a good way." The sun today is shining in a very good way on the audience, the dancers, on me, and on the eagle. Des Ta Te is an adult female bald eagle. She was found in the fall of 2000 somewhere in the state of Washington with a severe gunshot wound to the right wing. In order to save her life, the wing was amputated at the wrist joint. "It is the natural property of a wing to raise that which is heavy and carry it aloft to the regions where the gods dwell," Plato wrote. Denied her birthright to soar close to heaven by the selfish, cruel actions of a human being, Des hasn't flown since she was roughly three months old.

I met her when she was already three years old and newly resident at a nature center and avian rehabilitation facility where I took a job. Excited to be working with a bald eagle in the wildlife education program, I told a friend who had done many years of rehabilitation work with birds of prey. "Lucky you," she replied, her voice so disdainful and joyless that sarcasm almost dripped through the phone line. She could have been channeling the pre-Revolutionary War American naturalist William Bartram, who described the bald eagle—soon to become the national bird—as "an execrable tyrant: he supports his assumed dignity and grandeur by rapine and violence." Likewise, Benjamin Franklin—following the eagle's enshrinement on the National Seal by act of the Continental Congress in 1782—wrote to his daughter, "For my own part I wish the Bald Eagle had not been chosen the Representative of our Country. He is a Bird of bad moral Character. He does not get his Living honestly." My friend's disdain did not stem from such lofty moral high-ground; captive bald eagles have a reputation for being high-strung and irascible, they bite and grab with their talons, and they are infinitely well equipped to do damage with either the sharply pointed, hooked beak or, far more dangerously, feet that squeeze upwards of one thousand pounds of bone-crushing pressure per square inch. Shortly before I started working with

Des, she had a disagreement with her regular handler over some intended minor medical procedure. The eagle drove her talons through the handler's forearm in the ensuing debate and the two of them weren't really interacting much when I got there.

I had the luxury of several months to let Des Ta Te get used to me. I started our relationship by lingering outside her cage where she could see me. Once she was used to that, I went in with her and sat just inside the door. She was anxious at first, but as long as I didn't move toward her, she eventually got to where she mostly ignored my presence. As she became more comfortable with me, I would shorten the distance between us. Then I started taking food in and letting her see me put it on her feeding perch, but at first she wouldn't eat until I was gone. Within days, though, she would eat with me in the cage. It was then that I reintroduced her to her handling glove. She had developed quite a dislike of the heavy leather gauntlet, associating it with unpleasant medical activities—West Nile virus injections, baths, beak and talon trimming, and the like—and I needed her to start thinking of it as a good thing again.

One day someone from the Division of Wildlife Resources, the state agency that oversees hunting laws, and some of the permits that allowed us to have the eagle, brought in a load of ducks that they had confiscated from a poacher. Rather than waste them, they gave them to the nature center to feed to the resident animals. Des really liked fresh duck, especially the liver. These were so enticing that her desire for duck livers overcame any residual fear of the glove. First I hung the glove on her perch and put the liver beside the glove. Once she no longer feared that, I put the liver *on* the glove and waited until she would come to take it. From there it was only a short time until she began to take food right out of my gloved hand. I knew then that I had won her over.

When approaching her to feed I always crouched down so that she was taller than me on the perch. Some bird handlers suggest that you should never look straight at a raptor-in-training, as this is very aggressive to predators—it is how they look at their prey. But at this point in her training, I wasn't comfortable *not* keeping my eyes on Des; I did try to make myself small and unimposing, however. I clucked my tongue and talked quietly to her, tried to imitate soft eagle calls, and avoided locking eyes with her in staring matches, which she could invariably win in any case.

By the time the day came that I offered her a gloved hand to step up on, with the promise of duck liver as a reward, it was a small gesture that she was not reluctant to make. Granted, this was not an entirely new behavior for Des Ta Te. She had been trained to the glove and used in public education previously, but it had been at least several months since she had been worked with regularly. Ultimately, though, this training process was as much for my benefit as hers, teaching me how to move around her as I learned what her tolerances were.

After four months, and with Des readily stepping to the glove when it was offered, it was time for a public outing. The first was a group of retired professional women who chose our nature center for their monthly meeting and activity. It was my first experience with Des indoors, and doorways proved to be a significant first hurdle.

With an eight-foot wingspan when she was healthy, and six feet in her truncated condition, Des only fit through doors with her wings closed (preferably), or turned sideways. On this day she was too agitated to close them entirely, so we had to sidestep our way through the door. She nervously eyed the door jam and ducked awkwardly as we passed underneath it, apparently unsure if she would fit. Then the ladies spotted us, and all of them came toward us. Des saw the approaching mob and turned and cracked me on the bridge of the nose with her beak. This, I learned, was her favored way of expressing displeasure with a situation—she takes it out on the handler. This is only right. She did not ask to be in this condition or to be made example of in this way, and it is the handler's responsibility to keep the bird feeling secure. When she is feeling insecure she lets you know. The blow didn't draw blood—it was a calculated strike with the flat rather than the point of the beak, just painful enough to encourage me not to let it happen again.

Another early program was for an Eagle Scout Court of Honor ceremony. I prepared and read a little speech about the significance of the eagle and its symbolic representation. The whole show went off pretty well, and Des didn't seem to be upset by the commotion or being indoors. At the end of the closing prayer, just as the audience said "Amen," Des threw her head back and unleashed her crazy, unlikely barking cackle of a call. A startled lady in the front row looked up. "Does she spend a lot of time in church?" she asked. It turned out that as time went on, she did; we attended dozens of Eagle Courts over the next few years.

When she wasn't being used for educational programs—getting her living honestly—Des was on display in an outdoor pen. It had a water dish and several perches, and was big enough to accommodate her compromised mobility. But she still needed other diversions or enrichment to mitigate her captive routine. Bathing in her shallow, aqua blue, hard-walled kiddy pool was one of her favorites on hot summer days. This allowed her time out of her enclosure, tethered in the sun, with a 360-degree view of everything going on around her. She always started her baths shyly, eyeing the water in the pool nervously as though it concealed a potentially bottomless pit. She didn't like too many spectators, either, but a few people weren't a bother. She would hop to the edge of the pool and dip her bill to drink, clamping her huge talons onto the curled, hard lip. Sometimes gentle splashing or floating sticks—things in motion always fascinated her—would be enough to prompt her to get in. Finally she would ever-so-reluctantly half hop and half fall into the water, always looking a little astonished when it was only thigh deep. Then she would squat to wet her belly and undertail feathers, something we came to call the "butt-dip." After a couple of butt-dips she would bend first one wing and shoulder into the water, then the other. There would follow a series of forward dips, submerging her head and letting the water pool over her shoulders and back. Some days she got through the routine rather quickly, but other times she kept at her ablutions for twenty minutes or more, splashing water with her wings open and not getting out until she was wet through. Then she would hop out onto a perch, soaked and bedraggled. Lacking the waterproofing oils that, for example, a duck has on its feathers, Des's plumage would get completely limp and waterlogged. But après-bath meant sunning, and she would preen and stretch and flap her wings while she air dried. Her exuberance and obvious pleasure, though undignified for so august a national symbol, showed a gentle, playful side of Des that is rare in eagles, or at least rarely seen.

Things happen when you spend so much time with someone—feeding, bathing, and going out in public together; feelings grow, bonds deepen. There came a time when Des would call when she saw me pull in, and she started preening my hair and beard when I held her. "I'm nobody!," I'd quote Emily Dickinson to her, "Who are you?" and she would reply by boring into me with her heavily browed wild eyes and act like she was going to pluck my eyeball from its socket, delicately preening an eyebrow instead.

As with any animal, a relationship with Des Ta Te is based entirely on trust, mine of her as well as hers of me. Treated with respect and gentleness, she returns the favor. From the early days of our work together when I let her down and received a peck on the nose for my troubles, I learned to be more careful and she became more forgiving of me. Our relationship was special, though, and her other handlers always had to be conscious of the possibility of a lunging swipe with her bill if she thought they were becoming too familiar or complacent.

Des's serene appearance on the glove could lead strangers to the misconception that she was completely tame and docile, an impression she was quick to dispel. Once we attended a military awards dinner at a swank downtown hotel. To avoid crowds and congestion we brought the eagle in through a loading dock and up the elevators. The gentleman sent to escort us up was a big, burly military liaison with the appropriately masculine demeanor one would expect in the position. Another handler had the bird while I ran interference, opening doors, clearing the path, and keeping a controllable space around the eagle. The elevator was too small for all of us to fit at once, so the liaison decided to take the handler and bird up first while I waited for another car. As they stepped into the elevator, he reached across to push the button for their floor, leaning a shoulder dangerously close to Des's space. The handler felt the eagle tense and pulled Des back as far as she could just as the eagle made one of her lightning-quick feints with her beak. Des didn't make contact, but after that the escort crowded as far into his corner of the tiny elevator car as he could, rigid and submissive.

Considering the bald eagle, it is tempting to fall back on easy patriotic iconography and symbolic metaphors for rhetorical effect. I have used them myself in my court-of-honor speeches, equating the eagle's bravery, fidelity, and trust to admirable qualities in Boy Scouts who achieve the rank of Eagle Scout. The bald eagle is probably second only to the American flag as visual shorthand for capital *P* Patriotism. But for all this regard, eagles were driven to endangered status in the lower forty-eight states and, despite sufficient population recoveries to warrant their being delisted in 2007, continue to suffer from habitat loss, environmental degradation, and occasionally, as in Des's case, persecution.

Eagles are more than our ambition to better ourselves by celebrating those qualities we admire in them and disparaging the ones we don't like. Des Ta Te's deportment gave lie to the belief that because she was an obligatory carnivore she was "an execrable tyrant," supporting "assumed dignity and grandeur by rapine and violence." That description better fits the idiot who shot her. If eagles are only proxies for all the things we wish we could be—stronger, kinder, gentler, braver—we risk missing their real value to us and to our world when we fail to live up to those standards. What I hoped to evince in public programs with Des was that eagles are intrinsically grand and dignified, they don't need us to project it onto them; they are, in Wendell Berry's words, "Not raw sources, symbols, worded powers, but fellow presences, independent, called out of nothing by no word of ours, blessed, here with us."

Des Ta Te is still here with us, still blessed, although I am no longer with her. After being her chosen human mate for a number of years, I migrated out of Des's life. Like an eagle in the wild that loses its mate, she took me for dead and shifted her attention to someone else. We are told that animals live in the present, that past and future don't exist in their minds. If so, then she probably doesn't recall or miss me. I cannot say the same about her.

"I think I could turn and live with animals," Walt Whitman wrote in "Song of Myself." If it was Des Ta Te, so could I. She was "placid and self-contained," and brought "me tokens of myself," pieces that I didn't even know were missing, allowing me to expand my definition of myself. I would "stand and look at [her] long and long," and for that looking, and for the time I spent with her, know that I could never see an eagle the same way afterward.

White Wings Out of Dark Sky

✤ ALISON TOWNSEND

> *As of April 2007 there were about 340 whooping cranes*
> *living in the wild, and another 145 living in captivity.*
> *The whooping crane is still one of the rarest birds*
> *living in North America.*

All month I have wanted to speak of the cranes
and how they arrived one morning, floating
down out of the sky like a band
of five strange angels, landing in a farmer's field
beside Rutland–Dunn Town Road to browse
for a week among last year's corn stalks, each bird
picking its way through the mud, deliberate
as a meditating monk or nun. I have wanted
to say how white they were against the brown,
their feathers packed densely over their bodies
as snow had been over the land just a few
weeks before; how red their caps of pebbly skin
were, balanced on the top of each head
like a perfectly aligned beret; how their legs
were black as the bare trees (that same black
brushed on their wings' tips and mustaches);
and how elegant their necks were, the long
trachea coiled twice inside their breastbones
resonant as a French horn's *whoop*. I have wanted
to say how enormous our silence was as we sat,
staring at these creatures, trained to migrate south

behind an ultralight, then returning north on their own,
finding their way back to Necedah, red and yellow
I.D. tags and transmitters chinking around their legs
like Five & Dime bracelets. I have wanted to say
how they held us in their gaze, only seeming
to ignore us, the bright golden sun of each eye
watching as we watched them. And how,
when we least expected it, the cranes began to dance,
rising effortlessly then parachuting down, bowing,
jumping, flapping their wings in that movement
we call courtship, though it can happen
at any age and season. I have wanted to say
how silence continued to hold us in the small,
warm world of the car, how our hands
touched briefly at seeing this together,
and how all the rest of the day, as I bent
over my papers, the cranes seemed to float
inside my body, their great white wings
opening and closing like doors in the sky.

Between Green Flannel Sheets Splattered with Portuguese Roses

ALISON TOWNSEND

All night, in the middle of winter,
the great horned owls call around our hill,
their *who's awake, me too* drifting
through the bare branches, soft as smoke,
soft as their loosely packed feathers engineered
to move through air without making a sound.
Now, in the burnt-down nub, in the raw beginning,
they are mating, the murmurous calls flung out
in lassos of sound that seem to circle
our house as we lie awake, eavesdropping
on this primal call-and-response, this avian
love song. As if it can tell us something
about ourselves as we curl, impossibly human
and other, in the nest of our bed, our green
flannel sheets splattered with Portuguese roses.

When we first moved here, I thought it seemed
a hard thing, mating as owls do, in the dead
of winter, their eggs laid in February or March
in a nest stolen from crows, great blue herons,
or hawks. I pitied the female, protecting
the brood as the wind tore through the oaks,
wondering how she kept warm, though I knew
the male fed her. But now it makes sense, not
lonely at all but ferocious as they are,

and mated for life, winging through the dark blue
air, the country night powdered thick with stars
one cannot see in the city. The owls can hear
a mouse moving beneath a foot of snow,
and their eyes close from the top down, like humans.
Though they are not like us at all.
Though it is our luck to lie here,
overhearing the way the male calls out
in his low voice and the female answers,
the *I'm here, I'm here, I'm here* not
so different then when we call *Whoo-whoo,*
I'm home; where are you? whenever we enter the house.

You doze, falling asleep so quietly
it is as if you are moving through the air
on the owl's soft wings. I lie awake,
listening, straining to hear each *whoo, whoo,*
whoo-whoo in a way it seems I have not done
since I was a child, listening as the Perkiomen
River purled outside my bedroom window.
That was before I knew sadness, before
anything I'd ever known had ended, before loss
piled up inside me, a mesh of fur and bone.
And this is now, my life still large
with all that lies ahead, here, in the middle
of winter, in the middle of the country,
in the middle of the years I have been given,
all my wandering having brought me to this:
our warm bed and your breath, steady beside me,
the owls' beautiful and incomprehensible
music floating over our sleep.

Exaltation of Elk

⁂ Janisse Ray

Light rain had fallen most of the afternoon and the sky looked as if it planned on raining into the night. At night wild animals move and wounds heal and rain passes. This was not night, but an afternoon so dim it hardly seemed day.

Raven and I had been walking for five days through the Bob Marshall Wilderness of Montana. Since early morning we had come ten miles. We were wearing cheap rainsuits and were walking in plastic bags. Our packs were covered with trash bags. We had become so small we were almost invisible.

We had stopped to rest at the fork of Headquarters and Dryden Creek trails, a flowery bluff overlooking Headquarters Creek and the junction of the trails. A half hour earlier, we had crossed by packbridge over the North Fork of the Sun River, and were entering the territory of an old fire, wherein an incredible amount of biomass had turned simply to mass. The strange gray landscape was a tumble of timbers, a graveyard of trees. Older trees were standing dead, or were lying where they had fallen at the whim of wind, crossing and crisscrossing on soft slopes like toothpicks. Here and there young firs had begun the slow process of recovery. Life—beetles and ants and nestlings of cavity-builders—was returning.

Indian paintbrush and lupine bloomed in the grasses of the bluff. Silent rainy wilderness stretched for many miles on all sides, and fog crept in among the blackened sticks of trees. Above us Beartop Mountain rose. On top of that mountain was a lookout cabin, eight thousand feet high, and a lookie would be in it now, reading and glancing out his big glass windows. He would be alone too, and far from people, and maybe wondering about them, as we were. We couldn't see the cabin from the bluff, but we had seen it, smoke drifting from its chimney. We were invisible to the lookie.

Being invisible made us quiet, and that made us more invisible. Because of our invisibility, we were able to see more than if we had been large, in a small wildness.

We had a few more hours of hiking ahead of us, before we could make a fire, get dry, and sleep. Hungry and chilled, we needed food. We unpacked our stove in the rain and boiled water. Ground squirrels crept in, trying to pull off a food raid.

Within ten minutes, we sat on wet logs eating hot soup. Two deer were bedded down in knee-high grass below us, in the small valley; one doe faced us, the other faced away. They were both the red cedar color of summer deer.

For days my husband and I had seen almost no people. This early in the summer, mid-June, the snow had not melted from the high country and we had not been able to reach the Chinese Wall, a stunning formation of layered cliffs that marks a section of the western Continental Divide. We had turned back and pitched tent at the site of an old trapper's cabin, where we found a rusted enamel pot, tin cans, and all manner of bottles pitched over the embankment of Rock Creek. Two days we camped there, writing, painting, and reading around a small and constant campfire. Sometimes we would descend to the creek and watch a water ouzel, dipping its head in and out of the stream.

At dusk one night at the camp a pair of young men had passed on the trail—they had seen our smoke. I was crouched at the edge of a small muskeglike marsh, filtering water, and had watched them pass without being seen. The morning that we broke camp we met them. The young men had settled into the Forest Service cabin at Rock Creek, the one with log walls scarred from grizzly scrapes, the one bordered by indentations where bears had repeatedly passed, each time deepening their tracks. The young men were biologists, they told us, part of a huge grizzly bear study that would give a more definitive figure on the number of grizzlies left in Montana.

When we finished our soup, we proceeded down the steep little hill to the creek for water. The trail was muddy with earth that caked our boot soles and added a pound of weight to each step. We progressed slowly down the trail because of the mud and because we wanted to get close to the deer bedded down in the grass.

We were lucky to be downwind of the brace of deer, but one of them noticed us. Her ears lifted. We moved, easily. Another set of ears lifted. We stopped. The first doe lifted to her feet. We waited. She moved backwards, the other leapt up. We waited. One after the other they ran away from us, up a hill into the bizarre burned country.

Creekside now, Raven began pumping water bottles full while I washed pots and spoons. We hadn't brought bowls, to save weight. I was thinking about water. The air was full of it, the ground soggy with it, the creek swollen with it; our hands were in it; we were retrieving it to fill our bodies. Water rules the earth.

I glanced up from dishwashing. On the other side of the creek, the mountain rose into burned and returning trees. Just then I glimpsed brown movement through a small strip of fir trees eight to ten feet tall, halfway up the slope.

Our hike had not been without wildlife. On the first day three mountain goats roamed the rocks of Headquarters Pass, wishing to lose their shyness. We had seen a hoary marmot and a beautiful coyote, mountain bluebirds and nighthawks. We had seen tracks of moose and grizzly. One sunny day in a deep fir forest we had come face to face with a bear on the trail. The bear had been fifty feet from us when we rounded a bend and saw him; we could not tell to which of the two bear clans he belonged. We began to back slowly away, and to cajole the bear with sweet talk: "Good bear. We're just passing through. We won't bother you. Nice bear." The bear moved no muscle, but studied us, gleaming in sunlight, very big and very real. Finally, he had turned aside and crashed into the woods, and we saw then, with relief, that he was a black bear.

I touched Raven's arm.

"Elk," I said softly. Raven looked where I pointed but nothing moved. I shrugged and returned to my washing.

The next time I glanced up, minutes later, I saw flickers like brown ghosts behind a thin scrim of young trees twenty feet farther down. I watched, motionless, crouched by the creek. A couple of elk stepped into sight between trees, first one and then another, and I touched Raven again.

"I see three," I whispered. Our voices were washed away in the rushing of creek, and the stirring of rain.

"More," he said. "Five."

The elk were a couple hundred feet away, but they were definitely drifting downward, and they were multiple in number. They kept coming. I could see six now. Raven went back to his pumping and I kept watching the hillside. I could see more bronze flashes and random movement. Unbelievably, elk poured like molasses behind the scrim. The trees breached to make a clearing halfway up the slope and this fanned out in a wide grassy gap. Slowly, cautiously, one by one, elk stepped out onto the open hillside, onto the broad aperture that led to Headquarters Creek. After four minutes or so, I whispered to Raven: "How many do you think are there?"

Raven glanced up. He counted. "Seven."

"I think there are twenty-five."

Raven glanced at me. "Twenty-five?"

I couldn't see the elk, only an occasional russet movement, a flowing, but I had been watching long enough to know that animals were pouring down the slope, through the trees. They came and they came. One by one they moved downward. Now ten, if I had counted correctly, had reached the clearing. They moved slowly, warily, a step at a time.

We were crouched by the rushing, ten-foot-wide creek, which was lined with sapling willows. Now I saw that the willows were not young but cropped short by animals. We were invisible and there was no hurry. Ever vigilant in that wild country, I checked behind us for bears. I brushed my teeth and washed my face and Raven finished with the water pumping and brushed his teeth. We leaned back on our heels and sat in the rain, by the water, below the bank, among the willow. We were rocks.

The elk came down and down. I counted over and over, as they passed a certain stump, or moved down a patch of bare ground to creek-side, fifty feet upstream. They were hard to count: 24, 21, 25. Often they moved side by side. Every time I counted, their number changed. I counted 27.

An elk has a shape unlike most ungulates. It has no tail to speak of. Its head and neck are like that of a horse, its body like a zebra's. It has a long head and a dark neck. The hide is a richness of browns and reds and tans, moving like prairie grass in wind. Elk hair looks not like watercolors mingled, but like oils. An elk's body has the wet richness of an oil painting.

The herd moved slowly, older, bigger cows in the lead stopping to raise their long dark faces to the breeze: something didn't smell right, but what, they couldn't tell. The wind was in our favor. One young cow heedlessly rushed forward, eager to feed.

The herd was without bulls. As it moved, young spikes confronted each other, brandishing their short fuzzy antlers, less interested in food than relationship. Typically, one would head another off, until two were facing, then in slow motion, gracefully, the spikes reared at each other, pawing the air like horses but more slowly, carefully, not ever touching. Much of their activity was this heading-off, contact muzzle to muzzle, followed by a rearing-up and pawing midair.

I could not see Raven's face, only the back of his hat, and I hoped he could see what I saw. Turning, deliberate and slow, he whispered, "I bet that ground squirrel is tearing up our packs."

"That's okay. This is worth it," I mouthed more than whispered.

Neither of us wanted to mention the more fearsome possibility of bears. I surveyed behind us.

"They're very close," he said.

"Yes."

The water erased our words from the small valley.

The cows came down. The calves came. The spikes came. They moved by degrees toward the willows at the creek. We had been squatted now for fifteen minutes. I shifted almost motionlessly, slowly, onto my behind. My legs were falling asleep.

The nearest elk was thirty feet away. We were witness to the herd's intimacies: the sniffing, the coming forward, the pausing. And in the background spikes reared and stroked the air, the largest one snuffling and prancing all over the lower slope. Now I made no movement, only sat as still as still could be. Perfectly still.

The riskiest cow had reached the creek bank, twenty-five feet away, and was stripping willows of their leaves. A foot-long branch hung from her mouth as she chewed, then it fell—she bent down with her long-muscled neck to pick it up. The other cows came down and down.

One was in the water.

On the far bankside a cow pissed a stream of urine into the creek. She looked toward us, looked away. Another stared at us for a long time and did not alarm. Neither Raven nor I allowed even our eyes to move, but looked forward, thankful for peripheral vision. We were slowly being surrounded by browsing elk. Twenty feet away in the water a spike bull gazed directly and curiously at us, but he could not figure out what we were. Over the willow, leaves in his mouth, he gazed. Our raincoats were dark green like young trees. The spike bent down for more leaves and moved closer. He was fifteen feet away.

We were so invisible we were two spirits, crouched by a stream.

I wondered then if the elk would finally enfold us. What would they do when they discovered we were human? Might people be killed by stampeding five hundred-pound elk? How close would they come?

The spike was twelve feet from us, in the water, chewing.

We stared. We stared as long as we could, hidden by rain and wind and color and stillness. For ten minutes, then twenty, we sat still.

The lead cow, the biggest, foraged past us on the far side of the creek. She was farther away than some of the others, twenty-five feet or so, but a little downwind now. She breathed in the smell of us. She started. Somewhere close she smelled rank unbathed humans, perfumed with wood smoke and wet wool. Or thought she did. Unsure, she stared and stared, Raven and I locked in her gaze. She chewed, pondering. We were so close we saw beads of water dripping from her chin. We saw the black tips of her big velvet ears. We saw the huge, bottomless, brown orbs of her eyes, yet unafraid, gathering us into them. Her ears were up, her tail flicked gently. She chewed.

We never moved. We were hypnotized by wildness. We were grateful.

Finally wind brought enough smell that the cow moved backward, head up in an unmistakable position. She pumped her hooves in final ac- knowledgment that something was amiss. Interpreting her warning and relying completely on her instincts, the other elk immediately stopped pulling leaves and turned as a measured herd and headed back the way they had come. But not in a rush. Never did they charge or stampede. They went instantly but not chaotically.

Watching them go, we ached.

Even when we finally stood to leave the elk were far enough away to register our movements but not to bolt. We climbed the hill slowly back to our packs, which neither the ground squirrels nor the grizzly bears had bothered, and shouldered them. That night we would pitch our tent in a crevice among black and fallen logs, and by the evening of the sev- enth day we would be back at the edge of wilderness, and within two days, not even in Montana.

Raven said later that maybe we did the elk a disservice, letting them go thinking they could trust humans. Maybe we should have stood and shouted. But I don't think so. I'm glad we waited quietly among them, and saw what we saw.

Letter To Douglas

☙ TONY CROSS

Dear Douglas,

When I first made your acquaintance I admit I felt a little disinterested. I had known other fir trees, and my childhood recollections of Christmas and winter walking had put a shine on any thought of a fir tree. But when I moved to California, I had my sights on something bigger. It was predestined, or so I expected, that I would make my bones and join up with the big guns of the West, alongside your much-ballyhooed older sibling, the coast redwood.

Yes, *Sequoia sempervirens* was what I had my eye on. You can take those two words and bite them off and chew them like raw cabbage—crisp, and bold, and straight down in the body of the earth. But in contrast, look at your real name: *Pseudotsuga*, which translates to false hemlock. Who would ever align themselves with the cause of a false hemlock?

And look at your unexceptional cones. The only thing that really distinguishes them is the short wisps that pierce out like miniswords from between the layers. Now, consider the unfathomable cone of *Sequoia sempervirens*. It's tiny, a micro-cone, the appropriate scale for a doll house, a cone a mouse can relate to. This cone is a rebel. It says, "Forget everything you ever knew about pine cones and start over. There are no rules here. No one ever said that the smallest cone you'll ever see can't grow into the largest tree." Blasphemous! But Douglas, your cones take the middle path, they follow protocol, they do exactly what one might expect.

On top of that, *Sequoia sempervirens* dwarfs you in size. You're like the Spud Webb of the tree world, five feet tall and playing point guard at Madison Square Garden, dribbling the ball through a world of towering elders. What are you doing here? Why are you always coattailing it with the big boys?

The thing about you, Douglas, is that you are everywhere here. Your prodigious dispersion breeds an easy familiarity. The coast redwood may be the fire, but you are the stoker. The coast redwood may be the Hollywood celebrity, but you're the working class stiff I have a beer with every night. I admit that I may have moved to California with certain predispositions. So let me tell you about what has happened to all of that, Douglas.

I've spent hours watching the fog traverse your branches and settle on the other side of a ridge. I've seen you outlined against a three quarters moon at 2:00 a.m., and I've stood at the base of you, spreading my hands across your rough bark, working through the discomforting ridges and the gritty, splinter-filled river beds that cover your ancient interior. I know that you are probably hundreds of years old. I've inhaled the dust from your roots, making you a part of my own biology. And I've seen that the coast redwood is the neon sign attracting travelers to this way post in Northern California. It's the center ring of the woodland circus, a magnet for pilgrims with binoculars, or incense, or long measuring tapes. Don't get me wrong: there's nothing insincere about our friend *Sequoia sempervirens*. It's just that after a time, I am drawn to the quiet places that don't ask for anything, that don't require anything, but that simply endure, and in which I am invited to endure also.

For to call a place home, one must find a sense of solidity in that place. One must spend an afternoon melding into the curve of a tree trunk; recall the smell of the place and taste it on the tongue; pass moments of misery there, freezing from rain or overcooked from heat; one must never require a map, even in the night; one must spill blood or birth on the ground; one must bury things in the earth, or scatter ashes across it. And you Douglas, you are my solidity. You are the constant, the humble, the stoic, and the mighty. I would never utter the old adage, "You are my oak," because the oak has nothing on you. You may be labeled false by the prophets and snake oil salesmen of science, but I will call you by your true name: fir.

P. S. I've taken home a couple of your cones and set them alongside the cones of *Sequoia sempervirens*. Those cute little cones became brittle and are easily blown off my desk by a light breeze from the open window. But your cones, Douglas, they have aged, and opened, and the spiky crowns from within have softened and kept their color, and there has yet to be a rain, or earthquake, or gale force wind, or thunderclap that has budged them from their spot. I can open the window wide, and everything that the world wants to send in to me can come in, and we will go forth together.

This Ground Made of Trees

Alison Hawthorne Deming

—at the H. J. Andrews Experimental Forest

The giants have fallen.
        I think I can hear the echo
                of their slow composition

the centuries passing
        as note by note
                they fall into the forest's

silent music. Moss has run
        over their backs, mushrooms
                have sprung from the moss,

mold has coated the fungal caps
        and the heartwood
                has given itself to

muffled percussion
        of insect and microbe
                that carpet of sound

that gives the forest its rhythm.
        A nuthatch twits
                or a vole cheeps.

The scent of decay rises
    like steam from a stewpot.
        Anywhere I set my foot

a million lives work
    at metabolizing
        what has gone before them.

The day is shortening
    and the winter wrens have
        something to say about that.

I can almost give thanks
    that the soil will claim me
        but first allow me, dear life,

a few more words of praise
    for this ground made of trees
        where everything is an invitation

to lie down in the moss for good
    and become finally really
        useful, to pull closed

the drapery of lichen
    and let the night birds
        call me home.

To Liv

🌹 Jennifer Barton

We sit in a black plastic chair, her back to my chest, my elbows pressing in on her wings, bookends, my hands squeezing her tarsi in case her talons flare. My lips bow to her feathered head. On her perch in the aviary, I never wanted to kiss her, not with that thick, black beak clacking, not in the fire of her hiss. This is different.

The vet forces a needle through feather, skin, and breast tissue, pushes fluid out a syringe tip, releases, steps back, pauses, exits. I hold my breath and wait. Wait, we should be sitting under white pine and red oak, where mice skitter around pellets that house bones of their kind. She should be in a digestive tract, her own bones solidified with saliva, coughed up to the soil as an offering. I should have left her broken-winged in the sand.

I was told never to look a great-horned owl in the eyes. Some absolutes are meant to be honored; most invite questioning. I questioned. Her yellow eyes were suns: some days I looked straight into them, some days askance, others I didn't dare enter her world. Intuition stopped my feet at the cage door.

One afternoon, while testing her ability to perch on my fist, I encountered a five-year-old girl who asked an all-too familiar question: "What is her name?"

"She doesn't have a name," I asserted. "She is not a pet. We don't pet her. She is a wild creature." Five-year-olds need black and white—pet or wild, touch, no touch. In truth, this owl was something in between. She no longer sliced silently through her birth skies, nor did she come home with me and eat from a bowl with her name on it. Would she become an education bird, an employee, touched only when on duty, locked up when off? But the truth was that here in the aviary she did have a name. Olivia. I called her "Liv". She was teaching me how.

I don't know how to be intimate with her now. In life, it was call and response, action and reaction, this dance of distance making the closeness a privilege, like witnessing a lobelia blossom once every seven years. In dying, does she want the same distance she can no longer defend? How do I read her without eyes? Can I trust human to owl heart? I fear intimacy, yet it is what I most crave.

Her lids lower, the yellow light of her eyes extinguished. I imagine my daughter's closed eyes at birth, how I held her to my chest in just this way as life poured in, not out. The air is breathing me now, owl body so still I feel like I'm the one dying. I hiccup on an inhale for reassurance. I want to hold my breath in solidarity with her. But she doesn't hold hers. She is the sky allowing the clouds passage, she is a cocoon through which her spirit is escaping. I am still sitting in a black plastic chair in a white-walled room, palm sweat and feather oil forming their own feral fragrance.

Two months prior, when I retrieved her from the beach, the sun penetrated all things, rounding every bend, filling every shadow, shooting fire through my chest. Creature of the night, cowering in this light; I didn't know if it was right to approach. But "right" is a proclamation of the head. Meanwhile my body eased toward her. I tossed a torn blue towel over her head, bent and scooped. That was the moment of no return. She was my patient now. I would soon decide her fate—euthanasia due to irreversible neurological damage. She couldn't stand or eat without assistance. She turned away from the dead mice delivered daily at 4:00 p.m. She was parasite ridden and immobile, living in a box without flight, without sight, without purpose, or so I projected. But she didn't have a choice in directing her demise. She could not sign a consent form.

Her head flops onto my chest, yielding to the gravity of my heart. Her talons tighten. I can almost imagine she is osprey, the splash, snatch, lock of her talons, the faith that fish weight won't pull her down before she flies up to a branch to feast. Here we sit in this odd fusion of flesh and feather. I want to lift her lids. I want that one, last, haunting glare. I peel my thighs from the plastic chair; the window pulls me toward the pines, the cacophony of crow drowning out the traffic. In the absence of loon, crow wails for me, releases what I cannot because I don't want to scare the poodle owners in the lobby.

I return to the beach that afternoon. The evidence is long gone; black-backed gull tracks cut through the spot where the blue towel fell. Lying among sand fleas and crunchy kelp, I stare straight into a soft sun, until it bends and scoops me up, inside. Inside, the yellow light never fades.

Dispute with Thomas Hardy

⚶ SYDNEY LEA

> *The smile on your mouth was the deadest thing*
> *Alive enough to have strength to die.*

—Thomas Hardy, from "Neutral Tones"

It won't last long, this snow that sheathes
        the dooryard pine in April and lays
its pale doomed cover on the slope behind.
        Crocuses, just tall enough,
are poking their small blue noses through.
        It's clear they're alive enough to live.
Yes, April's gale is loud as bombers.
        What's left of ice around the pond
in town looks rough as predators' teeth.
        Somewhere a red squirrel is felled by a fisher.

There's much I too may try to cover,
        which is why perhaps I feel strange gladness
to watch the omni-inclusive white
        subsume the neutral tones that pushed
our brilliant poet to ponder death
        and love's deception, its cruelty.
We've been together, my love and I,
        near three decades, which have scudded by
like these sideways flakes. My mortal wife....
        There *can* come pangs. But freshets have started

to wander the brush and leave their signs.
      Soon we'll find the trillium,
the painted kind, in the hidden place,
      which I discovered ten springs ago
and which since then I've kept a secret
      from all but her—from even our children;
and the valley's white-faced Herefords
      dropped new calves while winter endured.
Mud and blood still cling to the cows
      but their calves shine clean as a colorful dream.

What dream would be mine? That life go on
      as ever. That all our lives go on.
No more than dream, of course, I know,
      the planet heating up, the cretin
politicians rattling swords,
      as if, by counter-logic, war
might transmute the earth into something saintly.
      The harder facts conspire against me.
Yet to know as much is to make me hang on
      the harder to gifts apparently given

without my having at all to deserve them:
      flowers, animals, glinting trees,
and a disposition that moves me here
      to disputation with my great better,
in spite of all my darker doubt.
      Inkling of something soon to come down
like rain upon mown grass, as showers
      that water the earth. Some Lordly power,
or at least new weather. Or the smile on the mouth
      of that lover-wife, which blinds like snow.

Or the road agent waving from his bright-red plow
    as it smoothes the drifted back lanes over.

Yellow-bellied Sapsucker, Craftsbury Common, Vermont

🐙 DAVID HASKELL

You and I do the same work, woodpecker.
Thumping our beaks on wood
Ja Ja-Ja-Ja Ja-Ja
Pounding desires on cellulose sheets
Barn boards, paper scraps. Resonate!

Weave of wood flexes and trembles,
Your call lobs through air. She'll hear.
Life tapped, and rising.

Pigment on paper.
Flexes? Perhaps. Trembles? Oh yeah.
But who will hear?

Breakfast.
We tongue the tree's sweet wound
Beak-drilled wells, metal spouts.
Sugar shacks burn the body to thicken the blood
Maple tree surges into animal flesh.

You and I are nothing without leafy temple pillars.
No substance, no fire, no drumskin, no song.

You and I do the same work, woodpecker.

Migrations

⁂ Glenda Cotter

> *The restlessness of shorebirds, their kinship with the distance
> and swift seasons, the wistful signal of their voices down
> the long coastlines of the world make them, for me, the
> most affecting of wild creatures.*
>
> —Peter Matthiessen, from *The Wind Birds*

It's autumn and so Peter Matthiessen's haunting and beautiful lines about shorebirds seem to be continuously in my mind. His words have been sitting shoulder-to-shoulder, neatly juxtaposed, with an image that I am holding close. It is of a wild day in October, the sky dark as evening though it is still afternoon, the wind spitting rain from the west, the marshes populated with shorebirds. I am looking out over a stretch of the wetlands that surround Utah Lake. Probing the mudflats with their characteristic sewing-machine motion—stitching the landscape together—is a flock of one hundred or more long-billed dowitchers. The urges of autumn have sent them this far south, down from their northern nesting grounds on the way to kinder winter habitats.

This flock is intent on feeding, for the dowitchers have a thousand miles and more left in their migration. The wind across the marshes keeps them unsettled—restless is precisely the word. At times they are picked up and blown about by the gusts; a few chase their fellows from place to place without reason. The whispered urging in the wind keeps them moving.

Little flocks of peeps, probably least or western sandpipers, sweep across my field of view, but they do not land and my look is too brief for anything but a guess. Their flight adds to the overall sense of autumn unease. Killdeer feed in the mud, and a few yellowlegs—some will stay and some will go. Long-legged avocets, pale ghostly versions of their summer selves, sweep their bills through the shallow water. Farther out, where the water deepens, are a few pelicans and coots; a Forster's tern glides and wheels overhead. Everywhere the air is filled—literally filled—with darting thousands of swallows. Cliff swallows, mostly, though I catch a few forked tails of barn swallows. They too are readying to leave, fueling for long flights that might begin tomorrow, or the next day, though not today, not in this day's wind and rain. Restless motion, chill and change, wind and flight—these define the day.

The snow-capped peaks—already in early October there's enough snow that it's likely to linger now until spring—of the southering Wasatch Mountains seem to hem in the birds, but a lovely sort of avian avenue between the mountain ranges gives them passage to the south. Passage. Whenever they are ready to leave, whenever the urges become insistent. Soon.

Bird migration may be one of the most inspiring facts of the natural world—the movement of millions of birds around the globe, movements begun largely by photo receptors inside each bird's skull—an internal light sensor like an alarm, the changed light alerting them to the season. A "certain slant of light" achieved and it is time to follow generations of the ancestors. It is time to fly steadily and with purpose. Are they going home, or leaving it? Perhaps it doesn't matter, for assuredly they are going.

Despite the need for real global thinking, we humans live in an increasingly fragmented and polarized world. Yet bird migration connects us—even the most sedentary of us—in very real and meaningful ways, with distant places, with foreign manners, with universal dreams and desires. It opens within us deep wellsprings of hope for the safe passage of these fellow creatures, and for the safe return that will signal our own season of renewal. It is vital that these greatly roaming species find many safe havens: the havens of arrival and departure, the expected and unexpected stopping places along the way. We now have some part in assuring their safety.

The restless shorebirds link us with places that we may never see. Scott Weidensaul, in *Living on the Wind*, described the nesting phalaropes that hatch their young on Alaska's coastal plain, then spend their winter on the vast Pacific Ocean somewhere off slender Chile's many miles of coastline: from cold ocean to cold ocean across thousands of miles. I have seen some of those phalaropes whirling and spinning in the briny waters of the Great Salt Lake, engaged in a feeding frenzy to collect the fat that will fuel the next leg of their flight. There at my land-locked lake, watching phalaropes, I have connected of a sudden with the Bering Sea, with the great rocky drainages of the Yukon River, with the ocean lapping at the sands of the Atacama Desert or even, a little wildly, with Easter Island. I am in Pablo Neruda's "enchanted place where we can dance our clumsy dance and sing our sorrowful song," a temporary member of the clan of the living. Solitude sits in our human souls next to this vast abiding world and all her wild things. And it speaks the language that both birds and humans speak, Matthiessen's "kinship of distance." Do you see how the light falls on the glistening wings of the shorebirds? Do you see how the Earth carries us all?

Spirits

❧ GLENDA COTTER

—with thanks to W. S. Merwin

I know that the only certainty has always
been that I'll grow older and the crazed
surfaces of my body speak to that truth I've
kept to the pace of my life without
learning much beyond a certain inclination to
tolerance and a reticence in
the matter of finding or telling fault
I feel much as I did at twenty or thirty
though happily the fretful anxieties of fifteen
have mostly fled at least the size of my breasts
is no longer something to fear and
I know that pain however great or small
is too persistent and love however
long is always brief and that until
such reason as I have deserts me
there will always be my grandmother
at her silent station in an old green
chair working puzzles by lamplight in
the dark nights of her many-widowed years
and a bedroom with a cold east
wall because of soldierly apple trees
too miserly in admitting the sun
even when leafbare and
avenues of cottonwoods

towering over my childhood and
raining their amber hearts each autumn on
the tree house that wasn't much a few
uneven boards but a rope
swing across the ditch below
my mother in her warm kitchen of
an afternoon after school and
my father in his garden with its peas and
beans and always corn and tomatoes
and my daughter who climbs trees and
builds houses for bugs and the men
who desire me and the men who don't
and the sunlight filling the alpine
meadows where I want only to
roll among the wild flowers or
stand with naked arms above my head as
though the sky could surely be embraced and
the wide desert spaces where breath and
sand and spines weathered and sharp are
whole empty continents of emotion
requiring no further meaning where
anything seems possible even that I
might never grow old but live always in the
self-same exuberance as when I began.

Fourth Night Magic

✤ ROBERT KIMBER

Our position is, roughly, 51 degrees, 56 minutes north latitude, 65 degrees, 30 minutes west longitude. To put that in more accessible terms, we're way out in the Canadian bush, still in Quebec but about five miles away from the southwestern corner of Labrador. It's Sunday, early August, about 6:30 p.m. We're pitching camp on the shore of one of the innumerable little ponds that make up the labyrinthian waterways of northern Canada, a country so densely laced with streams, rivulets, bogs, rivers, lakes, and ponds that no one could begin naming any but the larger bodies of water. But names the mapmakers cannot get around to, the wilderness paddler can, because any place you make camp and lay your head for a night becomes a home. Garrett Conover has already named tonight's resting place Camp Hummock for the obvious reason that hardly anywhere within a hundred yards of our campfire can you find enough level ground to pitch a tent.

We are eight: Hugh Stewart and Neil McDonald from Quebec and Ontario; Wendy Scott, Dawn Morgan, Anne Ingerson, and Dave Brown from Vermont; Garrett and I from Maine. Ages are as diverse as origins: Dawn and Neil are in their twenties; Hugh, late fifties; me, mid-sixties; everybody else, fortyish. We're making our way toward the Labrador border. Once we've crossed it, we'll be in Lac Assigny, the first of a chain of lakes that make up the headwaters of the Atikonak River watershed. From Lac Assigny on, it'll all be downhill, though "downhill" on a wilderness canoe trip is not always the equivalent of smooth sailing. Before this trip is over, we will have portaged twenty-one times. Four days ago, we climbed off the Quebec North Shore and Labrador Railway train at a whistlestop named Eric. Since then, we've already made seven of those twenty-one portages. We're only about forty miles into our 250-mile trip, and already Hugh has dubbed this "the trip that wouldn't give an inch."

Hugh is cooking tonight. "Ham au gratin or spaghetti?" he asks. Three voices say, "Ham au gratin." He puts a bag of mixed nuts and one of garlic sticks on top of a wanigan for us to snack on as we do chores. Garrett has cut a couple of dead black spruce for firewood. Dave and Wendy are sawing them up and tossing the billets over to him to split. I set up the galley poles for Hugh to hang his pots on, split some kindling, get the fire going. Neil, Anne, and Dawn are pitching tents. One of the joys of traveling with old hands is the ease, the utter routineness of routine. We set up a rotation of cooks, but nothing else is foreordained. Everyone knows what chores need to be done and automatically steps in.

Camp Hummock may not be ideal for setting up tents, but it's superb for lounging. All these hummocks padded with caribou moss make exquisitely comfortable backrests, and once camp chores are done, we kick back, pull out maps and journals, and start comparing notes on the day's travel.

The first joint on Garrett's thumb is equal to one mile on a 1:50,000-scale map, and he calculates each day's mileage in thumb joints. Before Dave Brown even leaves home, however, he lays out the route on his maps and marks each mile with a tick mark. He and Garrett rarely come up with the same daily tally.

"Eight miles today," Garrett says.

"I get nine," Dave says, so I write "8.5" in my notes.

"Which point was it where we had lunch?" Dawn asks me, "This one here, or the next one up the bay?"

Wendy is collecting our cups and lining them up on a wanigan lid. "Cocktail time," she says and tips a tiny flask lid of rum into each cup, about an eighth of an inch, not enough to induce even a mini-buzz but enough to warm the tongue and heart.

Hugh's pot of rice is bubbling softly. In a pot next to it, water is heating for after-dinner tea. The swarms of black flies that often keep northern travelers in headnets in the evening are blessedly absent tonight, and they will remain so for most of this trip. Why? None of us knows, but we speculate—an unusually dry summer, perhaps, or maybe just a low in a normal cycle.

A light northwesterly breeze has swept away the showers that drove us into raingear in the morning and at noon, and now the wind has dropped; the air is still and cool, promising a night of perfect sleep. We pull on wool shirts and hats. Hugh serves up heaping platefuls of ham au gratin and rice. We cradle the warm plates in our laps and eat.

The flow of talk that is almost as constant as the flow of the river stops for a few minutes. A moment of sweet stillness takes over in our little company. We look out on the glassy water and on the spires of black spruce rising around us, on clouds of translucent gold drifting across the sky. We grin at each other.

Garrett calls this moment fourth-night magic, a time that does indeed seem to come with astonishing regularity on the fourth night out, that moment when a canoe company coalesces into a clan. We've shared four days of wet feet and driving rains. We've waded and wallowed, tracked canoes up rapids and lined them down, chopped our way through blowdowns, humped canoes and wanigans and hundred-pound packs over portages. Four days of bruising adversity we've shared, and four days of fun surpassing mere fun. Bliss is the better word, beatitude maybe. Blessed are the wilderness paddlers, for they shall know heaven in the boondocks.

We are warmed by food and wool and a tot of rum, of course, but most of all by the presence of our brothers and sisters of the bush. When fourth-night magic descends, what goes unsaid but is understood by everyone around the fire is simply this: There is no other company I would rather share right now. There is no other place I would rather be. This, my friends, is as good as it gets.

Fishing with George

❧ Jim Collins

I lost a good friend recently. George Kingsbury was a store owner and sheep farmer and member of the Dartmouth class of 1938. A love of the outdoors reached into the heart of him, as anyone knew who sailed with him at his cottage on Granite Lake in Stoddard, New Hampshire, or walked his land with him in nearby Keene, the county seat. That hundred acres of open pasture was more valuable to him than money; he turned down a million dollars for it, defiantly protecting it from development that pushed against it on all sides. He was a patrician leader in the local business community, but it was the land—especially after he retired and turned to his farm full time—that rooted him here.

My time with him was spent mainly on trout water. We usually fished with my, our, friend, Steve Smith, the three of us sharing not only an interest in the hexagenia mayfly hatch on Sourdahunk Lake in northern Maine, but an interest, as well, in wooden boats and reading and history. We fished all over southwestern New Hampshire together: Willard Pond, Hunts, gin-clear Caldwell, Center Pond in Nelson, the Ashuelot River in Marlow. In the fall, when the foliage was peaking, we'd hike up to Lake Solitude on the back side of Mount Sunapee, where for a time we stashed one of George's old dinghies in the woods for our private use.

I met George in the mid-1980s at the Keene Country Club, at a meeting of the local Dartmouth alumni group. He had an Old World formality about him, and an air of class that intrigued me and intimidated me—I was a local kid from a regular family who was only just beginning to accept that I had belonged at a fancy Ivy League school like Dartmouth. Yet his eyes sparkled, and he smiled kindly, and we almost instantly struck up a friendship around fly-fishing. He was tall and lanky, white-haired, seventy years old, and I was just two years out of college. But the difference in our ages seemed not to matter. On our first long trip together, George, Steve, and I slogged down the inlet stream into Allagash Lake, deep in the Maine woods, wading through muck and hauling the canoes over beaver dams. The July air was humid and buggy, and in the afternoon the rain started. It was a discouraging way to begin a first trip together, but a good way to learn about someone's character. George appeared to be having the time of his life—I think he was tickled to be in the company of a couple of young guys, and he seemed to relish the hard work. When we finally made camp, he took some butterscotch candies from his pocket and said, "I suppose you fellows earned these." A little later he pulled off his wet boots and socks, and found some small leeches attached to his ankles. "Well would you look at that!" he said, laughing. "I thought I felt something funny!"

On our third or fourth night in, George took out his harmonica, and in his modest way told us that he'd been part of a pretty fair harmonica band in high school. He played beautifully for us—that sounds odd, I know, talking about a harmonica, but I'd never heard anything like it— as a fire burned at our feet and a soft rain pattered on the tarp above us. Talk about the band drifted into talk about high school in general and then college, and to two summers in the late 1930s when George had hiked in the Tetons in Wyoming. He sounded wistful as he described leaving that wild high country behind and returning home to Keene, to go into the family stationer's business. I know that a part of him stayed out there forever, and that his decision to settle back in New Hampshire was one of the great forks in his life. I understood his decision, and I admired him for it, because I had once faced a similar fork, and had gone the other way. I felt selfish for my choice, which had been a flip side of George's. He had chosen family obligation over a landscape that had enthralled him. I had turned away from my father's small medical supply business to find my own way, though remaining in a landscape I'd grown up in, and was growing to love.

George remained a Main Street merchant until he retired at sixty, when he got his sheep and at least a version of the western ranch he'd privately dreamed of owning. The flock eventually grew to 225 sheep, one of the largest in the state.

During long days sharing a canoe or wading alongside each other in streams, I felt a kinship in the way George appreciated our northern New England surroundings, the way we both loved being out there without caring, really, how many fish we caught. Yet there was much we didn't talk about. In that sense, George was a true Yankee. He talked at length about Zane Grey's novels and conservation easements, but little about the family tragedies he'd lived through, little about his field artillery unit in World War II, never about his health. For my part, I would have felt awkward letting him know that he gave me an image of what I hoped to grow into: a vigorous outdoorsman, a gentleman who never lost his boyish sense of enthusiasm, someone at home in both the country and the country club. And I could never have found the words to express how he helped me reconcile my sense of place and background and the possibilities of who I was becoming. He was a grandfather I never had. My New Hampshire forebears were silent, brooding, hill people, who fought the hard land and climate even as the Kingsburys, close by but a world away, sailed ice boats on Granite Lake, took in shows at the Peterborough Summer Playhouse, and cheered on the Dartmouth football team each fall.

The outdoors was the currency George and I shared, but we had Keene and Dartmouth in common. He had been a student at Dartmouth in a golden age, when west-central New Hampshire still bordered on wilderness and Dartmouth was building its national reputation as an outdoors school of the first rank. I pictured him as a leader in the Dartmouth Outing Club, a champion skier, an acolyte to Ross McKenney, Dartmouth's legendary woodcraft advisor who had been a Maine guide and river driver up in the Allagash. That picture I held of George somehow made me feel connected in a lineage.

In fact, he hadn't done much outdoors while at Dartmouth. George had majored in English, had run for the track team, been tapped into a senior society for student leaders.

Over the years, though, as our friendship deepened, I sensed that he may have wished that some of that outdoorsy collegiate image I held of him had been true. As his wife, Midge, gradually lost her eyesight and her memory, George no longer dared leave her alone overnight. Steve and I planned shorter fishing outings, with side trips so George could see—for the first time—the 26,000-acre Dartmouth Grant in northern New Hampshire; the Dartmouth Outing Club's Ravine Lodge on Mount Moosilauke; the Dartmouth–owned ski area. George seemed especially excited about the side trips. I think they meant something deep to him.

He was starting to slow down by then, no longer felt safe driving at night, and our friendship turned tender. He begged off on a trip because of a cold, and Steve and I bagged the fishing and brought store-bought salmon to his house for dinner, to cheer him up.

By the end of our time fishing together, George was growing too stiff to sit in a canoe for very long. He spent less time casting and more time simply watching. He offered me his arm for support walking over rough ground. I tied on his wispy 6x tippet and his tiny #16 dry flies for him; my eyesight was good. He accepted my help absolutely without complaint or apology. He accepted his aging as naturally as he'd accepted the friendship of someone nearly five decades younger than he was. He gave me the rare gift of grace.

And I see clearly now: It was never about the fishing.

Calling the Dove

🦋 Dorinda G. Dallmeyer

My grandfather taught me how to call doves. Growing up in south Alabama, he developed a repertoire of skills, some to earn money, like bricklaying or rafting pine timber all the way to Mobile, others to put food on the table. Doves could be called by imitating their round note. If you were good at it, the males would come to chase off the interloper they heard. If you could call and shoot, that was the start toward a meal. To sharpen his marksmanship, in his youth he learned to pick off bullbats—what you know as nighthawks—darting in the evening sky. Unthinkable as it is to me now—the grandchild who has raised catbirds and blue jays and mockingbirds lost from their nests—I have to admire his skill in pure observation. He watched nighthawks to learn their pattern of wing beats as they sweep the sky for insects—flap-flap-*glide*, flap-flap-*glide*—a waltz of predation in the dusk. If they are going to swerve, they do it on the flap, not the glide, so you shoot them on the follow-through.

That was his youth. By the time I knew him, his forays with gun in hand were strictly for the table, squirrels mostly, but mostly just walking the fields. One time he passed up the opportunity to shoot a cottontail he nearly stepped on before he saw it cowering in hopeful camouflage. But there was no skill in blundering into a rabbit. It never crossed his mind to raise his gun; he just told the rabbit to go on home.

He taught me how to call doves, and doves have been on my mind a lot lately. At home mourning doves frequent our feeders although they prefer to feed on the ground. The pairs whistle in on squeaky wings, dressed in subtle pearl-tones, the male rosier in the breast, both teetering on absurdly small feet atop the feeder roof. They pad around anxiously, unsure just how to make the transition from eave to platform as if, once landed, they forgot they could fly if they fell.

Their nests seem tentative as well, the eggs clearly visible through a minimalist lattice of sticks and straw, a Zen nest on a fan of pine. But if they were that flimsy, we'd have no doves. Although the male makes dramatic beelines to present the female with nesting material, item after item, he knows when to stop and she knows what's enough: that the flex and bend of the bough requires a supple nest, not a massive one.

Pity the doves, who come freighted with more symbolism than their narrow shoulders seem capable of bearing, much less delivering on. The dove of peace, the dove returning with the olive branch to signify God's reconciliation with man after the Flood, the billing and cooing of court-ship, doves released at weddings to symbolize marital harmony. What could they have done to deserve this?

And why have their cousins fared so much worse? The rock doves, "street pigeons," reviled and persecuted because they squat on the stat-ues of our ancestors, the same people who brought them here in the first place. The homing pigeons, so nurtured and bonded to a place, then dragged off hundreds of miles and released despite weather and pred-ators just to see if they can make it home. To me it's the equivalent of cockfighting at altitude.

Even the mourning doves we treat Janus-faced. My uncle with his purebred pointers, a man who called it "buhd huntin," was a chemist for a multinational clay company running an extensive mining operation in central Georgia. He was a man judicious and measured in life. But each fall the executives and major clients flew down from up North to take part in a Georgia dove shoot. No lawman questioned the baited fields, the birds shot by the hundreds; no one questioned that the doves were retrieved, plucked, and gutted by black men without guns; no one was rueful about the pitifully small carcasses packed into ice chests to be ready to fly (now with some assistance) back to New Jersey. Afterward, my uncle would appear at my great-grandmother's house with several dozen doves wrapped in newspaper. She would be gracious to his face, but once he left she had to pluck and clean them all herself, uttering mild oaths, knowing that each one would yield only a few tablespoons of meat most likely studded with birdshot. That kind of carnage took no skill. No one needed to know how to call doves.

Sometimes when I walk the deer paths in my woods, I spy on the doves drinking in the creek. Or worse, they flush from underfoot in a blast that trips my heart. The bird lover's rhetorical question, "How could you *shoot* them?" merges with the hunter's practical "How *could* you shoot them?" It reminds me that the dove of peace is a gambler who bets on surprise.

This year the doves are nesting somewhere in the woods away from my house, so mostly I see them at the feeder and hear them call from deep in the woods. And I remember my grandfather smelling of Prince Albert pipe tobacco, the white stubble on his cheek scratching my ear, his flannel shirt warm against my back as he bent and encircled me with his arms and shaped my hands just so—the fingers of the left hand bundled against themselves, cupped by the fingers of the right hand, hands pressed together to form a hollow, the thumbs parallel for the mouthpiece. Put your lips right here on the knuckles of the thumbs and blow. You'll get it. "Keep trying," he says, "you'll get it." And then I hear the round "whoo," as round as your lips are now, sounding a bit breathy at first and then clear as the dove itself.

Mine

✿ STEPHANIE JOELLE RENFROW

Went walking, yesterday.
Saw you sitting at your
        kitchen window;
the sunflower growing
        from your eye
looked warm and bright, leaning
        into the glass.

Can't talk to you much
        anymore,
so hard to concentrate with that
        Amazing flower
firm and tall, a green and yellow soldier,
        rooted in the finest soil
of your face,
        leaves dripping lightly down your lips
really no room for other kisses.

Wasn't there the day it
sprouted, tender and soft—
        and so weedable—but now no chance
of untangling its roots
        from the depths of your head.

Kept walking, of course;
        nothing left to do.

but keep watching;
    you know, though, nothing
roots me so
    like that plant, footed
in the flowerpot of your eye.

Over

Elizabeth Wynn Banks

The long stems of buttercups
weave together in the dark pasture
as clouds swallow any last stars,
and rain leaks over us all.
You and I slip in and out of dead dreams,
lost to each other and the field outside.
At dawn, we don't say a word.
Wind blows through us and
the buttercups, filled with rain,
tip and empty.

PART II

Speaking of Place

*What makes a place special is the way it buries itself
inside the heart, whether it's flat or rugged, rich or austere,
wet or arid, gentle or harsh, warm or cold, wild or tame.
Every place, like every person, is elevated by the love and
respect shown toward it, and by the way in which its
bounty is received.*

—Richard Nelson, from *The Island Within*

Hiking the Fakahatchee Strand

⚜ Linda Maree

First one foot, then the other. You step into water so cold you might believe you are sinking into a snowdrift in a frozen landscape, a sensation unexpected here in tropical south Florida, especially in the summer. The water seeps into your shoes and begins wicking up your pant legs. You shiver and suck in your breath sharply in surprise. The chill is unpleasant, although at the same time welcome after the long, hot, dusty walk along the deeply rutted trail that led you to this place. This is the South Slough, a gently flowing stream of tea-colored water—the lifeblood of the Fakahatchee Strand.

Unlike the Everglades's sea of grass, which is navigable by airboat, the Fakahatchee Strand is wooded and much of it is accessible only on foot. It is filled with trees, ferns, poison ivy, tangles of vines so dense you might wish, except for your environmental ethic, to hack your way through with a machete, and sharp sawgrass capable of tearing through your clothing and skin. You cannot come to this swamp unprepared; it is unforgiving territory. If you want to enter it fully, you must be willing to get more than your feet wet. Waders are not advisable, not even chest waders. You could fall, or step into an unexpectedly deep pool, and once those waders fill up with water, you are immobilized, subject to hypothermia and other, more terrestrial, perils—think snakes, alligators.

So, you have come today well prepared, wearing high-top sneakers with good traction that will not be sucked off your feet in the muck; you wear a sturdy belt to ensure your water-laden jeans will stay where they belong. You have learned how to eat lunch standing in waist deep water if necessary; you know to move slowly (although, to be honest, there is no other way to move in the swamp), and you know that tall walking sticks are essential for maintaining and regaining balance when slippery surfaces and submerged logs cause missteps, slips, and near falls. You have been warned not to bring anything with you into the swamp that you are not willing to lose. You wonder, momentarily, if this includes your life.

From where you stand now all you can see is dark water, surrounded by an exoskeleton of green vegetation, like a giant terrestrial coral reef that seems endless and impenetrable, and no sign that it will be easy—or even possible—to find your way out again. There are no readily recognizable landmarks from this vantage point. Maybe your sense of direction is not the best—you can get lost in a parking lot; maybe you have the internal compass of a fighter pilot. Either way, you must be careful. This watery landscape covers approximately 80,000 acres—a big place to get lost in—and some of it has not been trod by a human foot in more than half a century.

American alligators, once endangered, and venomous cottonmouth water moccasins live here in abundance. So, before stepping into the water, before you can know how cold it is, you tap your walking stick loudly on one of the large metal culverts that run at intervals underneath the trail and through which the waters of the slough—and its resident critters—pass. You do this to get the attention of any alligators that might be resting in there. Better to startle them while you are still standing on high ground than to frighten them as you step into the slough and, possibly, right into their path. This is how you hike the Fakahatchee Strand.

After the first shock of cold water on hot feet has passed, you move forward cautiously, one slow step at a time, probing with your stick and watching carefully for any sign of reptilian menace.

The Fakahatchee Strand is an elongated swamp in southwest Florida, twenty miles long and five miles wide, not part of Everglades National Park, but an essential component of the larger Everglades ecosystem, which includes land within the park boundaries as well as outlying swamps, strands, sloughs, lakes, and rivers that feed into and drain out of Everglades National Park. The Strand was formed by the dissolving of an underlying limestone base by subterranean water currents; the resulting subsidence caused elongated depressions to form above ground, a mirror of the underground flow. The subsequent accumulation of water and organic material that occurred over many thousands of years in these above-ground depressions make this area one of the richest ecosystems in North America, home to many of Florida's endangered and threatened species, including charismatic critters like the Florida panther and the Florida black bear, as well as numerous plant species, such as the clamshell orchid, threadroot orchid, and the ghost orchid.

The Strand's unique climate, created and moderated by water flow, allows a widely varied combination of both temperate and tropical plants to exist and thrive side by side; it is thought, by some, to be the closest you can get to the feeling of a tropical rainforest in this country. In addition to orchids, it is rich in bromeliads and other epiphytes, ferns, and the largest stand of native royal palms in Florida. Royal palms are aptly named, stately trees that can grow to a height of nearly one hundred feet, taller than three three-story houses stacked on top of each other; they tower over the forest canopy. In fact, only here in the Fakahatchee will you find royal palms growing with bald cypress trees. It is the only forest of its kind in the world.

You step into deeper water, the cold shock progressing up your body as you move deliberately through what looks and feels like flowing iced tea. Your calves, your knees, and finally your thighs are submerged in the chilly liquid. How much deeper does this get? you wonder, but you already know the answer: it's hard to say. So much depends on uncontrollable variables: the weather, human intervention, the water level of Lake Okeechobee to the east. Perhaps you should be concerned with this uncertainty, but surprisingly, you are not. In fact, any discomfort or concern you might have had earlier soon dissipates as you move deeper into the swamp, replaced by an awareness and appreciation for a wild habitat in which you are beginning to feel yourself a welcome guest.

You scan the landscape with appreciative eyes: gnarled, knobby cypress knees poke out of thick muck here and there like mischievous children playing hide and seek, and bright red splashes of flowering bromeliads nestle contentedly in the crooked arms of trees. There are pop ash, pond apple, bald cypress, dogwood, and a half-dead oak scarred with woodpecker holes. A hint of sweet and spicy floral scent hangs in the moist air, and you wonder what smells so good. Sound in this place is muted, like the hush of a winter evening after a heavy snowfall—cavernous quiet evoking a Zen-like peace. Words like holy, mystical, and magical come to your mind. Here, you think, is nature in perfect balance—a balance that shifts and changes, coming back to equilibrium over and over again in a dynamic dance of life. To be here is to recognize that you are not a guest after all, but a partner in the dance.

The Fakahatchee Strand has faced problems in the past, mostly from the excessive cutting of cypress trees by timber companies. The bald cypress is a conifer that, unlike most of its cone-bearing relatives, loses its leaves in the winter; hence its descriptive name. It is a slow-growing tree that is also both termite and rot resistant. In the early 1900s, timber companies descended on the Fakahatchee, intent on taking as much cypress as they could. They built raised earthen beds at regular intervals on which to run rail lines for bringing harvested trees out of the swamp. When lumberjacks first laid long saws to the giant trees there seemed to be an abundant supply, so they felled virtually every mature cypress in the swamp to fill the need for durable lumber for a growing human population. Trees that were found to be unusable (too small, damaged) were either left standing or, if already cut, were abandoned in the gently flowing waters of the slough, where they still lie, decades later. Once all the harvestable trees were cut, the timber companies took their saws and rail lines elsewhere, leaving a bruised and ailing ecosystem behind.

Although badly damaged, the Fakahatchee survived this trauma. The old rail lines were pulled out, but the raised beds, called tramways, remain. These now form a series of trails that traverse the preserve from east to west. Some are suitable for hiking but most are so choked with vegetation that they are unrecognizable as trails. The metal culverts under the trails assure a somewhat truncated, but mostly sufficient water flow from one end of the Strand to the other, which ultimately empties into the Gulf of Mexico in the vicinity of the Ten Thousand Islands. The royal palms that have moved in on their own and populated the edges of these tramways stand like tall sentinels, silent witnesses to the ability of the land to heal—if we just give it a chance.

You've been told that more species of orchids can be seen here in the South Slough than anywhere else in North America and you imagine a veritable greenhouse of corsage-orchids hanging on the limb-wrists of every tree. Unless you know what you are looking for, though, you might think someone has played a mean trick on you. It turns out that not all orchids bloom at the same time, and when not in bloom some orchids are no more than thin, green ropelike roots with an inconspicuous leaf or two clinging tenaciously and unobtrusively to the trunk of a host tree. One of these tree-hugging orchids, the threadroot orchid, a Florida native whose numbers are in decline, when not in flower is just an inconsequential little thread (hence its name), much smaller in diameter than a pencil, with no leaves at all, that has cleverly adapted to produce chlorophyll within its skinny little root-body. Luckily, because some species of orchids prefer to grow on specific types of trees, once you know this and know what to look for, orchid sightings quickly become more plentiful. Until then, even though abundant, most go unnoticed, except by poachers and those like you who are training themselves to see them, admire them, and leave them be.

Shadow witches and ghosts. Many orchids have fanciful and imaginative names like these. Today, the shadow witches stay hidden, but there, before your eyes, is a ghost—orchid, that is. Very rare. The ghost orchid (*Dendrophylax lindenii*), a finicky creature that has resisted easy cultivation, prefers just the type of warm, humid climate the Fakahatchee

Strand provides, and it grows in the wild almost nowhere else on the planet. It dances before you now, its white frog leg petals dangling from a shoot so thin it is barely visible, even in the daytime. At night, the flowers seem to hover in the air, tiny apparitions that attract the gustatory attention of their primary pollinator, the elusive giant sphinx moth (*Cocytius antaeus*), a creature that, given its six-inch-long tongue, you can only assume has a well-defined sense of taste.

Beyond appreciation now, you're absolutely smitten. You've fallen in love with this place. You don't know for sure when it happened, but it did. Maybe it was after lunch, which you ate standing up in knee-high water, with your backpack turned around and hanging from your neck like a feedbag. Maybe it was when you first noticed those unobtrusive yellow flowers over there—a dingy-flowered star orchid in bloom—or the needle-leaf air plant up above, growing on Spanish moss, which itself is sporting extremely tiny, very fragrant, pale yellow flowers, delicate as a butterfly's wing. You didn't even know that Spanish moss, which is ubiquitous in Florida, is a flowering plant. You might have overlooked it completely if you had not been paying attention. *That's* how you fell in love. Paying attention to the little, seemingly insignificant details. You don't even want to think about nearly missing your first glimpse of a clamshell orchid, an endangered species that brings tears to your eyes when you spy it decked out in its rich, yet delicate, wine-and-butter floral finery. This dainty bloom becomes for you a symbol of your growing love for the Fakahatchee Strand and your commitment to doing what you can to convince others that this is a place worth preserving.

The Dividing Spring

🦂 BRENT MARTIN

> *There is another world under this, and it is like ours in every-thing—animals, plants, and people—save that the seasons are different. The streams that come down from the mountains are the trails by which we reach this underworld, and the springs at their heads are the doorways by which we enter it, but to do this one must fast and go to water and have one of the underground people for a guide. We know that the seasons in the underworld are different from ours because the water in the springs is always warmer in the winter and cooler in summer than the outside air.*

—James Mooney, History, from *Myths, and Sacred Formulas of the Cherokees*

Within the heart of the southern Appalachian Mountains, where the Cowee, Nantahala, and Blue Ridge mountains converge, lies a rich tapestry of human and natural history, woven over the millennia from a myriad of interactions between the plant, animal, and inanimate worlds. It is the homeland of the Cherokee people, whose cosmology is a layered interpretation of the complexity of season and geography, the explosion of spring from the grey and stark shadowy world of winter, and the incalculable number of birth and death experiences within one of the oldest mountain ranges on earth. And it is a land of water—water which is present throughout the landscape in powerful and profound display. Mysterious springs bubble forth in small and hidden grottos; waterfalls cascade down narrow and impassable gorges; rivers carve their way through wide and alluvial valleys. As it has shaped this land, so has it shaped the consciousness of its inhabitants.

The journey leading me to these ancient mountains begins with the springs that emerged from the hollows surrounding my boyhood home in the once wild forests of Cobb County, Georgia. One spring that has remained a particularly strong memory was located near an abandoned old farmstead where I squirrel hunted and where I would stop for cool drinks after long autumn and winter sojourns. It was marked by a large spring box, made of roughly worked square stones fitted perfectly into the hillside, its setting completed by a large beech tree full of pocket-knife doodles and arbor-glyphic strangeness. A quartz arrowhead once emerged from the loose soil near its edge, my first such find, which has motivated me to this day to pay attention to the soil beneath my feet. The spring is now gone, submerged beneath a terminal landscape of over-sized suburban homes and decaying strip malls, along with every vestige of that once rich cultural landscape. I will never know its history, nor whether the Cherokees who once inhabited that sacred place revered it, or knew it by name.

However, I am hopeful that such is not the story of the spring that I and three equally interested friends are searching for today. Located near the tiny town of Mountain City in the extreme northeastern cor-ner of Georgia, the spring is said to flow from a point below the spine of the eastern Continental Divide, where the Blue Ridge Mountains drop to a low point of 2,044 feet. This wide and low-lying gap is so indistin-guishable that, were it not for a sign on State Highway 441 signifying its crossing, most travelers would never give it a passing thought. In an 1892 report from the Chief of Engineers to the U.S. Army, which was then considering a canal through the gap, it is described as "one of the most remarkable depressions in the Blue Ridge...and to the traveler passing along this road, it has the appearance of a narrow valley separating two parallel ridges, rather than a gap in a great dividing ridge."

Eighteenth-century explorers mapped and described the gap as a marshy savannah, but today it is a tomato field of several acres that spreads behind a short row of storefronts where bronzed Hispanic workers bend to the task of harvesting under a dazzling autumn sky. On this particular October day, the town is silent but for the endless and steady drone of automobiles and tractor trailers, which occupy this ancient major north-south pathway both night and day.

The significance of this spring derives from the fact that for many thousands of years its waters flowed down into this wide and shallow area where it mingled with waters of other springs, leaving on its journey in opposite directions into two major river basins. Water flowing south from this point winds its way for several miles to the southeast to join the Chattooga River—the rugged mountain setting of James Dickey's controversial novel and film *Deliverance*—where it flows on to the Savannah River and the Atlantic Ocean. Water flowing north forms the Little Tennessee River, which makes its way into the Tennessee River and the Gulf of Mexico.

This in itself is a rare and interesting geographical and geological phenomenon, but the cultural overlay is equally intriguing. To the colonial traders who settled among the Cherokees in the area, the spring was enchanted. This belief was first chronicled by the noted Indian trader James Adair, who passed through the area in 1775 and wrote a vivid description of the spring's mythical powers in his classical work, *History of the American Indians*. By Adair's account, one drink from its waters and the recipient would lose his or her ability to leave, and would spend the next seven years living within the wilds of the ancient Blue Ridge Mountains. This belief was also documented by ethnographer James Mooney, who described the spring in his *Sacred Myths and Formulas of the Cherokee Indians* in 1891.

However, the name that was bestowed upon it after its first documented European encounter was Herbert's Spring, named after Commissioner of Indian Affairs John Herbert, who travelled through the valley in late 1727 and early 1728, and who mapped the Carolinas in 1744. Though Herbert's journal from the period makes no mention of the spring, he spent several months in the area meeting with Cherokee headmen and attempting to rouse them against the Lower Creeks, who had attacked colonials near the Altamaha River in southern Georgia. One can only speculate that Herbert must have described the area's geographical features somewhere in some detail, with this significant gap and spring registering with particular vividness in his consciousness. Herbert's Savannah, however, does not show up formally on a map until 1764, when British Army officer and historian, Thomas Mante, mapped the area in great detail.

Mante's map shows Herbert's Savannah and spring prominently on the map. It is drawn in as a large savannah, signifying the low-lying marsh that existed there before the era of draining, channelizing, and filling. America's great naturalist William Bartram also passed through the gap in 1775, and though he does not mention Herbert's Spring, or the savannah, he describes in some of the most rapturous language of the time the location's lush meadows, waterfalls, and streams.

Well over two hundred years later, there are four of us who are passing through this gap in search of the remains of its rich history. Dr. Tom Hatley is the recent past chair of Cherokee Studies at Western Carolina University, and author of *Dividing Paths*, a seminal work on Cherokee people and their interactions with colonial South Carolina settlers. Tom has corresponded with me for some time now about the significance and possible location of the spring. He tells us that there is only one other such spring in the eastern United States, and that its significance was so profound that the two tribes that were connected to it culturally had refused to include it in land-cession treaties in the early nineteenth century.

Carrie McLachlan teaches Native American history at Western Carolina University, and is in the final stages of a dissertation on Cherokee religion. She is meticulous in her search for the spring's location, and she and Lamar Marshall pore over the maps like bloodhounds, searching for every geographical and topographical nuance, determined to place us in the proper location. Lamar works for the nonprofit organization Wild

South as cultural heritage director, where he identifies and protects cultural heritage sites.

We have determined that a prominent spring on the USGS map for the area is our most likely candidate. The spring is noted as Darling Spring, and it sits astride the divide in a well-defined nook that should not be hard to locate, especially since Darling Spring road is one of the few roads that make up the town's small intersection. We drive the road slowly until we determine that we are at the curve where the spring should be located. An older home sits directly across the road from where we believe the spring to be, tucked away and invaded by an overgrown thicket of nonnative privet and multiflora rose.

Just to the west of the spring's location, a modern new home sits in a manicured and well-hidden setting. The gravel road that parallels the drainage the spring bubbles from is a string of broken-down singlewide trailers and dilapidated automobiles. Uncertain as to whether or not we are in the right place, we push our way through the thicket to where we believe the spring to be. It is only a few yards before we see a small PVC pipe emerging from beneath the soil, water flowing steadily despite a debilitating drought. Our excitement is not enough to disguise what is a depressing little sight, with exotic vegetation and a worn-out and eroding hillside above us.

We decide it best to inform the locals as to what we are up to, so I advance to the older home in hopes of meeting the occupants. The woman who greets me warily becomes more curious once I spew out our strange inquiry, and explains that her husband is busy but will be out soon to talk with us. While we wait on Mr. Dotson I decide to approach the owner of the much larger new home, who is immediately interested in our excursion. He explains in an accent that is not of this place that the spring is on his property and that we are welcome to explore, and would we like something cold to drink on this warm October day?

We climb back into the privet thicket and quickly find above the spring pipe a brick tiled floor that is covered with a carpet of vinca and

English ivy. It clearly was a significant location in recent times and the reasons for its disrepair and current insignificance are a mystery. At about this point we see Mr. Dotson emerge from his home and amble towards us, squinting in the bright sunlight. He is perhaps seventy years old, maybe a little older, and tells us he has lived here all of his life. We explain our search for the spring and he seems mildly impressed that anyone would care. He explains that the spring was once a gathering place where people would come to get water and that a pavilion once protected it. We have clearly found that floor today. According to Mr. Dotson it has always been called Darling Spring, but when I ask him if he has ever heard it referred to as Herbert's Spring, he shifts and cocks his head and says, "Yeah, I have," in a way that seems slightly uncertain.

However, as we study the maps more closely, along with Adair's description of its location, we become increasingly certain that Darling Spring, despite its significance, is not Herbert's Spring. Adair's original description reads:

> From the head of the southern branch of Savannah river it does not exceed half a mile to a head spring of the Mississippi water that runs through the middle and upper parts of the Cherokee nation about a northwest course, and, joining other rivers, they empty themselves into the great Mississippi. The above fountain is called 'Herbert's spring,' so named from an early commissioner of Indian affairs, and it was natural for strangers to drink thereof, to quench thirst, gratify their curiosity, and have it to say they had drank of the French waters.

Since we have determined that Darling Spring is clearly a head branch of the Savannah, Herbert's Spring and the once-French waters of the Mississippi must lie somewhere within a half mile to the north.

On our second trip, we return to examine the large area where the savannah would have been had it not been ditched, drained, and filled.

It is a spectacular autumn day, and we decide to stop and ask the workers who are finishing up the tomato harvest if we might walk around the large field for a bit. I know enough broken Spanish to determine that the *jefe* of this group leases the field, and has no problem with us walking about. The low-lying area is ringed with watery ditches and one small bold stream that bisects the area. Hatley examines a bit of clay that he describes as common to hydric soils, which signifies historical water coverage. River cane, once abundant and culturally significant to the Cherokees, is attempting to creep back in, though it will have a difficult time with the constant clearing and alteration of water flow.

Back in the car, we follow the divide's undulating contours around to where we find the large stream called Black's Creek on our topographical map, which flows out of a deep hollow and is clearly a headwater stream of the Little Tennessee River. We stop to look at a small pond that is full in this record drought, and a small stream that feeds it. It is next to a rambling old mountain home, which was most likely located here for the constant flow of clean water. We also visit another farm with a small sign out front that reads "Tennvannah Farm." A small stream parallels the driveway, and since the home sits next to the old trade path that is now State Highway 441, it is a good candidate. We drive slowly up the gravel road, and when we reach the farmhouse at its end to find its occupants not home, we decide it best to leave rather than taking the liberty of walking around.

Traveling slowly back for one last look at the Darling Spring and the drive beyond it, we search the slopes for any hint of another spring. Even in drought we speculate that surely such a significant spring would have some water or moisture to mark its origin. If the Darling Spring was the head of the southern branch of the Savannah River, then Herbert's Spring must lie somewhere along the route to Black's Creek and the Tennvannah Farm.

On the drive back to Darling Spring, we go slowly and look closely at the pasture land just to the north. At about a half mile north of the spring, we all remark upon a small pond, about twenty feet long, that lies excavated out of a hillside with no apparent water source. A coppice of scruffy trees obscures our view and since we cannot see it closely, we are uncertain as to whether this is a spring. But it is getting late in the day, so we must return for a third visit.

Once I return home, I e-mail Carrie to ask about her interest in the spring. She tells me about her dissertation and sends an excerpt that includes a quotation from noted nineteenth-century librarian and historian Charles Lanman's *Letters from the Alleghany Mountains* (1854):

> Long ago, a Cherokee Headman, Kostoyeak, Sharp Shooter, fell in love with a Yamasee maiden. But because of her great beauty and family connections she was desired by many suitors of various tribes. Her father, a Yamasee chief, devised a contest to try the suitors. The man who succeeded in finding the common source of the two great river systems that flowed in opposite directions from the continental divide, the Savannah River and the Tennessee River, would marry this Yamasee maiden. According to Lanman's account, Kostoyeak succeeded in finding the source at "a gorge—now called the gap of the Blue Ridge as well as Rabun Gap—where the two great rivers 'shake hands and commence their several journeys.

Accounts such as Lanman's, as well as Adair's and Mooney's, seized the imagination of nineteenth-century American novelist Mary Noailles Murfree (1850–1922), who wrote under the pseudonym Charles Egbert Craddock. In the March 1900 issue of *Harper's*, Murfree published "A Victor at Chungke," a fictional account of the Cherokee ball game "hungke" and of the attendant colonial traders who lived among the Cherokee during the difficult years following the French and Indian War. In describing one such trader and his life among the Cherokees, Murfree writes:

He was possessed by that extraordinary renunciation of civilization which now and again was manifested by white men thrown
among the Cherokee tribe.... Whether the wild sylvan life had
some peculiarly irresistible attraction; whether the world beyond
held for them responsibilities and laborious vocations and irk-
some ties which they would fain evade; whether they fell under
the bewitchment of "Herbert's Spring," after drinking whereof
one could not quit the region of the Great Smoky Mountains,
but remained in that enchanted country for seven years, fascinated, lapsed in perfect content—it is impossible to say. There is
a tradition that when the attraction of the world would begin to
reassert its subtle reminiscent forces, these renegades of civilization were wont to repair anew to this fountain to quaff again of
the ancient delirium and to revive its potent spell.

Murfree borrowed heavily from Adair's account, written more than
seventy-five years earlier. Adair's description of Herbert's Spring, which
might have had its own fictional qualities reads:

Some of our people, who went only with the view of staying a
short time, but by some allurement or other exceeded the time
appointed, at their return reported, either through merriment or
superstition, that the spring had such a natural bewitching quality that whosoever drank of it could not possibly quit the nation
during the tedious space of seven years. All the debauchees readily fell in with this superstitious notion as an excuse for their bad
method of living, when they had no proper call to stay in that
country; and in process of time it became as received a truth as
any ever believed to have been spoken by the Delphic oracle.

On the third trip back to the area, only Lamar and I remain from the
original crew, but we are joined by another interested party, Honor

Woodard, a local painter and photographer who draws inspiration from the cultural and natural history of the area. It is a dreary and soggy day when we gather at the Mountain City post office. A thick cloud bank hangs over the Blue Ridge and the recently plowed savannah is a wash of mud. We drive up the road to the farm where we think Herbert's Spring might gurgle into the small pond we had noticed on the previous trip. The house that sits at its edge is fairly modern, and though we are doubtful that they are the owners, it is a place to start.

I am elected spokesperson for the group and so walk to the door alone, a stranger with a strange tale. The woman who greets me is friendly, curious, and talks rapidly as I sit before her long bookshelf and a collection of old blue Ball Mason jars. Her silent husband appears to be in poor health, and he stares steadily ahead as we talk, sipping from a small carton of lowfat milk while we prattle away about the spring. She seems interested in the history, and tells me that the family who owns the pond is most likely at work. Although she thinks the Hooper family would have no problem with us walking around, it is a farm with dogs and farm animals to consider.

She is so intrigued by our story that she thinks it best to call the Hoopers at work and see if it is possible for us to take a look around. After a few minutes of chatting, she hands the phone over to me. No, Mrs. Hooper knows nothing about Herbert's Spring, but will be happy to have her husband give us a call if we would like to have a look around. We leave, and I agree to return with the story when it is complete. Since we haven't been given permission to look around, we drive back out to the road and park, standing in the rain and peering about for a better view of the dip in the pasture, where a small grove of trees sits above the pond and where the spring might indeed be located.

After a few minutes, Lamar declares that he thinks the spring is on the other side of the savannah, at Tennvannah Farm. We had considered this possibility before, but could not look around because of its absent owners. Lamar has researched all of the historical maps, and the old trading path through the gap clearly was on the west side of the savannah. It would make sense that travelers passing through would stop to get water and rest at a spring that was close to their path. We drive the road up to the old farmhouse at the top of a knoll, and find that it appears to be empty. An old log smokehouse sits on the hill behind it, and a corn crib of similar appearance sits just beyond it. A crew of motley looking dogs gather about me and sniff.

As I am approaching the door to knock, a small car pulls in to the driveway behind me and a woman of about sixty gets out. She is friendly, trusting, and invites me in. As I am explaining to her why we are there, I begin to realize that I am in one of the oldest mountain homes I have ever been in. Sitting at a desk within is Ray Connor, her husband, who has a friendly grin and speaks with a rugged mountain accent. He tells me quickly that he is a pastor at the Church of God in nearby Hiawassee, and that he is only the caretaker of this property, not the owner. He has been there for eleven years, though, and has studied the place over pretty well. He points to a hill behind the house where the Scruggs family, who built the home, lies in eternal rest.

"The Scruggs built this place in 1825," he says. Cherokee land, I think, the home built only fifty years after Adair and Bartram passed through. Only seventy-five years after Herbert himself passed the winter here and claimed it with his name. I tell him about our search for the spring, and he instantly begins telling me of a spring on the property that was renowned for its quality and appearance. "It was such a good flow that they made a log flume from it down to the railroad tracks to fill up the trains," he says, as we exit the house to retrieve Lamar and Honor.

The spring is there below the house, in a small amphitheatre of stacked stone, gurgling forth on this wet December day much as Herbert himself must have seen it. Our instincts and research tell us that this is the place. From where the spring leaves the dark earth from beneath large stones, a small circular pool has been carved from rock to serve as a basin. It is perhaps two and a half feet across and six inches deep. Its water is warmer than the outside air and perhaps there is an underworld beyond its entrance that we will never know. We kneel to drink from the spring, one at a time. The rain is steady, and the hemlocks and rhodo-dendron sag with days of saturation. We take photos and plan with Mr. Connor for a return visit.

On our way out, we stop to look at an ancient and enormous beech tree, just a few yards from the spring, covered in undecipherable scrib-blings. Lamar thinks it is at least three hundred years old, and that with powdered chalk we might interpret some of the carvings grown wide with age. Did a boy stand here once who pulled artifacts from the soil? Are Herbert's initials somewhere buried in that tree's old gray cambium layer, grown thick with the widening gulf of time?

Two more stops before we drive back home—one to locate a possi-ble Indian ceremonial mound that Mr. Connor has told us of not far down the river, another to partake in the local fare at Country Vittles. We drive to the river and walk downstream through a recently plowed field, where old potatoes lie rotting in the mud. Agriculture, houses, and roads have taken their toll on the river in this low-gradient section, and the steep and collapsing banks are far from their original condition. The rain is growing heavier, but we see what we think is the mound, and stare across the river at it and wonder. There are large trees growing from its summit, and stones scattered about. Despite our shared knowledge of the mounds within the Little Tennessee River valley, we have heard nothing of this mound until today, and are mystified.

What we know is that this dark and silt-laden river has traveled be-tween these long-worked fields for many, many years, and that many have come before us and drunk deeply from its source a few miles up the road. There are plans to widen this section of state highway, as they have to the south of here, where Atlanta's sprawling metropolis has pushed growth out deep into these old and majestic mountains. Real concerns abound about Atlanta's need for water and the possibility of interba-sin transfers out of the Little Tennessee River. Vacation homes ring the ridgetops, and tourists come from all directions to enjoy the area's na-tional forests and whitewater paddling.

Walking back to the car, I reflect upon my years of living in this magnificent valley, and on the layered and rich history that I walk upon and inherit. It feels like home, and it feels like a home worth protecting. Now I have drunk from the sacred spring, and am perhaps confined to these mountains even against my will. But should hope begin to fade, I will *repair anew to this fountain to quaff again of the ancient delirium and to revive its potent spell.*

Aubade

🏵 JULIA SHIPLEY

An aubade is a goodbye song sung by a lover
to the beloved upon parting.

This one-lane road was not so much laid down as worn into the sand, dragged through a shrubby thicket of branches interlaced like hands holding hands. My brother and I are sprawled in the middle of the sand track, spelling our names in the sand with our fingers. We pull the letters through the inch-thick dust. I, the elder, can make my letters more legible. I write my name over his. When he lurches to rewrite it, I begin to draw a circle around an ant, revising the circle as the ant crawls off each island. Neither of us hear the engine—a quick honk from the car jolts us. There are tiny white pebbles stuck in the tread crevices of its tires. Its grill has skinny plastic tubes attached, with fishing poles rising whip thin from them. Above the hunkering hood, above the windshield wipers and steering wheel, at the top of all we can see, a smiling man waits for us to stand and scramble out of the road into the dust-covered scrub oak, poison ivy, and bayberry to let him pass. His tires crush our names and replace them with diamonds and zags.

I won't name a beach, although their names are beautiful: Miacomet, Pocomo, Monomoy, Polpis, Wauwinet. I won't say it was a vista with waves unfurling into foam. I won't claim any of the three lighthouses, their beams lancing each other through dark or fog-choked nights. It isn't the feel of jouncing over cobblestones, nor is it going to the grocery store in flip-flops with hot stinging skin and the bathing suit's dampness leeching into my shorts. It isn't a morning glory slinking up a white picket, and it's not standing under a warm outdoor shower interrupted by gusts of breeze.

It is halfway down Shimmo Pond Road, turn right, then most of the way down South Valley Road. It's the place between the house my parents rented throughout my childhood, and the house they bought when I started high school. This spot of blonde grit that isn't a spot, the way the river isn't the same river with water sluicing through every moment, is part of it. But what I pick is the middle of the road where we sank to our knees to look at a broken shell, then lowered further till the sand shifted and filled the space between the backs of our knees.

Why a road, why the middle of the road, why the middle of a one-lane, sand-packed track? Because it was ours. Our concentration enveloped it, and it absorbed us, offering us one ant hole and a stunted prickle of grass. We were ignorant that the rabbit-infested scrub behind us would one day be scuffed and scraped for more houses, that a tract of grapevine and beach plum would sell for almost a million dollars. It was simply that there we squatted in the middle of our childhood, in the almost quiet road that was ours that hour, the way the topmost twig belongs to the bird that sings from it.

Hornbills o'Plenty:

Birdwatching by Bike in West Africa

✳ PHILIP JOHANSSON

The first paradise flycatcher I saw was undeniably in its element. This stunning bird appeared in the dappled sunlight of a dense riverine forest, a deep green Eden that flows into Kenya's Rift Valley. I saw the bird for only an instant, a blaze of red and turquoise hawking into the clouds of butterflies that hovered over the water. But it was enough to confirm my suspicion: I was in paradise.

The second sighting was not so clear. Then I found the paradise flycatcher on the outskirts of Ouagadougou, Burkina Faso, by a waste-choked rivulet where citizens tended their rice patties and washed their clothes. The bird was all white this time, with a dangling snow-white tail that doubled its length. He defied the dirtiness of his environs against all odds. The paradise flycatcher is a striking bird in any setting, but here he represented to me a vestige of paradise lost.

West Africa does not enjoy the reputation of East Africa as a haven for unusual wildlife. A particularly cruel colonial history, fueled by trade in gold, ivory, and human beings, left the modern West African nations with depleted wildlife populations, and with little infrastructure to preserve what was left. The removal of dwindling forest resources, desertification, and growing human populations continue to put a strain on wild habitats. But despite its history, West Africa still hosts a diversity of wildlife that astounds most visitors from temperate climates, like me.

My wife and I spent five months bicycling around West Africa, experiencing its varied environments and the people who live in them. Our trip took us through Côte d'Ivoire, Mali, Burkina Faso, and Ghana. We biked through rain forest, savannah, and sahel, and past more humble little villages than you could possibly shake a bicycle spoke at. But our visit would not have been complete without an appreciation for the birds that still make their home there. While paradise may be a distant memory in West Africa, there are still more than one thousand species of birds to welcome anyone paying attention.

Showy flycatchers are fine for flourishing introductions, but hornbills are more helpful in defining our bicycle voyage. Hornbills are uniquely tropical, uniquely visible—even from a bike—and, well, just plain unique. Often we would see them settling in haughty flocks among the fronds of an oil palm, or preening themselves like African queens in a sheernut tree. Sometimes we would just hear them. But they were always there, scimitar-billed harbingers of our progress along bumpy roads, reminders that we were not in Kansas anymore.

We saw four species of hornbill during the course of our adventures: piping hornbills, black-and-white-tailed hornbills, grey hornbills, and red-beaked hornbills. All are on the small side by hornbill standards, ranging from seventeen to twenty-one inches, and lack the grotesque boney beak protuberances, called casques, sported by some. They are neither as massive as the ground hornbill, nor as elegant as the white-crested hornbill, with its long, tapered tail: they are just your average Joe Hornbills. But each of the four species is unique in its own right, and each characterizes a particular habitat we passed through on our trip.

The first hornbill we saw was perhaps the most distinctive, the piping hornbill. We were in the parking lot of an Abidjan supermarket when we saw a flock of eight pipers beeline overhead with determined flaps of their white-blazed black wings. This hornbill has a heavier build and beak than the other three, and is the most social—one could say raucous. We continued to see them, and especially to hear them, as we biked our way through the fragmented forest along the coast and into the interior of Côte d'Ivoire.

Where continuous rain forest once sprawled north from the coast, we found only patchy secondary growth or plantations of palm, cacao, and coconut. Eroding red hillsides and village gardens were punctuated by truly giant trees, reaching more than 120 feet over the landscape, reminders of the forest's former magnitude. In the weedy scrub skirting the roads and farms there thrived a coterie of opportunistic birds. Senegal coucals, large members of the cuckoo family, swooped from scrub to ground like silent shadows of chestnut and glossy black. Small, glossy finches called bronze mannikins dangled from grass heads, and pin-tailed wydahs gathered finicky harems with their sexy but cumbersome tails. Spooky bald-faced harrier hawks clung to epiphytic staghorn ferns to drink the trapped water. Palm vultures labored with broad white wings over lagoons and ridges, specialists with a uniquely expanding habitat in the sprawling palm plantations. Along the rivers and lagoons, the song of the red-eyed dove was unarguably the prototype for the "Cuckoo for Cocoa Puffs" commercial. And in the dense foliage of the highest trees, the piping hornbills gathered in conspicuous flocks to quarrel and squawk.

Largely overlapping with the range of the piping hornbill, the black-and-white-tailed hornbill was present in the fragmented upland forest but also straggled well into the savannah region of northern Côte d'Ivoire. They have a lighter build than the former and a weaker, more undulating flight, cupping the humid air with their lanky wings. Ironically, they have a more "piping" song than the raucous piping hornbills, a querulous descending laugh reminiscent of gulls. We found them laughing their hearts out on the tops of palms and flying in floppy flocks across the road.

As we biked north into the upland forest, and the domain of the black-and-white hornbill, a new menagerie of birds welcomed us and expanded our horizons. Senegal fire finches became so common that an hour would not pass without seeing them ornamenting some thicket like bright red berries. In the ponds and reservoirs we found chestnut-winged lily trotters, with their improbable spidery feet that they use to walk on pond vegetation, Jesus-style. And on the margins, the most striking of the many birds we saw in the weaver finch family, fire-crowned bishops fluffed their crimson plumage for maximum effect. Fine-spotted woodpeckers, with handsome green backs and red crests, made their way up and down snags in forest clearings. And at the edge of cacao planta-tions, where enormous sebele trees marked the northern extent of the former rain forest, pairs of hawks called shikras glided between short wing beats.

The wooded savannah of northern Côte d'Ivoire and Ghana, and into Mali and Burkina Faso, marked the domain of the inimitable grey hornbill. Lacking the apparent formal pretense of its forest cousins, this mottled grey-and-white bird is a hornbill's hornbill. Grey hornbills are haughty to the core, and lanky to the appearance of dislocation. In flight they climb clumsily and then arc with wings closed as if shot from a can-non, only to brake with their rounded wings and climb again. Their song is more plaintive and broken than the black-and-white-tailed, and ut-tered joyfully with beak held high and wings ajar.

As we biked through the wooded savannah, vast reaches of waving grasses or burnt stubble were broken by scraggly sheernut and dawadawa trees, affording many glimpses of grey hornbills and their many winged neighbors. African golden orioles nested in roadside scrub, appearing remarkably like giant goldfinches. Blue-bellied rollers perched alertly on power lines, looking as drab as a crow until the sun caught a flash of their turquoise and cobalt wing-patches and gave them away. Grasshop-per buzzards swooped on rufous wings from their low perches, or just stood alongside cattle egrets at the edge of shrinking puddles, awaiting the jackpot of stranded aquatic critters. Carmine bee-eaters fairly soared overhead, and red-cheeked cordon-bleus flitted in and out of grass tufts like sparks of ethereal blue flame. Patches of woodland were haunted by the sonorous song of the wood hoopoe, sounding like the forest's finger on the rim of a wine glass.

Beyond the savannah, where the grasslands stretch thinly toward the Sahara Desert, the sahel region was the extreme of the lush forest in which we began. It was a barren, parched landscape, with only an oc-casional unearthly baobab tree or mango grove to break its spell. Here, red-billed hornbills stood out in brilliant white, black, and red among the somber earth tones. This smallest of the hornbills we saw was as at home sagging from a leafless shrub as a piping hornbill was perched in the canopy of mighty forest giants. Their flight was lanky and undulating like the grey, but the fire of their bright red bill added a certain self-consciousness to the act. Their song was more monotonous and melancholy than the others, a tooting rather than a fluting. Perhaps their red-billed throats were as dry as ours.

The arid monotone of the red-billed hornbill's habitat made other birds stand out as well. Little green bee-eaters hung like emerald light from the boughs of mango trees, and flocks of long-crested helmet shrikes brooded among bare saplings as if they were contemplating some misdeed. White-crowned cliff chats swaggered on the ground between giant stones, kicking among the dry grass for insects. Long-tailed doves shot across the dusty horizon with their stiff comet tails, and chestnut-backed finch-larks fussed among the roadside stubble, their white ear coverts and collars looking like faces on the back of their heads.

These feathered citizens, and many more than I can mention, ushered us through West Africa's extremes, from the coastal rain forest to the barren edge of the desert. Our bicycle tour was brightened by the diversity of birds that hailed us along the way. Every sighting, from the bright pygmy kingfisher near the coast to the big-headed hammerkops on shrinking sahel ponds, was a colorful incentive to go on. But the hornbills, those well-beaked icons of tropical exotica, accompanied us all the way. As we headed south again from Burkina Faso through Ghana and finally back to Côte d'Ivoire, the reverse succession of familiar red-billed, grey, black-and-white-tailed, and piping hornbills was like a welcome home.

The Bench

♪Ȉ Aɴɴ B. Dᴀʏ

There is a smile on her face and beads of perspiration on her forehead when she finds me with some of our guests in rocking chairs on the back porch of the farmhouse.

"I made it all the way to the bench this time," she says, her sense of victory clear in her eyes. She drops her cane to receive our hugs as we file down the porch steps to congratulate her.

The bench has been a goal, a destination for hundreds of people who have come to our farm over the last fifty years. This sturdy wooden seat is about 1,500 yards above our farm guest house on a south-sloping hillside in the Green Mountains of Vermont.

A mowed path leads up through the field to the upper pasture fence. A small wild apple tree, several thorn apples, gray birch, and steeplebush grow along the fence line, where beyond Scotch Highland cattle graze and doze under a grove of white pines.

From this spot there is a wide view of the Mad River bending north through the valley below. Hay fields and ski lodges line the banks and Vermont Route 100 runs from north to south into Granville Gulf. The Northfield Ridge rises to the east and Lincoln, Glen Ellen, and Stark mountains rule the western side. Just below is our big red barn, the barnyard, and pastures with horses and cows.

In any season a climb to the bench to sit awhile and watch the east glow orange-pink and then the sunlight spreading long birch-tree shadows across the snow or grass fills me with peace.

The solid wood seating space was created during the 1960s by my husband, Frank Day, in his converted horse-barn workshop. He used five two-by-two sugar maple pieces four feet long and laid them lengthwise, side by side, on two cross boards, leaving an inch space between each two-by-two.

He then cut two, six-foot-long maple four-by-fours for the legs and sealed them with several coats of stain. The seat was stained and then shellacked to protect it from the weather.

Frank and I and our two teenaged children walked around the upper field and pasture to decide on the place with the best view, next to the wild apple tree and cattle fence.

He dug three-foot holes for the posts. I held the post upright in the hole for him as he back-filled and tamped stone after stone into the hole to make it tight. When both posts had been set, we installed the seat of the slatted two-by-twos and secured it with bolts.

It was done, and a tradition was born. Our guests, visitors and family could walk to the bench to watch the movement of the day, to meditate, to talk one-on-one. There was ample room for two.

One Quaker couple from Long Island stayed at our farm each summer for thirty consecutive years. They would hold hands as they climbed the hill. During the last years of their visits, it took them much longer to make it to the bench. I can still see them sitting side by side looking out over the valley.

A blind woman, Linda, lived at the farm with her family for six years in the 1980s. At first her father or brother would guide her up to the bench. After a few months, she could go by herself. She knew many of the bird songs and would come back to the farmhouse to tell us what birds she had heard.

When a guest came into the kitchen, Linda would introduce herself and ask if they had just arrived at the farm. If they were new people, she would tell them to be sure to go up the hill to the bench to see the birds and take in the gorgeous view.

In 1966, Frank had a mental breakdown. Four years later, on July 28, 1970, he took his own life. That night the moon was full. Our two children, Deb and Alan, Deb's future husband, Mike, and I took blankets and a bottle of wine and walked up through the duskiness to the pasture corner. We lay on the blankets next to the bench and gazed at the deep purple-blue sky. We could hear the Highland cows on the other side of the fence as they moved about, lowing softly to their calves.

We talked about Frank and his creative way with wood. We remembered how he encouraged everyone to climb the hill, not for the view but because of the challenge and the reward.

A shooting star flared across the sky.

"There he goes," said Alan, "he's free."

Now, as I give a congratulatory hug to our elderly guest who made it up to the bench and back by herself, with only the use of her cane to help her arthritic knee, I ask, "How was it?"

"Wonderful, wonderful! I made my goal," she answers with a glow. "I sat there a long time, just to take it all in."

The valley is changing. There is increased traffic, encroaching noise, migrating tourists, huge houses, scarred mountains, and the river drained down for snow making.

But the path to the bench remains for those who want to climb the hill, sit and listen to the bluebirds, the pileated woodpecker, the black-capped chickadees in the winter birches. Or see the sun strike the tops of the frosted mountains, glimpse a red fox crossing the pasture only a few yards away.

The bench will be there, waiting.

Leaving Dorland Mountain

ALISON TOWNSEND

*I have before seen other countries, in the same manner, give
themselves to you when you are about to leave them, but I
had forgotten what it meant.*

—Isak Dinesen

On the last night,
when I do not dare to hope
that I might see them again,
they come to me, the beautiful
mother and her long-legged daughter,
drifting into the clearing
in coats of tawny smoke.
When I put my book down,
blow the final lamp out and pad,
barefoot through the kitchen
for a glass of cold water,
I see them, lying down together
on the rough grass outside
my window, like two dreams
kneeling on a carpet
of finely woven light.

The moon is everywhere.
Almost full on this warm night,
rising above oak trees in a brief
swell of abandon before autumn,

she shows them to me
—what I have seen by day
but must meet in another
way before leaving—
this pair who browse there
beside me with no other purpose
but pleasure, moon-bathing
and waiting among the chirr
of crickets and hoots
of the horned owl,
resting, but not asleep.

They're so close I can see
their flanks moving, each breath
rippling like water beneath their ribs.
I can see their ears, translucent
as furred shells, flicking at sounds
I do not notice, and feel their gaze,
lambent as the moon itself,
turned deeply upon me
until the window melts
and there is nothing between us
but breathing measured
by the night's slow pulse.

The forest heaves
within my body, completely herself
in the guise of these lithe,
delicate women who come to say
that she will take me.
The reward for silence
and attention is acceptance.
The moon will do the rest.

And as I watch, the doe
begins to lick her daughter's face
softly, so softly I can almost
feel her tongue caress
my pale cheek into
russet velvet layered
over wands of slender bone.
All I want to do
is lie down there beside them,
slipping free of this tight skin
and letting that wild mother
lick me and tongue me and
polish me into a new life,
glistening and raw
as any naked creature
brought to birth from darkness
and baptized by the moon.

I want to go out there.
But because I want to keep them
this way; because the sound of my
foot on a loose board alarms them,
because I've been permitted
entrance into a secret world, I don't.

I just stand here, for a long time
drinking cold water
and watching, while the deer
watch beside me.

The forest holds me.
In the hushed, nearly imperceptible
pause that comes between each breath

I am her own daughter,
innocent again and holy.

I have never felt so safe.

Prairie Skin

✿ · SUSAN FUTRELL

I have driven past the brown sign along the highway at the Colfax/Mingo exit a hundred times: Neal Smith National Wildlife Refuge, this exit. I'm usually in too much of a hurry for meandering, and I drive on down the interstate, taking the fast route.

This time when the sign beckons, my husband and I take the exit and turn south. We wind through Colfax, home of the toy train museum and Colfax Mineral Water, following small brown signs that lead us like a treasure hunt along the county roads for another ten miles to Prairie City. It's a rundown little place, paint peeling off all the houses except one at the edge of town, where the yard and driveway are filled with bright wooden lawn ornaments for sale. There is a dairy and a school, a gas station, and an ice cream shop that looks as if it could get busy on a summer evening.

On the south edge of town, a narrow asphalt road leads off into a curving expanse of what looks like pasture. Farmhouses, silos, and electric towers thin out to wider sections of open horizon; at first, there's nothing much to notice. We wind down into gentle hills, still mostly shades of brown as winter slowly lets go. A mile or so in, we see a small herd of buffalo, bulky and rugged, grazing slowly across the field.

I can see the marketing challenge here. Vision has to be wide, but you have to look close, and not much is moving—certainly not anything you could ride on or float down or climb. The postcards will definitely need captions.

When we reach the Prairie Learning Center at the wildlife refuge, we are still within sight of two farms, off to the south and east. Between them, a dark swath of trees along a creek bed and the light brown hills rolling off to the west hint at being wide open. The parking lot has only a handful of cars.

It is quiet here, or what passes for quiet in this modern, well-inhabited time and place. Birds are trilling, there is the occasional sound of a distant car, and an almost constant drone of jet airplanes overhead, the approaching flight lanes to the Des Moines airport twenty-five miles away. Flies buzz, a hot early spring sun bakes winter-pale skin, a breeze makes soft strumming on the leaves of grass.

A sign along the path instructs us to look out over the hill and savannah, once the farm home of Arthur and Leona Bolvier. "Jasper County prairie land developed over thousands of years; in less than seventy years it was nearly gone." An old photo of a man with a plow is positioned on the sign next to a drawing of prairie flowers in bloom. I wonder if the irony is intentional; was it his plow that tore those flowers from the soil?

Farther down the path, we stop to sit at a wooden bench dedicated by the relatives of Aunt Leona on her one hundredth birthday, soaking in the quiet and the warm smells of vegetation and earth. From this vantage point you can see the grain elevators of Prairie City on the horizon beyond.

Virgin prairie remnants in the Midwest survive mostly in places too small or useless to have been plowed—cemeteries, schoolyards, and along railroads and fencerows. The land in the Neal Smith National Wildlife Refuge is not virgin prairie. It's been plowed and grazed and built on, and is undergoing a slow reclamation. Still, it may be that some bits of the virgin prairie are scattered here, along the fences of what was once Aunt Leona's yard.

As we follow the loop of the trail back toward the visitor center we encounter a man and a young girl, his granddaughter perhaps. She is wearing a little red hat with ears that make her look like a tiny devil in costume, but up close she looks more like a kitten. "Beautiful place, isn't it?" we say by way of greeting. "It sure is," he nods slowly. " I come here whenever I'm in Iowa, unless it is the dead of winter." He tells us he is from Idaho and asks if we will take a picture of them. He hands over his instamatic camera and we snap a photo, the little red kitten smiling obediently, the prairie rolling out to the vacant sky behind them.

A few years ago, there was a proposal to build a rain forest just outside our town. At least, it was going to have some of the plants of a rainforest, and some of the animals, and perhaps even birds, although presumably not the ones that migrate. And it would have some soil with the same properties as soil in the rainforest, and moisture would be added to the air and soil at the same rate as in a rainforest, and sun would shine, although it is Iowa after all, so sun would shine only when it shines in Iowa. All of these things would make this place enough like a rainforest to put up a sign calling it such. It would be enclosed in glass and metal, and surrounded by a building and a parking lot so it couldn't be easily seen from the outside, and so the animals and birds couldn't get out. Because it would in essence be indoors, it would be possible and necessary to convince people to pay money for the privilege of going inside to see and experience it.

A rainforest is a rich and diverse ecosystem, home to thousands of species of insects, plants, lichens, birds, animals. The Rainforest Action Network says only 20 percent of the Earth's tropical rainforest is left. The story is familiar by now: The forests are being cut and burned and harvested at a rapid rate, and species are becoming extinct as quietly as we breathe in and out. Reservoirs of biological knowledge, medicines for untold ills, all are being lost even to those of us who have never been to the rainforest. What else is being lost to the people who live there— languages, places, home?

That Americans know about the rainforest at all is no accident. It is part of a calculated strategy, with costs and risks of its own, to preserve what is left of the tropical rainforest by turning it into a commodity that has value only if intact. Rainforest products—shade-grown coffee, brazil nuts, buttons made from tagua seeds—are marketed, and ecotourism is promoted, and donations of 1 percent of profits to rainforest causes are used to sell all kinds of products, from toys to clothes to juices and snacks—all part of a campaign to create economic value in the forest so it will be saved.

It is the prospect of loss, and the fear and fascination of loss, that would presumably compel so many people to stop off at the glass-walled version of the rain forest on their way through Iowa, and pay money to go inside. Meanwhile they are driving over the remains of a landscape that was once even richer, more diverse, and just as exotic, one that is now even more unreachable, and more lost.

Less than one-tenth of one percent of the tallgrass prairie that existed in the entire United States in 1800 is still intact, and only *one percent* remains of the tallgrass prairie that once covered what is now the Midwest. In the Prairie Learning Center we tour an exhibit designed to teach children about prairie. We see a column of deep topsoil and the long roots of prairie grasses, six feet or more, next to the shallow roots of corn and wheat plants that go barely two feet down. We walk through a human-sized prairie dog tunnel and listen to the amelodious chimes of an instrument that adds and subtracts tones and notes while a little girl, mesmerized, slides a "scale of plant diversity" up and down. We watch a film of a prairie fire, and learn that the suppression of fires to protect human settlements led to the suffocation of the prairie: without the cleansing sweep of flame to blanket the deep prairie grasses in ash, trees and shallow-root species took hold and took over.

Around the corner is a display extolling the virtues and hard work of the hardy souls who farm the prairie. We see that tallgrass prairie soil is the richest soil in the world. And that the tallgrass prairie region now boasts one of the most dramatically altered landscapes to be found anywhere. The invention of the steel plow in 1837 made prairie farming possible. Before, nothing could cut through the heavy rich topsoil with its thick web of roots and plant matter. The land was seen as empty and hostile, too harsh to sustain trees, too desolate to sustain permanent settlement. It was land to pass through.

I turn away from the photographs of old farmsteads that look like my grandparents' house and come face to face with a pole. It is painted brown to show that the depth of the topsoil at this place was over six feet in 1840. A thin line marks the level the topsoil had shrunk to by 1994: less than twelve inches, halfway between my knee and ankle.

Much of that topsoil has gone down the river, filling in the Mississippi Delta with silt, leaching minerals and organic matter out of the thin crust that's left. The soil has been washing and blowing away since the plow came. Since the advent of chemical farming after World War II, something else has been washing down the river with it: millions of pounds of pesticides, herbicides, and nitrates, added to the gradually depleted soil to coax more bushels of corn and soybeans out of the nation's breadbasket. So much of what is put into the soil washes back out again that there is a blossoming coloration spreading out from the Mississippi into the Gulf of Mexico, so large and distinct it can be seen from space. Another altered landscape, so altered it is called the Dead Zone.

The prairie has been covered over by asphalt, corn and soybeans, washed down the Mississippi by rain and floods and wind, left to crumble and fall apart in thousands of abandoned farmyards. These days the word "prairie" is used to conjure up images of a place in the world that is a homestead, a settlement, a fertile community: associated with words like immigrant, pioneer, nourishing, peaceful, quiet, poetic, rich, sustaining, fertile, humble, serious, kind. Not virgin prairie, only prairie remnants.

I want to see what this used to look like. First to know it, and then protect it—from subdivisions, and monocropping, from groundwater run-off, soil loss, genetic contamination of native plant stocks, boom-bust agriculture, declining population, consolidation of agribusiness, destruction of agricultural heritage, and now, for heaven's sake, from the encroachment of the rain forest. I want to feel in my bones what is being lost. I want its poetry to overtake us while we still have the sense to notice what losing the prairie might mean.

One of my favorite paintings is a landscape by Grant Wood called *New Road*. It is what you would expect of Grant Wood: rolling hills, rounded trees, a farm in the distance, a road winding in the foreground, fences marking out an orderly patchwork in between. I can imagine standing at the crest of that hill, looking out at fields and pastures and old farms, rolling and wide, broken by gravel roads and lines of trees and the changing colors of the fields from soybeans to corn to grass. Every other landscape that has made its deep imprint on me starts with this one: the wide fields, the broken and divided expanse, the ability to see to the horizon. There is no question that part of what seems nostalgic, and beautiful, and worth preserving about the prairie landscape is the sentimental image of that landscape in its most altered form: rolling fields, outlined by fences and trees, and a red barn with a silo poking up toward the sky.

Driving through the countryside I look out over the familiar, beautiful patchwork of fields and farms and tree lines, and try to imagine all of it gone, and nothing but grass rolling out before me. It is impossible to get a sense of it. There are brief spots where nothing vertical breaks the view, but they don't even fill the eye. The plowing and settling and roads that have obliterated the grasslands and sent the prairie soil downriver are the same processes that have made it feel like home.

This comfortable vision is what the prairie has been turned into. It will take something much more wild to achieve urgency.

According to early accounts of travelers through the tallgrass prairie, the wide-open expanse was so unbroken and unrelieved by trees or settlement as to be unbearable after just a few days. Some pioneers were reported to go crazy in the vastness, breaking down into tears and incoherence, turning back. No easily visible landmarks by which to locate the self. Too exposed, too direct a view into the void.

Architect Christopher Alexander, in his book, *A Pattern Language*, describes common elements that are found in dwellings and public spaces all over the world, and that are recognized as what makes those spaces comfortable. Pattern Number 239 is called Small Panes. Alexander says of it:

The smaller the windows are, and the smaller the panes are, the more intensely windows help connect us with what is on the other side.... It is the extent to which the window frames the view, that increases the view, increases its intensity, increases its variety, even increases the number of views we seem to see—and it is because of this that windows which are broken into smaller windows, and windows which are filled with tiny panes, put us so intimately in touch with what is on the other side.

Perhaps this impulse to frame our view is the human response to too much unbounded wildness, the kind of wildness that sends the arctic explorer howling into the open ice after spending too many days looking out over nothing but whiteness, or the settler thrashing and wailing into an endless sky. The same instinct that tells us we will go mad upon looking directly into the face of god—or an endless sea of tall grass.

If that frame around the view allows us to look upon it in comfort, surely only a glimpse of the vastness beyond the frame allows us to know what is really out there. The rain forest behind glass, the prairie cut by fences, they may be comfortable but they limit what we see.

The last display before the exit at the Prairie Learning Center, after the diorama of prairie wildlife and the push-button tour of the restoration process, is a row of animal pelts. The skins hang down on two sides of what looks like a wooden coat rack; small white tags identify each animal. They are gruesome and lifeless, and my first impulse is to walk quickly by and head to the gift shop. But I can't; it seems disrespectful somehow. I turn back, walking down one side of the rack and then the other, reading tags, at first just looking. After awhile I reach out tentatively to pet the fur, and it is so soft I circle around again, touching each one. The otter is so smooth and glossy, the fox thick and unbelievably full, soft as our cats at home. When I slow down to look closely, the pelts are unbearably, almost painfully beautiful.

It would never occur to me to confuse the shiny beckoning furs with live animals, with their wild flesh and bone and beating hearts. Glimpses, remnants, stand-ins for the real things, not wild themselves, but as close as most of us will get to the real thing, like trying to imagine the horizon beyond the hillock of prairie grass or hear thundering hooves coming from the dots of buffalo wandering across the nearby field.

It is the row of limp, supple skins, hanging from the rack like ties or sweaters, that stays with me as we walk back to the car and drive slowly out to the highway. I search the horizon for places where the frame has widened—where the gap between power lines and silos is wide enough to hint at the vastness that once pulsed beneath this skin of grass. I imagine this prairie remnant stretching wider and wider, out to the horizon until there is nothing to break the view. When it breaks the frame at last, I imagine it calling out; a cry so wild that those who pass by are compelled to stop, lie down in the tall grass, and join the howling.

Settling

♨ RACHEL SHAW

A whirlwind rose in my path, dusty red and towering like a demon of malign confusion. Flaxen tumbleweeds spiraled up into the light, and my thoughts followed. I looked in the rearview mirror at Dan's car, and I knew I'd never live in San Diego again. Only the god of the whirlwind could confirm the truth of that belief, and dust devils are notorious for lying.

We'd left California two days before, a two-person caravan headed for the Middle West, a misnomer to a person born west of the Great Plains. At a rest stop outside of Needles, I had to lean on the door of the bathroom, feeling light headed with heat-induced palpitations. I grew up in deserts, baking and sweating in the hot metal interiors of four-by-fours with vinyl seats. Was my Western blood already beginning to thicken with Eastern humidity?

In Amarillo, Texas, where the humid aroma of the stockyards permeated the dry air, large families of large people splashed in the pool in the courtyard of the Motel 6. Three states and two time zones lay in our wake, and when we rolled into town we were exhausted. The next day, we would cross the hundredth meridian, the line separating the land of irrigation from the land of rain. The dry knowledge in my bones would give way to a humid uncertainty.

What would the United States look like, had it been settled from west to east? When American explorers first encountered the desert Southwest, they were rendered literally speechless. Our words for arid landforms come instead from the Spanish: *arroyo, canyon, mesa.* Their cadences and rhythms roll over the rocks and ravines, hard as stone, as subtle as dust. I was filled with their gritty truth. The West is not defined by absence, if it is all you have ever known.

The problem I faced in the Midwest was not lack but excess. The tropes of our national culture, the dreams of brilliant autumn and lazy watermelon summers, were as foreign a country to me as the red rock and dusty chaparral would have been to my pioneering ancestors. The vegetative Crayolas in my childhood box were olives and pines, and the bright light green of new spring growth. The strange waxy Green, the green of a thousand Midwestern childhoods, had no place in mine. I entered a geography filled with words and other people's experiences, a country where a nation's assumptions hung as thick in the air as water.

In Indiana, I struggle to adapt to an alien landscape that is as familiar as childhood. The seasons, the insects, the thunderstorms, the fast-growing grass, the lush green summers and the golden falls, the stark white winters and bare-limbed trees were the subjects of coloring books and calendars, schoolbooks and after-school specials, the iconography of a nation. They were the essence of America and I, native born, was adrift in their strangeness.

Do insects generate spontaneously from air, from water? If the latter, that might account for the size and number of them here compared to home. Perhaps, in the case of lightning bugs, they spring from both fire and water. The line of the aridity meridian cages them in the humid zones as surely as a child captures them in a jar on a warm night. When I was a girl, I spent a summer with my grandparents in Illinois. My brother and I were astounded by the glow of lightning bugs, only having heard about them in stories. As an adult, I laughed when in the course of my dissertation research I read a "translation" of a California Indian place name as "home of the fireflies." I knew, more than the man who purveyed that fiction, that nowhere in the West was any such thing. Yet, having seen these phosphorescent miracles, I could see how one might wish for such a place. Perhaps this man was, like me, trying to find home in an unfamiliar world.

If William Least Heat-Moon saw the transition from west to east in the increasing juiciness of the insects bespattering his windshield, I saw it in the glowing corpses of lightning bugs on mine. Dan and I had flown out earlier, in June, to find and reserve housing in Greencastle for the two years we'd spend working for DePauw University. Every night I would dance about, giddy, like a child with a Fourth of July sparkler, with the delight of those green sparks flaring in the soft warm darkness. We drove up to neighboring Crawfordsville one afternoon, charting the contours of our new home. On our return, the light was fading from the sky and reappearing in the thick clouds of lightning bugs billowing over the road. With a rhythmic slapping that brought me to the brink of tears, firefly after firefly flared into piercing green death before my eyes, faded, and died. Flared, faded, died. Brilliance, decline, death. Mile after mile, until we reached the sanctuary of our motel, this cadence beat at me. I don't believe in omens, but this felt like one.

Home, it turns out, is as large as a region. Skittering from locale to location within its expanses, I stood on mountains and gazed across ocean and desert, and could not see it. Now, uprooted, out of place, I *can* see it. I see it as clear as sunrise, as clear as stars in an arid sky. I see it, and feel it, a deep aching that runs through bone and marrow. Dislocated, I face the challenge of orienting myself to a world of humidity.

I am from the West; the West lives in me; the West is my home. I did not understand this until I tried to adapt to life in Indiana. I sat in my green chair and scratched and watched ants, seeking at least a form of fidgety peace, or salvation in the form of the mover's arrival.

"Grow where you are planted" was an adage that fell into my life early. We moved around a lot, my family, during the years of my childhood. Eventually we settled down in the San Francisco Bay Area, staying there for over a decade, the longest time in my life I've lived in a single location. The pattern had been set by then, and even now, by dint of Dan's and my academic careers, to live in a place for more than a year or two is unusual. Is it any wonder then, that I quest for home? My life growing up was shaped by nomadism, by impermanence. Friends and places were seemingly brushed away as easily as dust, each time we moved. Flipping through old address books, I see my homes and experiences and relationships reduced to a few lines on a page, black and blue shapes bruising the paper, graphite lines fading into gray meanders and scratches.

A moving truck is a curious thing, a box on wheels filled with other boxes, each containing the material elements of a life. The boxes are sufficiently alike in their mass-produced brown cardboard that it is impossible to distinguish between Bedroom and Bath, practical utensils and playful whimsies. A child's treasured collection of stuffed animals and a container of old clothes for donation are the same in the indifferent eyes of the moving company. So too places seem these days; we are reassured with the sights of familiar chains and neighborhoods everywhere we go—why, then, should we fear transplantation? We carry our boxes with us, and buy more things for our boxy houses in big-box stores when we arrive.

To keep sealing parts of one's life away in anonymous cardboard is a peculiar activity. Is the screech of the tape dispenser an echo of the sound of displacement? Cardboard is the color of dull earth, of clods that form on the drying roots of plants ripped out of place. Cardboard itself is the product of trees rendered down into abstraction—instead of knocking on wood for luck, I knock on cardboard.

I have been surprised to discover that I did put down deeper roots during my nomadic life west of the rainfall line. Desert plants often combine a network of fine, surface roots with a deep taproot; the fine roots spread wide like a net to catch any moisture that might fall, while the taproot reaches deep to pull up water that was stored since the last full rain. Growing up, I assumed that all I had were surface roots, easily broken, and I longed for a deeper attachment to place. It turns out that the taproot ran so deep I did not see it until it lay exposed on unfamiliar ground. Regrowing a taproot, a root that reaches deep into the soil of a region, has proven far harder than regrowing the surface roots that connect me to my immediate surroundings. This is the secret cost of living deeply, in a society that praises the willingness to migrate. Transplanting deep-rooted plants is hard; if you break off too much of the taproot, they will die, yet that vital lifeline is hidden below the land, invisible until the separation.

Opening one of the boxes, I discover that some of my belongings have been spoiled with mildew and mold while in storage. I must discard them, having become allergic to my own past.

How do other people make these transitions? From its founding, the United States has been a nation of rovers and ramblers, of people who uprooted themselves generation after generation, raising children in worlds and places strange to them. It is true that places change through time—no parent raises a child into the same childhood, even if they stay fixed in place for generations—but I wonder if the movement from place to place might be more profound than the movement through time. What did those eastern parents think, seeing their children grow up to be westerners? Watching them tossing pebbles into upturned hats under a slanting afternoon sun, seeing them grow reddish brown with dust and the sere heat of drylands summers? What did it mean to those parents to know that they'd never share the joy of a firefly summer with their children, even as they watched those cheerful little bodies racing about in the dry grass or shrieking at the coldness of the ocean?

I grew up in a world of tans and yellows and ochres and rusts, of dusty waxen leaves and sere brown sticks. Mountains stopped the horizons, the ocean exhaled moisture with the tang of salt, the deserts grew pregnant with heated air that they birthed into dry winds and scouring fire. Seasons slid gradually into one another, while the ground leapt and shook. I inhaled the petrichor that chased new rains, the smells of creosote and sage and eucalyptus. I walked on dry dust as soft as sleep, sand as gritty as salt, through grass turned brittle by the touch of summer. I reveled in the miracle of new spring grass, lifted my chin to scent the coming of fall. My brother, my first cousins, and I are the first generation of our family to be born west of the Plains. My parents' families are from the Midwest; my parents' generation was seduced westward by the scent of orange blossoms in winter, by jobs and opportunities not found closer to home. Extended networks of cousins and aunts and uncles remain here in Illinois and Indiana, embedded in the heartland. Like the Midwest itself, they are familiar-unfamiliar, a part of childhood but not a part of daily life.

I have declared my desire for cremation after I have moved on from the ultimate home, my body. Cremains resemble rocks and sand and dust, calcium phosphate eroding into powder, the floured and gritty remnants of a meal ground in a metate. The veiny teeth in a burro's jaw jut out from the smooth curve of bone, the slickness of desert pavement alongside the gritty velvet of sandstone. Car-struck forms lie flat along the roadways, baked into pancakes of feathers and skin. The assumed aridity of death, the lightness of sunlit husks emptied of life, brushes tenderly against my soul like drifting motes of dust.

The clean lines of stately bones take on new connotations in the moldering darkness, mold-slick with the humidity of flesh. Wet death is heavy, sinking, somber. The subterranean passage of damp things, the humid imbalance of ergot and smut, mildew and mites, turns my eyes into itching, weeping redness, pink nose into dripping rain. Wet sand clings to the skin, damp and abrasive.

At Wildbranch one year I found a dead mole beneath a picnic table. It lay limp and heavy in my hand, its pelt gritty from being rolled back and forth in the wet sand. When I picked it up, it molded to the cup of my palm, warm and gravid with the weight of death.

In the yard lay a heavy rock in the shape of a *metate*. Entombing the mole beneath the stone, my knees pressed into the wet moss, I arose stained with water and soil. I envisioned the ants rendering the darkness of

the mole into wet redness and slick gray-white bone, breaching the barrier
of the mole's somber coat in the lightless world from which it was torn,
precise as a mortuary of coroners. The mole and I lay pressed down by a
metate out of place, flattened into the humid soil, reborn into the chitin-
ous bodies of ants. The mole sank back into darkness, into the deep womb
of the earth, unblemished by dampness. I rose up, shedding the moisture
of moss, comforted by the hopeful dryness of sunlight and air.

My blood and bones are in this soil, this strange wet soil, in the form
of previous generations. The body of my father's father, a widower and
a suicide, lies in a graveyard only ten miles from Greencastle. His grave,
like his death, is a strange and lonely one, several counties distant from
that of his young wife, my grandmother. He is the only Shaw in the
cemetery.

As I grow older, I wonder about raising children in this wet land,
of living intimately among natives of a land to which I do not belong.
I worry about being an expatriate within the nation of my own family,
a westerner among midwesterners. I fear the liquid eyes of my potential
children, brought to fruition in the dark wet world of my womb, gazing on the landscapes of my childhood and finding them barren and
ugly. My maternal grandmother joined her children on the West Coast
in death, her ashes swirling in the waters off the Santa Barbara shore, but
she was only a sometime visitor there while she was alive. My maternal
grandfather appreciated the warm winters and fresh oranges, but he remained in Illinois after her death, and after his. Only my parents and
their siblings moved West and stayed, their final places as yet unknown.

Will I return to the West only after death, a floury bundle of ashes
and bones neatly sealed into a plastic bag with a twist tie? Will I, like my
father's father and my mother's mother, go to earth or ride the waves far
from the grave of my partner? Or will my remains settle into this new
land, merging wetly with the rich mud and warm summer rains?

At the end of our two years in Greencastle, the summer rains of the academic cycle washed us to Virginia for a year, then back to the eastern side of Indiana. This time, it looks like my displacement may be lifelong. It is good then that, slowly, I have learned small ways of coping with it.

Lately, I have been photographing rust. I've been wandering around the city of Richmond, camera in hand, looking for patches of it, large and small, to pin beneath my lens. Some odd blemish caught my eye one day, and now I can't stop looking for others.

It turns out that rust is variable and often quite beautiful. I'd previously thought about it, if at all, in terms of small patches on tools, or as solid masses of decay, as when oxidation claims a tractor entire, leaving its hulk to crumble into the sand among the sagebrush.

That happens here too, but most of these rusty areas strike me as the industrial equivalent of skin disease. Some are rashes, some are bruises, or cuts or scratches. Along the edges where paint is breeched, rust blooms. It runs along the sides of dumpsters and waterpipes. It stains white walls with iodinic streaks. It peels up old iron in flaking layers and crumbling chunks. It forms complex patterns inside garbage cans, shapes pits and protrusions on bridge railings. I see it at ground level, transforming a wrinkled drainpipe from zinc blue to rusty terracotta. It greets me at eye height, crackling and shedding beneath a layer of breaking paint on a flagpole. It is above me, winking from the eyebolts that pin a bridge to its concrete supports. We weep rusty blood, ooze iron-laden moisture, the city and I, when we are damaged and our vulnerable interior is revealed. Rust is all around me, within me, a dance of water, oxygen, and iron.

Out of a protruding faucet, a scarred dumpster, and peeling patches of paint I create a web that binds me into place. I walk around the neighborhood, up streets in the city center and along the brick back alleys, encountering rusty signposts of earlier passage. There I spotted a pattern of starbursts on a wall. There a scratch in the dumpster bleeds ferric secretions. A rusty nut juts from the high-tension cable of a phone line. I find my way navigating from decay to decay, from wound to wonder.

The water acts on us all. Water erodes my sense of place, running through my very bones, betraying me from within. On this side of the Continental Divide, water carries me away from home.

Return

🐾 ANDREA M. JONES

Years have passed since I've traveled these roads, but the route is in-
grained like an instinct and the topography matches my recollections with comforting precision. As the road bends and dips into a
shallow canyon, my eyes seek out the curves of buff sandstone that define
the rim of the drainage. I feel starved for slickrock, for landscapes where
the greenery of piñon and juniper gives way to a dominance of sandstone. I crave the stripped-bare landscape both for its beauty and for the
way it focuses my attention on first principles: water, earth, sky.

Where the road begins to climb the gentle eastern incline of Comb
Ridge, petrified dunes stretch into the blue haze of distance on either side of the road. Millennia of fierce weather have simultaneously
smoothed the pale stone into sensuous curves and etched the swells with
fissures and drainages. The highway follows the slow rise of the land
partway up the slope and then plunges into a deep road cut. Emerging
from the perpetual shade of the gash, I take the corner too fast and drift
into the oncoming lane. The error is partly due to the fact that I'm peering out the passenger-side window, trying to see the rampart of cliffs that
defines the abrupt western edge of the ridge, but it's also a simple mis-
calculation of the appropriate speed. As the car accelerates downhill into
the broad depths of Comb Wash, I realize that in spite of my acquaintance with this road, I've never actually driven it myself. Until today, I
have always been a passenger.

The first trip was in the early 1970s, and I would have been riding in
the back of the pickup with my three older brothers and the dog, our
boat bouncing on its trailer behind us. This incongruous trip—into the
desert with a boat in tow—was destined to be repeated many times over

the years, as Lake Powell became a favorite destination for our family camping trips.

Today, I'm making the journey on my own for the first time. As the path of the road breaks free of the low piñon forest and begins a long straight run across sage-covered flats, the contour of red cliffs against the sky to the north clicks neatly into alignment with my memory. At Clay Crossing, I stop for a pee and to admire the outcrop soil eroding into badlands of green and gray.

I draw in a lungful of the dry air and breathe it out slowly. I feel slightly giddy, a strange mixture of exhilaration and disorientation: it does not seem possible that sights I have not seen in so long look the same as they did years ago. The ubiquity of development in my home state of Colorado has left me unprepared for such continuity. It's been more than twenty years—half my lifetime—since I've been out this way. Once I left home after high school, I camped with my family less often, replacing such trips with college, travel, and the paired intimacy of marriage. I also began to explore the Utah desert on foot, on its own terms, without the luxuries afforded by the reservoir. Although I always had vague plans to come back, a trip never came together, and after my father died in 1997 the idea became tainted by loss. I have recently celebrated my fortieth birthday, however, and this trip is my gift to myself: a few days in the slickrock desert for solitary reflection.

Back on the road, which bends and begins to climb at Clay Crossing, I know exactly where to look for the remains of the narrow wagon track carved by Mormon settlers. A few miles farther along, I effortlessly locate the little Indian ruin tucked in a south-facing overhang. Then, after driving another ten minutes or so, my eyes and the landscape conspire to jostle a long-forgotten detail into consciousness: with abrupt certainty, I know that the left-hand bend I'm approaching marks the place where I used to eagerly scan the middle distance toward the north, looking for scraps of turquoise blue nestled among the sandstone hills, trying to be the first to holler, "I see the lake!"

Today, there is no blue.

It's true that I've come to this place, in part, to revisit territory from my past, but I'm also drawn by a slightly morbid curiosity. It's an April morning in 2005, and after several years of sustained drought, Lake Powell is lower than it has been since the reservoir began to fill in 1963. The delight I feel at being back in the desert and my happy nostalgia at seeing familiar landforms now churn against queasy apprehension at what the reservoir's falling water might reveal. As I round the curve where the expanse of Bullfrog Bay used to be revealed to arriving visitors, I'm presented with a vista composed of more sandstone than water. In this scene, familiarity and novelty collide.

These things I know: the form of the horizon, with the angular pile of the Henry Mountains in the western distance; the curved walls of pale sandstone that form graceful cliffs and amphitheaters downstream from the boat ramp; the low-slung stone dunes heaped into a long pink and lavender vista toward the north; the smudge of green cottonwoods across the bay. The sandstone mesas on my right, slab sided and round topped like loaves of bread, are as familiar as oft-viewed snapshots.

But the water that used to sprawl across the low basin in front of me is mostly gone. The landforms have reasserted themselves over what I'd always known as a waterscape; what I remember as islands and peninsulas have taken on the authority of mainland. The sheltered cove where the floating marina used to be anchored is a murky puddle. The concrete lane of the boat ramp has been stretched like something from a cartoon, reaching crazily down, down, down for the water's edge.

To my brain, primed on the drive in by the assurances of well-remembered landscapes, the shrunken reservoir is startling. I park in the nearly vacant lot at the top of the ramp and walk slowly, as if to compensate for the frenetic pace of my thoughts. I had decided to drive to Halls Crossing both for practical and sentimental reasons. I am boatless but unwilling to take my aging little car onto the more isolated and remote roads that access the shoreline. More than that, though, I needed to gauge the reservoir's fall in a place that was familiar. We camped in many different places over the years, but for me almost every trip began and ended here, at Halls Crossing, with this vista.

One of my father's rituals, once he had launched the boat and parked the truck and trailer, was to take off his watch and stow it, along with his wallet, in the wall cabinet of the boat cabin. The wallet sometimes came out to pay for gas or beer, but the watch stayed put: time spent at Lake Powell was time apart, a sanctuary from the day-to-day. We hiked and fished and swam—the water icy during springtime trips, warm as bathwater in the fall. We prepared elaborate meals—crab legs with artichokes, marinated shish kebabs of venison tenderloin, pancakes and fresh-caught fish for breakfast—and chuckled smugly as we ate, imagining other campers nibbling pathetically on charred hot dogs. We spent afternoons playing cribbage in the shade, talked in the orange circlet of light around the fire. When darkness fell, we counted falling stars and watched satellites trace their silent path through the night. Often, when the bright light of a late-rising moon woke me up, the murmured voices of my two eldest brothers, talking while they waited for catfish to bite, lulled me back to sleep.

Now I scramble down the rip-rap of boulders at the edge of the parking lot and step onto the slickrock. Striding up a steep incline, I revel in the familiar grip of the gritty stone beneath the soles of my tennis shoes. I descend a bulging formation, stopping just above the point where its curve accelerates to freefall. Violet-green swallows veer below my feet, offering a clear view of the white markings on their backs. I sit down and gaze out over the canyon and its burden of slow-moving water.

The beauty is unconventional. Rather than the verdure of forest or field, the blue-green water laps against stone in hues of rose, lavender, and tan. From atop a cliff such as this one, the view is expansive, with stone dune fields, lurid red mesas, and purple mountain ranges punctuating the distance, but I know how it is deep in the canyons' fissures. Down there, one seems to move through, rather than across, the land. Flat water meets vertical cliffs on the perpendicular; in the narrow channels, the sheer walls pull the horizon in close, pinching the visible world down to some fraction of a mile in any direction.

It's convenient to characterize a large body of water in the desert as an oasis, yet here there is none of the lushness one associates with the word. Mapped on paper, Lake Powell squiggles, twists, kinks, loops, and branches in a manner suggestive of organic forms—amoebas, taproots, networks of swollen blood vessels—yet on the ground it is characterized by a dearth of the organic. There are no reedbeds, no marshes, no grassy pockets where animals congregate. Greenery is rare: the verdant ribbon that occupied the river channel was drowned when the reservoir began to fill, and new growth along the water's edge is hampered by the harsh desert climate and rapidly fluctuating water levels.

The place is austere, but that is—and was, for me as a girl—the point. My parents took my brothers and me camping in the mountains from the time we were infants, and a love of the woods feels like part of my genetic makeup, an inborn affection. The sensibility that took root at Lake Powell was a harbinger of the more difficult and changeable love I would aspire to in adulthood: the kind of love I had to work at, the kind of love that demanded changes of me. When I began to think, later in life, about the foundations of my relationship with the natural world, impressions from Lake Powell were always prominent. The barren landscape framed objects and invited contemplation: a circle drawn in sand by wind-spun grass, a lizard doing push-ups, a petroglyph.

Yet the land, in its harshness and verticality, also demanded respect. Romantic notions of beneficent nature evaporated in the kilnlike heat, slipped away with the clatter of falling rocks, were scoured and pitted by blowing sand. The knowledge that Lake Powell was, in spite of its raw character, a man-made reservoir further complicated idyllic reveries about nature and my relationship to it.

I'm thinking about old campsites and what their vistas might look like now, when I hear a boat down below. The mechanical buzz of its engine, which I would normally dismiss as noise, is today oddly sweet to my ears. The vessel glides past the base of the cliff marking the far side of the channel. I contemplate the fact that the cliff looming over the boat is at least a hundred feet taller than it would have been at any time I gazed up it from water level.

From where I'm sitting, the change in water level is easy to see; the chalky stains of Lake Powell's high water mark are one of its infamous attributes. The residue invites the inevitable comparison to a bathtub ring, and it baits my eyes into focusing on the water that is gone rather than the desert that is present: the bottom two-thirds of the cliff opposite me is encrusted. The upper portion of the stone face was beyond the reservoir's reach, however, and is thickly streaked with black-brown desert varnish, mineral deposits left by precipitation cascading over the cliff's top. The reservoir hasn't been full in so long that the stains are beginning to overpaint the high water mark.

In my body's sensibility, Halls Crossing is unchanged: same texture to the sandstone, same smell of water and gasoline, same hot sun on my skin, same dry air in my lungs, same sounds of wave-lap and motorboats. This sensory conviction is sharply countered by the visual evidence presented by the shrunken reservoir, as well as the details my mind keeps offering up as gauges of time's passage between then and now: I didn't know they were called violet-green swallows when I was here as a kid, although I did know tamarisk is a weed; I have earned college degrees, lived abroad, become a wage earner since last I set foot in this part of Utah; have courted and married a man who has never been here.

Eventually, I return to the car and drive toward the once-bustling marina complex. Dozens of rental houseboats are parked in dry dock; the protected basin where they used to be anchored now harbors a graying pile of tumbleweeds. Strips of dock lie akilter, grounded by the shrinking reservoir. The parking lots are empty and their walkways point listlessly toward the distant water.

I climb in the car and leave, but melancholy trails me as I retrace my route up out of the canyon, through the stony hills, past the little ruin, down the pass at Clay Crossing. I stop on the flats for a picnic lunch and take a hike. When I originally planned this trip, I had pictured walking as a meditative, contemplative time, but at the moment I am hoping the rhythm of my legs' cadence will simply slow the whirl of thought and memory that continues to spin through my head. I understand that tearing out the Glen Canyon Dam will restore the flow of the Colorado River, but my mind fixates on the high water mark, Lake Powell's ghost lingering in the canyons for generations. I imagine a concentrated sludge of algae, silt, oil, and effluent in the bottom of the canyon, along with forty years' worth of dropped and wind-blown beer cans, ice chests, baseball caps, fishing poles, waterlogged trees and life vests, snarls of fishing line, bait buckets, and food wrappers. I think about my family.

Two hours later, I am sweaty, tired, and more calm. Back in the car, I arrive at the junction with the highway and, rather than turning right toward the mountains of home, I steer left and head deeper into the desert, on a road less traveled and less burdened by memories.

After a while, I see signs for a road offering lake access. I turn and follow the bumpy unpaved track as it winds among buttes and pillars of angular red sandstone. The road descends into a shallow valley, ending at a huge parking area. A lonely looking fee station and a hut housing pit toilets stand at the edge of the gravel flat. I cross the expanse and see tracks where other drivers have driven off the edge of the lot. I creep my car down the slope and park on a broad flat which would, at some point in the last twenty years, have been under water.

I'm thinking I may try to hike to the water's edge, but this whim is short lived.

There is no reservoir. There is no sound of lapping water, no hum of distant boat engines, no scent of wet sand or the slightly fishy mustiness of damp silt. The only signs that water has pooled here in any recent epoch is a faint chalkiness on some of the rocks and a fuzz of weeds greening the drainages. The reservoir is gone, and it feels like it has been gone for a long time.

Where the air was pensive at Halls Crossing, the atmosphere here is that of abandonment and desolation. I think of the loneliness of ghost towns, but this is more forlorn: there isn't even a town. If I did not know that Lake Powell's waters once stood here, the huge parking lot and fee station would seem like a practical joke.

The feel of the place is utterly different from that of the unadulterated desert, where vast geographies, enormous skies, and the harsh climate intimidate but also inspire and invigorate. The desert is not beneficent, but it has a quiet integrity that makes the human presence seem incidental. What is unnerving about this dry cove is the air of *absence*: that the lack of people can be so profoundly felt. The lonely parking lot and weeds and litter of vehicle tracks and trash evoke vacancy so that my sense of the desert's integrity is overpowered. I wander around a little, increasingly unsettled as the air of loneliness resolves into something more personal.

The confusion of thought and memory from this morning's visit to Halls Crossing rises again, but what comes to the fore is the wistful realization of how much of my emotional attachment to Lake Powell is centered on my family. Camping—that time apart—was our time together. At home, school and work schedules seldom allowed for everyone to sit down for meals at the same time; at home, my older brothers and I played together only occasionally. Our collective experience here forms a distinct storyline in our shared history, but since those days the ties of my family's kinship have frayed and in some cases snapped. Some of the wear has been typical of the evolution of a nuclear family: kids growing up and moving away, spending their time with companions other than siblings or parents. Other stresses are more abrupt or more complex—divorce, separation, death, lives grown apart.

In spite of my sympathy for the movement to decommission the Glen Canyon Dam on environmental grounds, my history here has always made me ambivalent about the effort. Lake Powell holds tender memories, and even though we have scattered, I've held on to the notion that echoes of those times may be found in its narrow watery passages. In this dry cove, I sense what it would be like if Lake Powell was to disappear, and the emptiness of the place presses into me. Although I grieve about all the tattered relationships, I am thinking now of my father, the engineer and driver of the family camping custom. A thought finally completes itself, after lurking as a fragment in the back of my mind all day: I have never before been to Lake Powell without my Dad. The loneliness of this place sharpens the blunt fact of his absence to a cutting edge, and I lean on the roof of my car and cry.

And yet the tears do not last long. Abruptly, standing in what once was an arm of that much-loved reservoir, I realize I can live without it. My father has been dead more than seven years now. I still miss him, and I wonder how my life would be different if he were still alive, but I have learned to let him go. I know I can also let go of Lake Powell.

As my sobbing subsides, silence presses in again. I take a few deep breaths, wipe my eyes, blow my nose, and leave.

As I approach the turnoff for the Hite Marina, I hesitate. I'm exhausted. The day has tipped toward evening. I'm not equipped to camp and still have a drive ahead of me. But I feel that I've come too far to leave this errand—of witnessing? of remembering?—unfinished, so I make the turn. Here, too, the reservoir is gone, but a scattering of campers in the RV park holds the ghost-town atmosphere at bay.

I park and walk to the top of the long concrete incline of the boat ramp. There is no visible water: the ramp peters out into sand. Rather than sorrow, though, I feel growing excitement. What I sense here is not *absence* but *presence*: the air is full.

Full of the sound of moving water.

Beyond the boat ramp, a plain of greenery has sprung up. In the distance, from deep within its tangle, I can hear the susurration of the Colorado River. For the first time in my life, I stand in the declivity of Glen Canyon and listen to the river that carved it.

I'm thrilled. I almost laugh out loud. Even though Lake Powell is gone from this place, Glen Canyon and the river that gave it form are present. To my childhood memories, in which the twisting arms and orthogonal planes of Lake Powell seemed uncanny and timeless, I now add this sound, which whispers of the ongoing changes of the planet's rhythms. I suddenly see Lake Powell as a passing phase in the inhumanly long timescale that has shaped—continues to shape—Glen Canyon. The analogy to my childhood experiences is unmistakable: those days at Lake Powell should not be thought of as time apart, but rather as a stage in a life passing through its necessary temporal arc. As I stand on the ramp and listen to the distant river, I am oddly comforted by the knowledge that the transience that defines my life also defines an entity many orders of magnitude larger and longer-lived than I am.

It's no longer enough to hear the river—I want to see it. I look doubtfully at the green thicket from which the river rumbles, calculating its distance in relation to the impending sunset. On the west side of the canyon, I see a slash in the rock: a road dipping into the tangle. Once again I climb into the car and once again I head west.

Glancing down as I cross the bridge over the Colorado River, I see water the color of putty and the consistency of milk: the spring runoff is on. The muddy flow cuts through the green plain I saw from the boat ramp; from this height I see that the verdure sprawls over hundreds of acres. I locate the dirt road angling toward the river and follow it to where a line of trucks and vans stand parked, each with an empty boat trailer behind it. The trailers are all similar—low-slung and wide—and I realize they are designed to haul river rafts, not motorboats.

I walk toward the riverbank, crossing a patchwork of slickrock outcrops and eroding clumps of silt. I wander among thickets of tamarisk and Russian thistle, realizing that the green plain I saw from the bridge is composed of these weeds. It also occurs to me that I'm standing among the Grand Canyon's missing beaches: the sediments of the upper Colorado that have been settling out of the water as it stalled behind the dam for four decades. The newly reinvigorated river has already cut deeply into the deposits, and I follow a lane that's been bulldozed down the bank to provide a put-in for rafts. The sediment looms thirty feet above me as I approach the river.

At water level for the first time all day, I put my hand in the chilly murk and savor the river's flow over my skin. I feel the ancient walls of the canyon around me, listen to the river churning quietly in its silty bed. Bent over the water, the sense of repose the desert offers me at long last settles in.

My hand numbs, and I straighten. There is snow in the mountains and the Glen Canyon Dam still stands: the river's current may well stagnate as the reservoir rises again. Eventually, though—perhaps in my lifetime—the Colorado River will again rumble through a landscape I've always known as a reservoir. I'll surely never live to see Glen Canyon without the rime of Lake Powell's high water mark, but that, too, will someday vanish, scoured away by wind and painted over by desert varnish.

Later, I'll think about how much harder it will be to restore the health of the watershed than it will be to restore the water's flow: ecosystems so long buried by silt and garbage and the patient seeds of weeds will not rebound quickly. Later, I'll be struck by how much the crumbly sediment of the fresh-cut riverbank resembles the canyon's ancient sandstone walls. Later, I'll think about how currents of time sometimes curve back on themselves, re-exposing what we thought was gone and reminding us where we've been, what we're made of.

For now, though, I simply linger at the water's edge, watching from deep within Glen Canyon as amber light plays across the river's gray-brown ripples and saturates the colored bands of the sandstone cliffs toward the east. I cannot ignore the silt or the weeds, but I can see them for what they are: features of the canyon at this stage of its existence. They alter the integrity of this desert landscape, but they do not destroy it.

Water. Earth. Sky.

Poised at the boundary of fluid and stone, in this moment between river and reservoir, I am filled.

Meditation on My Hometown

✤ HEATHER FITZGERALD

Plano, Texas, is a suburb fifteen miles north of Dallas on Highway 75. In 1960 it was still largely cotton fields, but since then it has been developed to its full capacity—"reached build-out," in the parlance of urban planners—with a population that hovers around a quarter-of-a-million people. I feel a strange mixture of pride and horror whenever I see it mentioned in the media as an example of a "supersuburb" or an "edge city," the wave of the future.

It's wealthy, with good schools. The neighborhood where my family lives, which is solidly within the realm of middle class, is in one of the poorer areas. Just before we moved there in 1982, it made the national news because of a wave of teen suicides, and about ten years ago it got a bit of attention because of a heroin problem in town. Mostly what it is, though, is houses. Rows and rows and rows of subdivisions, a grid of them as far as the eye can see (which, in north-central Texas, is pretty far). Strip malls and shopping centers punctuate the grid at regular intervals. It's a place made for cars. There are very few public spaces. I have trouble figuring out how to think about it: an extreme example of everything humans have ever done wrong, or just an extremely well-executed example of the way most Americans live every day, all over the place?

When we first moved to Plano, my mother would get lost driving me the eight-tenths of a mile home from my elementary school. All of the houses looked the same to her, although there were at least five different ranch-style floor plans in our subdivision, all built by a developer named Fox and Jacobs. (A silver sticker on the back of the door to our coat closet read, "This quality home built by Fox and Jacobs.") I could find our house because we lived on the block with the corner house that had all the prickly pear cactus in its yard. My mother hadn't wanted to move to Texas. She told me last year that when she cried about moving, my dad said in response, "You can stay or you can go. But I'm going."

I like to say I left Plano about thirty seconds after graduating from high school. Although it's not literally true (I left that August to go to college in Pennsylvania), it serves as an effective shorthand to convey how I feel about the place. I know teenagers everywhere can't wait to leave their hometowns, but I've always felt that my need, and justification, were greater than most. It wasn't just the aesthetics. When I lived there it was largely southern and white; overwhelmingly, evangelically Christian; and had a congressman who—I'd heard from someone who thought this was great news—had by some measure or another been rated the most conservative member of Congress. My family was from Boston, marginally Catholic, and thought Jimmy Carter had been a good president.

My parents are still in Plano. I've been back to see them almost every year since I left. These visits improved markedly when I started bringing Ben, the man who is now my husband, back with me. Part of their success, I think, was limiting them to approximately three days around Christmas.

This Christmas I'm returning for five weeks with Ben and our one-year-old son, Jesse. Ben and I want to give my parents some quality time with their grandson, and we also, I admit, are thinking that while the three of them enjoy their quality time maybe the two of us, who are self-employed in Vermont and have struggled to maintain our productivity since Jesse arrived, might get a bit of work done.

The day after our arrival, as we drive around from shopping center to shopping center to complete a few simple errands, getting lost in vast endless parking lots, Ben says, "I don't find this landscape inspiring."

I agree, from somewhere deep in the aggrieved teenage part of my soul, but I am surprised by an urge to defend this scruffy landscape.

I settle for saying, "You mean you don't find this *streetscape* inspiring." I look up. "What about the sky?"

Later we are supposed to get a thunderstorm, and I'm looking forward to some excitement—crashing thunder, vivid lightning, and water coursing dramatically over impermeable pavement to flooded creeks. All we get, though, is a little bit of rain and one boom.

I love the sky over Plano. I used to joke that I loved it because it was the only beautiful thing around. In truth, though, I have never seen sky that shade of dangerous gray anywhere else, never seen thunderheads with quite that contrast of angry white and gray-black, never seen front lines as sharp and endless anywhere else. It's the kind of beauty that can make you stare at it, while driving in a car, in a dangerous sort of way, as you might when driving on a bridge over a dramatic gorge or seeing a great horned owl on a telephone pole on the side of a highway. I've spent some time in the Midwest—I came close to a tornado in Iowa and huddled in a basement in the middle of the night during several particularly violent thunderstorms in Minnesota—but those storms didn't have the same colors in their clouds. I don't think it's all in my imagination, either, because when I go back I still start in recognition when I see that particular darkness coming toward me from the horizon.

When I was a kid I used to ride my bike along the Bluebonnet Trail. It mostly ran under high-tension power lines next to a cement-lined culvert of a creek. When I was younger, I would watch the fire ant mounds next to the path in fascination and fish for crawdads in the creek with hot dog chunks stuck on pieces of string. The path's location had been determined by power rather than transportation needs, so it couldn't actually be used to get anywhere. But it offered a good view of the sky. In the summer when I was in high school I'd get up before six so I could ride out and watch the sun rise over the football stadium, careful to leave for home again before the sun got all the way up and the temperatures reached too uncomfortably high into the nineties.

After the front that was supposed to produce thunderstorms fails to pass through, all we can see is fog, a thick and heavy blanket of it as far as the eye can see, and Ben says, "This is pretty inspiring." I appreciate his conciliatory move and decide to take him and Jesse on a drive out to the horse farms near my high school. My high school used to sit in the middle of nowhere, though development has since come to East Plano. Still, some places retain their original vegetation, and we pass through some creek bottoms that, I am relieved to see, have not yet been lined with cement. The fog lies even thicker in these lowlands. The three of us park and get out of the car to look over the landscape in silence.

When my family moved here in 1982 our house was about two miles west and one mile south of the end of development. When I left in 1991, the development had crept three miles north and four miles east of our house. Now our old house is smack in the middle of developed land for miles around. It no longer makes sense to describe its distance from undeveloped land.

While I lived here I don't remember feeling much of a sense of loss as development claimed the fields. The fire ant mounds, barbed-wire fences, and extreme weather (in winter, forty mile per hour winds that I pictured, on a map in my mind, as starting in Canada and blowing all the way down across the plains, unobstructed till they hit my body; in summer, heat that felt "like crouching too close to a campfire," in the words of John McPhee) kept my exploratory desires in check. In fact those fields seemed like grassy wastelands, no great loss. I remember being rather pleased at finding some fields that already had cul-de-sacs and streetlamps built in anticipation of future subdivisions.

There were little bits of nature that I cherished. I would slow down to look every time I drove past Baffin Bay Drive, which on one side was an ordinary street with a row of nondescript ranch houses, but on the other was a line of tightly woven trees hugging a fence. This fencerow exists because it is next to the still-functioning Haggard Ranch, which, while I'm sure a fraction of its former size, still claims enough area to hold 775 typical Plano house lots. There was also a vegetated creek near my house that I biked wistfully along. But I saw these special places as entirely separate from the fields. I didn't even think of the fields as green spaces; if pressed, I would have said they were beige, or brown.

Today, as an adult and an ecologist, I feel much the same about the fields, although I now recognize them as ecologically boring monocultures known as oldfields. But it's still a shock to see all that open space filled in.

A few days before Christmas my son and I ride north with my dad through all that former green/beige/brown space to Frisco. We are heading for a patch of green amidst the relentless brick of new subdivisions, strip malls, and schools, a nursery in Frisco that sells living Christmas trees. We pull in to the parking lot and park under mature cottonwoods. My dad and Randy, the owner, discuss the various merits of Afghan pines and Italian stone pines in Plano's Blackland Prairie soil, which is a vertisol—thick clay that regularly collapses in on itself as it goes through dry periods and, so the story goes, expands so much during wet periods it would crush basements—if there were any in this land of ranch houses built on slabs.

"We don't carry any trees that won't grow in the soil here," Randy says proudly. I wonder to myself if there were any native pines that grew here, biting my tongue while deciding probably not. My dad settles on an Italian stone pine because he likes the look of the saplings on display and Randy runs in to the office to Google pictures of the mature tree, so we'll know what we're getting into. The mature trees look nothing like the saplings we've been looking at; the needles are completely different and the Christmas tree shape transforms into a form fitting its other common name, umbrella pine, but my dad still wants one. When Randy tells us that they grow to be sixty to eighty feet tall, my dad's eyebrows rise.

Randy rubs his beard, points at Jesse. "Well," he says, "maybe he'll live to see it." We buy the one with the best Christmas tree shape and head back through the sea of brick. When my dad plants it on some seventy-degree day in January, it will take its place in my parents' yard beside live oaks that were sticks when we moved in. When we get back to the house I go out to look at the live oaks. They look like they might be approaching sixty feet tall.

Ben, Jesse, and I ride the new light rail to Dallas one day and look out at the vegetation when we stop at a station by a stream. Before we pull away I have time to wonder if there are bois d'arc trees down there, a species (pronounced "bo-dark," with a Texas drawl) that is endemic to the Blackland Prairie and has knobbly bark and giant, green, brain-shaped fruits. I wonder if the vegetation that's still green might be live oak, or invasive mistletoe. Whatever's there, it looks wild and verdant, even though it's next to a train station.

Jesse loves the train and stands for the entire ride, entranced by the movement, the people, and the bar on the seat in front of us. So do I. I could get used to this, I think. I could live near the downtown Plano station in the recently built New Urbanist neighborhood, which surely attracts more liberal types than Republicans; could walk around to do errands, and take the light rail in to the city. It wouldn't even be like living in Dallas. In fact, it would be like living in Vermont, except with public transportation. That night on the return trip we look out together on the endless sea of lights. Although I know it's just porch lights and Walmarts, I think to myself that it looks beautiful.

One day in January we drive north to the Heard Museum, a natural history museum with a few acres of native prairie and woods, several cages containing injured birds, and a small gift shop with bird feeders and field guides. In the January gray we meander on a short path through some mammoth trees. It surprises me to see them.

I know bur oaks from my time in Minnesota as plucky, scrubby, fire-resistant little things on the oak savannah, but these Texas bur oaks are something else, tall and stately. They are magnificent. Their scientific name, *Quercus macrocarpa*, means "big seed," and these acorns are the size of my fist. Farther along the path we come upon a small section of prairie. Even in January, I recognize the seedheads of old friends that I met in Minnesota: *Rudbeckia hirta*, black-eyed Susan, and *Lespedeza capitata*, bush clover. I learned to love the prairie when I lived in Minnesota, and I'd never really thought about Plano's landscape being related to it in any way, never thought about it beyond how it happened to be just now. But it's always been there.

When we get back to my parents' house I look up the Blackland Prairie and begin reading about its ecology. If I were reading about it while living anywhere else, I'd be fascinated and want to go see it. I read descriptions of familiar species of the tallgrass prairie: *Schizacarium scoparium*, little bluestem; *Sorghastrum nutans*, Indiangrass. I read about the vertisols and the bois d'arc trees and nod in recognition. A lot of this I already know, I realize. I'd just never connected it to the subdivisions and shopping malls of life in Plano.

While reading I come across an 1849 description by Dr. John Brooke, an English settler: "It was the finest sight I ever saw; immense meadows 2 or 3 feet deep of fine grass and flowers. Such beautiful colors I never saw." He said that he could "sit on the porch before my door and…see miles of the most beautiful Prairie interwoven with groves of timber, surpassing, in my idea, the beauties of the sea." A settler named Smythe, however, described it in 1852 as "a boundless plain scarcely broken by a single slope or valley, and nearly destitute of trees."

I think to myself that perhaps people saw what they wanted to when they looked at this place. I blush and squirm a little. Me, too. Sure, I still don't love Plano, but it's possible that it's improved with age. I still don't much like the prevailing architectural ethos or other surficial trappings. Given a choice, I'd prefer a more liberal political climate and cooler summers. If anything, this meditation on my hometown has made me sadder about the fate of the oldfields here, as I imagine them for a moment as restored prairie rather than subdivisions. But I think that over the years, what I've seen has been more about me than about Plano. I don't mean to say that what I saw before didn't exist, only that what I chose to see was not all there was to see.

The day before I leave town, walking Jesse around the block, I notice a redbud tree budding next to a house across the street, and see a hawk land on the roof. When I get back to my parents' house I notice, in the sidewalk, the perfect imprints of a red oak leaf and several live oak leaves that must have landed in the wet cement when the sidewalk was poured. I look around. The sidewalk is cracked and buckling in places. I'm certain this is the same cement that was here when I lived here. Buds, hawks, and leaves are very small things. I still don't love Plano. But I'm delighted by the budding, startled by the hawk, and astonished that I never saw the leaves before.

Pink Ribbons

❧ EVE QUESNEL

O ut our back gate and across the street my daughter and I often
wander with no direction or purpose into the ponderosa forest.
First in the backpack, then on her own two wavering legs, she enters a
world of undisturbed nature, a place transcending time. In the summer and fall as an unsteady toddler she stumbles along on the uneven
forest floor gathering her forest cornucopia—ponderosa puzzle bark,
minibroom pine-needle bunches, and a variety of sticks and stones.
Sometimes a prickly pinecone twice the size of her hand catches her eye,
which prompts her to pick up the prized item and carry it gingerly as if it
is glass and could shatter.

In the same forest in winter I harness our yellow Labrador to a child's
wooden sled and carefully place my daughter inside, snugly tucked in between too many blankets. Following behind in snow boots or on cross-
country skis and connected to the newly assigned sled dog, I slowly
guide the small team through the silent woods. While gliding through
a series of bends the little winter traveler stretches her arms in front of
her, turns her palms upward, and receives slowly drifting snowflakes in
her hands. After her mittens fill with a soggy white snow cone she sets
her snow snack on her protruding tongue and giggles with delight.

In the same forest in spring my daughter and I jump from one snow
patch to the other to avoid spring's muddy overture; we hopscotch
on white squares. Determined, we scrunch up our faces and ready our
bodies for flight, and then leap. And leap. And leap. We laugh and
grunt from patch to patch, making sure to keep our boots from getting
covered with squishy mud, although they fill up with melted snow anyway. Our gaiety is arrested when we reach the boundary between forest

and valley and stand in awe overlooking a sprawling meadow. There, winter graciously bows to its replacement, allowing spring with its brilliant colors to pronounce a colorful world, once again. Penstemon drags blue from the sky down to its whorled flowers. Lupine casts shadows of light blue onto the wildflower pool. An occasional snow plant peaks out of the ground like a layered conical piece of red coral, a bright red bulbous jewel as a special gift from the sea earth. Mule's ears with elongated tobacco-shaped leaves proudly display chunky yellow corsages like prom flowers pinned on green suits.

Spring smells pungently with mint-earth-sage and I tell my daughter to lean into a clump of sagebrush. "This is sagebrush," I tell her, "it smells like Thanksgiving with a bit of mint." She looks at me with lowered eyebrows, questioning. "It's sage," I say. "It smells like the spice we add to stuffing and pat on turkey, even sometimes mix into the gravy." "Oh," she says, and leans into the sagebrush a little closer.

As we step out of the forest and stand at the edge of the meadow, I notice a pink ribbon tied to the end of a branch of a ponderosa pine. A few steps farther, I see additional knotted ribbons protruding from sagebrush and bitterbrush limbs, synthetic pink plastic poking out of dusty gray-brown. Walking on, I begin to hear a faint rumble in the distance and turn to my daughter, who's clinging to my leg and holding my hand with trepidation. We walk gingerly toward the meadow, in the valley that stretches from the forest to the nearby mountain pass, when we finally see what all the commotion is about. Gears grinding, reverse gear beeping, a large yellow tractor jerks back and forth to gain enough momentum to pull up determined and willful roots of sage and bitterbrush. Back and forth it rocks, like a bucking bull, the yellow beast roaring its authoritative command dictates, kicking up clouds of dust and leaving in its path a sea of holes. I am stunned at what I see and even more surprised at what I didn't know. I soon learn, however, what will happen next.

I drive up to the sales office near my house, park the car, and timidly enter the building filled with salespeople and a mini-scaled model of a development centered in the front room. Forest lots, meadow lots, Jack Nicklaus eighteen-hole golf course, clubhouse and pool, sauna and restaurant: the beginnings. I pick up a brochure, which reads:

> An unprecedented variety of year-round family recreational amenities and 910 acres of Sierra parkland, [this new development] has been meticulously crafted to offer an incomparable golf and living experience rivaling the finest private golf club communities in the nation.

Though I hesitate to learn more, at home I click on the website and read the description of the golf course:

> Hole #1. Stop for a moment and take in the dramatic views of the thick carpet of conifers in the foreground and the Pacific Crest range between Tinker's Knob and Silver Peak with Granite Chief in the distance.
> Hole #18. The backdrop of neighboring Lookout Mountain is a spectacular sight you will take with you into the clubhouse.

What I learned, in the sense of being able to walk freely in areas surrounding my neighborhood, was that a new attitude had moved into town. The development that stopped my daughter and me from our seasonal wanderings—"What part of 'no trespassing' don't you understand?"—was the first of many similar developments. Expensive lots and look-alike "cabins" were sold at exorbitant prices that not many locals could afford. Numerous affluent housing projects moved in. Numerous locals moved out. What shocked us, all along, was that we hadn't seen it coming. We hadn't interpreted strips of pink surveying tape tied to ends of brush and pines as a foreshadowing.

Pink ribbons tell the story of the removal of one environment in exchange for the building of another. Pink ribbons say that *this* will become *that* and that soon you may not recognize the place you've been;

you may not even be permitted to enter it. Which is unthinkable. I have
been walking this land for years, and while it never belonged to me it was
part of my journey into nature, as well as my daughter's, who sensed the
magnificence I'd come to know.

To tie us to the Earth, we often tie ourselves to the land. This root-
ing, this adhesive bond from our wanderings, whether out our back gate
and across the street or on longer journeys into the mountains, desert,
or plains, instills a protectiveness. Yi-Fu Tuan describes this sentiment as
"topophilia," a love of place, a need for affective bonds with particular areas. But that bond comes with a price. What price could *I* pay to continue my seasonal explorations in the forest, meadow, and valley near my
home? Clearly, I was unable to pay *this* one. I had lost my freedom to
walk in the neighborhood woods and to overlook the valley at the edge
of those woods; I had lost a connection to nature.

Like many others who stumble upon pink ribbons tied to ends of
branches, I was confronted with a dilemma of topophilia, that of becoming familiar with and endeared to a piece of land and everything within
its domain, and accepting its new "off limits" status. The most difficult
part of the dilemma, however, is the part of loving a place too much and
in the end…having to let go.

Blackroot River

⚜ Mira Bartók

A poet once said that Heaven is not
like flying or swimming, but has something
to do with blackness and a strong glare but
how can one say that here where the water
glides green light over stones and the small bird
above calls who-*wheet* who-*wheet* telling me
to enter the river, hurry myself
to the sea, the place where all waters meet
a place like flying and swimming that
has nothing to do with blackness or the
unbearable glare of grief, nothing but
luminous fishes, bright stars in a sea
that resembles the sky, a chorus of
blue sleepless waves, white wings of cherubim.

PART III

What Comes from the Land

And the real name of our connection to this everywhere different and differently named earth is "work."... The name of our proper connection to the earth is "good work,"... It honors the source of its materials; it honors the place where it is done; it honors the art by which it is done; it honors the thing that it makes and the user of the made thing.

—Wendell Berry, from "Conservation is Good Work"

Fetching Water

✤ GARRETT CONOVER

Water in a pail
is exactly that
it's true.
But there is more
to gain with
every brim-full stride
to spring and back.

I dug the hole myself,
placed rocks to line
the sides—
places for leopard frogs
to hide,
a stone ringed sequin
for the color of sky.
My cares do not include
the hum of electric houses,
or mysteries
of pumps and pipes.
Structures I can't fix.
Easier to favor
buckets awash in self-reliance,
spilling freedom
with every sip.

There is no useful language
for those certain
of inconvenience.

Nor any for me
to speak of greeting days
with eager nose and eyes,
ears tuned,
expecting gifts
with every step.

You must already believe
there is news within the pail;
departing ripples from
a startled frog,
split sky streak
of a goshawk passing,
dippers of stars by night,
new green in summer leaves,
fleeting dimples from
snow falling,
bellies of clouds.
All this heaven
and earth crowding
the surface
of a simple drink.

If there is a joke
it laughs in the cost
of convenience.
There is nothing to trade
worth more
than one cool touch
of water to tongue
that loves purity,
such taste,
plump fullness from

these ritual minutes
that spice each day.
Carrying water
home.

Meat

🦂 STEVE BODIO

> *How, given the canine teeth and close-set eyes that declare the*
> *human animal to be a predator, had we come up with the no-*
> *tion that oat bran is more natural to eat than chicken?*

—Valerie Martin, from *The Great Divorce*

My life has been built around animals and books about them. They have been in every book I've written and most of my essays. I was imprinted on *The Jungle Book* and *Peterson's Field Guide* before I was four, fated to be a raving biophiliac as long as I lived. I fed myself a constant diet of books with animals—Darwin, Beebe, Lorenz on the one hand; Kipling, Seton, Terhune, Kjelgaard on the other. I read bird guides like novels and novels about pigeons. As long as I can remember I kept snakes, turtles, insects, pigeons, parrots, fish; bred them all, learned falconry and dog training, kept life lists, raced pigeons, hacked falcons for the Peregrine Fund, did rehab, joined conservation groups, supported veterinarians, partnered for life with bird dogs. I would say I "loved" animals but for the fact the word is so worn out in our culture that I distrust it. (Valerie Martin again: "…a word that could mean anything, like love. At dinner last night Celia had said, 'I love pasta. I love, love, love pasta,' and then to her father who had cooked the pasta for her, 'And you Dad. I love, love, love you.'") Suffice it to say that some animals are persons to me as well as points of focus, subjects of art, objects of awe, or quarries.

And…yet?…I eat meat, and always will. Which today is not only becoming vaguely suspect in some civilized quarters but also might be one point of dissension with what I understand of Buddhism. Although the Buddhist poet Gary Snyder once grinned as I handed him my copy of his book, *Turtle Island*, to autograph, opened to the poem "One should not talk to a skilled hunter about what is forbidden by the Buddha."

I recently announced too loudly at a dinner that I would no longer write anything with the purpose of convincing anyone to do anything. If writing essays means anything to me it is as an act of celebration and inquiry, like, if perhaps lesser than, poetry and science. With that in mind, let this be an inquiry into meat and, as my late friend Betsy used to say of the Catron County Fair, "a celebration of meat." I will try to be honest, even if it means admitting to crimes. Maybe this is about love after all.

Personal history does shape us all. I was born to blue-collar stock in the post-War suburbs. My mother's people were Irish and Scottish and English and German. Some had been farmers, one a revolutionary, and many had been fishermen, but by the time of my birth, they had escaped the land and become respectable, things my animal-obsessed intelligence rejected without analysis. McCabes tended to react with disgust to the messier parts of life. I still remember with delight my outspoken little sister Anita, who used to help me clean game, when she came to visit me with our grandmother and found me making a study skin from a road-killed woodpecker. She was all of eleven at the time, when many little suburban girls think they must be fastidious, but she scooped up the carcass and tossed it in the wastebasket. "You'd better get that covered up," she giggled, "or Nana McCabe is gonna puke all over the kitchen floor."

But the Bodios, who came over from the Italian Alps in their and the century's late teens, were from another planet than the lace-curtain Irish. My father had a furious drive toward WASP respectability, but his folks were Italian peasants who happened to live in Boston. Less than ten miles from downtown, they maintained until the ends of their long lives what was almost a farm. I believe their Milton lot contained a half acre of space. On it they had twelve apple trees, grape vines, and a gigantic kitchen garden. They also kept a few pigeons and rabbits. (No chickens—even then, Americans objected to the happy noise that half the planet wakes up to.)

Nana McCabe could cook pastries and cakes, but the Bodios *ate*. Eggs and prosciutto and parmesan, young bitter dandelions and mushrooms picked almost anywhere, risotto and polenta that, when I was very young, would be garnished with a sauce I learned ("don't tell nobody") was made from *uccelini*, little birds—I suspect sparrows, ambushed in the pigeon house. Eels, and mussels—which, back then, had to be gathered rather than bought. I tasted real vegetables there, not like the canned ones at home—tomatoes and corn eaten in the garden, warm from the sun, with a shaker of salt; zucchini and eggplant soaked in milk, breaded, and fried in butter like veal. Tart apples, stored in the cool cellar where Grandpa kept his homemade wine. Wine, served at every meal, to kids and adults alike.

And, of course, meat, interesting meat. My father hunted and fished and kept racing pigeons, but has always been indifferent to food. I suspect that, until his own old age, he found his parents' food too "ethnic," too reminiscent of the social barriers he wore himself out trying to transcend. As for my mother, she hated game—the mess of cleaning and its smells, the strangeness of its taste. She passed this down to most of the kids: my sister Wendy so abhorred the idea of venison that my brother and I would tell her steak and veal were "deer meat" so we could get her portion, a subterfuge so effective that she would leave the kitchen, claiming to be nauseated by the imagined smell.

So the good stuff often went to the Bodios by default. Really good stuff—black ducks with a slight rank taste of the sea, ruffed grouse better than any chicken, white-tailed deer that would hang swaying in the garage until the meat formed a dry crust and maybe a little mold. Bluefish, too rich ("fishy") for my mother's taste, and fifty-pound school tuna.

I don't know if my parents ever realized that I, tenderest-minded and softest and most intellectual of their kids, was also the one being trained to the delight of strange food, strange meat, even if the eating of it conflicted with my other principles. My father would snap a pigeon's neck without a thought if it was too slow in the races, but he wouldn't eat it. I would cry when he "culled" (never "killed") a bird, then eat it with delight at my grandparents'.

I thought then that I was weird, and felt guilty. Now I think it was my father who was weird, and my tender-minded sisters, who would be vegetarians if they had to kill their meat. They "love" animals, deplore my hunting. Only one of the six of them keeps animals, which are messy and take work to keep and know.

All these as yet unexamined attitudes and preferences went with me when I left home at seventeen. I became seriously weird at that point— to my parents, of course, because I grew my hair long and cultivated a beard and disagreed with them on sex, religion, politics, drugs, and money—but also, to my surprise, to many of my new friends. They of course shared my beliefs about all of the above. But at that time I usually lived in freezing shacks in seaside outer suburbs like Marshfield, with trained hawks and my Dad's old .410 and 16-gauge shotguns, and "lived off the land" in a way rather unlike that of rural communards. I spent so much time in the salt marshes that one girlfriend called me, not without affection, Swamp Wop.

I shot ducks and geese all fall, gathered mussels and quahogs and soft-shelled clams. You could still free-dive for lobsters then without being assaulted by legions of vacationing boat thugs. Squid swarmed in the summer and would strand themselves in rock pools on the spring tides. In summer we—my uncivilized blue-collar work mates and I, not my friends who agreed with me on art and politics—would use eelskin rigs and heavy rods to probe for stripers in the Cape Cod Canal. Winter would find us on the sandbars, freezing but happy as we tried for a late season sea duck for chowder or an early cod on a clam bait for the same.

Gradually I achieved some small notoriety—not just as some sort of nouveau primitive, but as a guy who could serve you some serious food. In the late seventies I was a staff writer for a weekly post-counter-culture paper in Cambridge and began to introduce occasional animal and/or food pieces to its pages. We had entered the age of debate on these subjects, but I still had fun. Just before the paper died, the food writer Mark Zanger, who still writes under the nom-de-bouffe "Robert Nadeau," and I were going to do a game-dinner extravaganza, to be titled "Bodio Kills It, Nadeau Cooks It," complete with appropriate wines and between-the-courses readings from my game diary. But the owners folded the paper and I left for New Mexico, a more hospitable ecosystem for my passions.

I present the above as a partial recounting of my bona fides, but also to present you a paradox. America and American civilization are still "new" compared to, say, France, Italy, China, Japan. France and Italy and China (and even Japan—fish, after all, is meat, the "meatless" Fridays of my youth notwithstanding) eat everything. They eat frogs and snails, eels and little birds, dogs and cats (and yes, deplorably, tigers and bears), snakes, whales, and poisonous puffer fish. They actually eat less bulk of meat than our sentimental in-denial culture of burger munchers, but they are in that sense more carnivorous—or omnivorous—than we are.

People who eat strange meat are considered "primitive" by our culture, whether or not theirs has existed longer than ours, or created better art, or happier villages.

So are our oldest ancestors, hunter-gatherers, who ate thistles and birds and eggs and grubs, roasted large game animals and feasted on berries like the bears they fully realized were cousins under the skin. Hunter-gatherers knew animals as persons, and ate them.

Can it be that we are the strange ones? We, who use up more of the world's resources than anyone, even as we deplore the redneck his deer, the French peasant his *grive*?

Can it be entirely an accident that in the wilds of southern France the wild boar thrives in the shadow of Roman ruins? That carefully worked out legal seasons for thrushes exist alongside returning populations of griffon vultures, lammergeiers, peregrines? That you can eat songbirds in the restaurants and look up to see short-toed eagles circling overhead? Just over the border, in Italy, they still have wolves, while in wilderness-free England and Brussels, Euromarket bureaucrats try to force the French to stop eating songbirds.

Three years ago I spent a month in the little Vauclusien village of Serignan-du-Comtat. Animals and books brought me there—in this case the insects and books of the great Provencal naturalist and writer Jean Henri Fabre.

The Fabre project I envisioned didn't come off. But upper Provence finally gave me a template, or maybe a catalyst, to crystallize my disconnected thoughts about nature, eating, wild things, and culture into a coherent form.

The thing is: I had expected insects, sure; stone medieval villages, good food, wine and vines, lavender and broom, Roman ruins and the signs of long occupancy of the land.

I hadn't expected anything like "the wild." But on my first walk into the dry oak hills behind the town I looked up into the brilliant yellow eyes of a hovering short-toed eagle, a *circaète Jean-le-blanc* bigger than an osprey, with the face of an owl and long dangling legs. The snake eater soon proved common, as did red kites, almost extinct in Great Britain. A week or so later I was hiking on the flanks of Mont Ventoux in a landscape that reminded me enormously of the Magdalenas at home when I saw a soaring hawk suspended over the deep valley between me and the next ridge. This one resolved in my binoculars into the extremely rare— but returning—Bonelli's eagle, a sort of giant goshawk.

More evidence of the paradox kept coming in through the month. Restaurants like the Saint Hubert—it was named after the patron saint of hunters—sold boar and duck; the proprietor told me to come back in the fall and eat *grives*, thrushes. A nature magazine discussed the reintroduction of griffon vultures west of the Rhone. Birders directed me to the bare stone teeth of the Dentelles, south of Ventoux, where the bone-breaking lammergeier or bearded vulture was nesting. I didn't think they existed any longer west of the Himalayas! I caught a jazz concert in the Theatre Antique, a Roman theatre in Orange, in continuous use since before the time of Christ. I looked down from wild hills with signs of badger and fox and deer into the ordered lines of vineyards.

One morning at dawn I came over a little rise and surprised two middle-aged men in camo fatigues loading two hounds into the back of a 2CV. The larger man was moon faced and moustached. The smaller, like many Provencals, could have been a blood relative of mine; he was dark and wiry, with curly black hair. Both smoked unfiltered cigarettes; the black tobacco was pungent in the still-sweet morning air. The short hunter's dog was sleek and black with long bloodhound ears, not unlike a black-and-tan coonhound; the big man's dog was also huge, white and shaggy, with a whiskered muzzle like a terrier's.

They replied curtly to my cheery "Bonjour," but I was fascinated. "Je suis un chasseur Americain," I began: "I'm an American hunter." The transformation was instantaneous; they both shook my hand and began speaking over each other in quick French made even tougher to understand by their heavy local accents. "You're American, that's good.... We thought you were from Paris…those northerners, they think they're better than us. They don't hunt, they hate hunters…they are all moving down here to their summer houses." I felt like I was in New Mexico. Then I caught, "Did you see the boar, m'sieur?"

The boar?

"Oui, the boar. We train our dogs here in the summer…It ran just where you were coming from, down near the village."

I must have looked skeptical, because they led me to its track in a mud puddle across the path. The soil hadn't even settled from the water; the great beast (its tracks were huge) must have crossed the path just seconds ahead of me.

They hung around to show me game waterers to allow the animals to drink during the dry summer months, to invite me to share a *pastis* at the bar in town, to ask me to return in the fall when we could eat truffles and partridge and *bartavelle* (a kind of chukar) and grives, and boar. I realized that, unlike in England and Germany, everybody hunts in rural France—the butcher and baker and mechanic as well as the local personages. Maybe it's the French Revolution, maybe the Mediterranean influence. I doubt that the sign on the tank, posted by my new friends and their fellow members of the Serignan hunter's society, would have appeared in England or Germany or the U.S.: *Nature est notre culture*: Nature is our culture, our garden.

Nature is our culture. Our "permaculture" if you will; something a part of us, that we're a part of. Nobody in rural southern France is ignorant of what food is, or meat.

I had been trying to live something like this for as long as I had been conscious. I hunted, and gathered, and gardened, and liked it all. I spent my rather late college years in rural western Massachusetts, put a deer in the freezer and cut cordwood, some of which I sold to professors. I ate road kill for two years, cruised the roads at dawn for carcasses of cottontail and snowshoe hare and squirrel, praising whatever gods when I found a grouse (I barely had time to hunt except during deer week), learning you could cook snake and make it good. I even ate a road-killed hawk once—it was delicious.

But the French visit gave me a more coherent vision. Having confessed to one crime (yes, roadkill picking is generally illegal) I'll tell you of a worse one. Or—no, let me tell this in the third person.

A naturalist recently returned from France awoke one fall morning to find his rowan trees full of hundreds of robins feeding on the red berries. He went to feed his goshawk and found the cupboard bare. (Goshawk: the French falconers call her *cuisiniere*, cook, because she is the kitchen's best helper; she'll keep you in diverse meat all winter.) But season hadn't started.

He thought long—well, maybe five minutes—about France and food and his hungry hawk. Opened the window. The robins flew up, then returned to their gobbling.

Robins are true grives, thrushes of the genus *Turdus*. In the fall they grow fat on fruit.

He tiptoed to the gunroom, got out an accurate German air rifle, cocked it, loaded it. Stood inside the open window, in the dark of the room. Put the bead on a fat cock's head, and pressed the trigger. One thrush fell, the rest fled to the higher trees. He walked out, collected the fallen bird, admired its lovely colors, felt its fat breast. Made sure the pellet had passed through the head, took it to his gos's mews, where she leaped on it with greedy delight.

Now, though, he is really thinking. He gets down his copy of Angelo Pellegrini's *The Unprejudiced Palate* and reads, "People now and then complain that their cherries, raspberries, strawberries are entirely eaten by the birds.... When this is true, the offending songsters should be captured and eaten." Well, he hardly considers the robins to be "offending," but they certainly were eating fruit. Pellegrini adds that they are "delectable morsels unequaled by any domestic fowl or larger game bird." Hmmm....

He goes to his copy of Paul Bocuse, which features a dozen recipes. He likes the one that adds sautéed potato balls and garlic to the briefly roasted whole thrushes.

He goes back to the window. Fires six times. Six times a bird falls; six times the others flee for a moment, then return to their feasting.

He plucks them, but leaves the head, feet, and innards. Roasts them in a 425 degree oven for ten minutes. Combines them with the potatoes and sautéed garlic. Shares them with his wife, a kindred spirit, accompanied by a red Italian wine.

He tells me that they were delicious and that he doesn't feel guilty at all.

Delicious, of course. Food should be delicious, and inexpensive, and real, which last two keep it from being mannered or decadent. My hunting and gathering and husbandry are driven both by principle and by pleasure—why should they not be driven by both? But because the "good people" in our northern protestant civilization-of-the-moment are so often gripped by a kind of puritanism even as their opposite numbers rape the world with greed (did I write "opposite"? I wonder....) most writers do not write of the sensuous pleasure of food. Okay, a few: M. F. K.

Fisher, first and always; Patience Gray; Jim Harrison; John Thorne. But even they don't write enough about the pleasure of meat. So before we return full circle to principle, to guilt and remorse, to "why," let's take a moment to celebrate the delights of our subject.

If we weren't supposed to eat meat, why does it smell so good? Honest vegetarians I know admit they can be forced to drool by the sweet smell of roasting birds. No food known to humans smells quite as fine as any bird, skin rubbed with a clove of garlic, lightly coated with olive oil, salted, peppered, turning on a spit over a fire.

Why do we Anglo-Saxons overcook our meat? Another residue of puritanism, of fear of the body, of mess, of eating, of realizing that death feeds our lives? Do we feel that guilty about not photosynthesizing?

Nobody could tell me wild duck tastes "of liver" if they cooked it in a 500 degree oven for fifteen or twenty minutes.

No one could say that venison does, if they dropped thin steaks into a hot skillet, turned them over once, and removed them and ate them immediately.

Hell, nobody could tell me liver tastes "like liver" if they did the same, in bacon fat, with onions already well-cooked piled around it.

A cowboy I know used to say he hated "nasty old sheep." We changed his mind when we bought a well-grown lamb from the Navajos, killed and skinned and gutted it, and let it soak for a day in a marinade of garlic, honey, chiles, and soy sauce, turning it frequently. Then Omar and Christine, Magdalena's prime goat and lamb roasters, cooked the legs and ribs over an open fire, until a crust formed over the juicy interior. The smell could toll cars passing in the street into Omar's yard. Omar and I, especially, are known to stab whole racks of ribs off the grill with our knives and burn our mouths, moaning with pleasure.

Stock: I put all my bird carcasses in a big pasta pot with a perforated insert. I usually don't add vegetables. I cook them for ten to sixteen hours, never raising the stock to a boil...never. The result perfumes the house, causes shy friends to demand to stay for dinner, ends up as clear as a mountain stream but with a golden tint like butter. Then you can cook the risotto (we say "risott" like northern peasants, to distinguish it from the yuppie version) with it. But you only need a little—the real stuff uses more wine or even hot water, and a lot of parmesan.

I love my pigeons, but have you ever eaten "real" squab, that is, five-week-old, fat, meltingly tender pigeon? I keep a few pairs of eating breeds for just that. You could cut it with a fork....

How about real turkey, the wild kind? It actually tastes like bird, not cardboard, and has juice that doesn't come from chemical "butter." Eat one, and you'll never go back.

How about the evilest meats of all, the salted kind? How about prosciutto, with its translucent grain and aftertaste like nuts? How about summer sausage? Old-style hams with a skin like the bark of an oak? How about real Italian salame, or capicola?

Good things could be said about vegetables too, by the way. We here at the Bodio household actually eat more veggies than meat; meat is for essence and good gluttony, not for bulk. We eat pasta and rice and beans, cheese, good bread, garden vegetables by the ton, roast vegetables, raw ones. But these things don't need a defender. Meat, improbably to me, does.

Let's veer in through that sensuousness once more. Last month I was preparing five domestic ducks for a feast with friends. To cook it the best way the breast meat had to be blood rare, the legs well done with a crispy skin. Which of course involved totally dismantling the ducks, hard work. You had to partly cook them, then skin them, getting seriously greasy. (The skin would become crackling, or as my wife Libby called it, punning on the pork-crackling *chicharonnes* of New Mexico, *pata-ronnes*.) You had to fillet the breast meat from the bone, and disjoint the legs. The carcasses had to go back into the oven for browning, and then into the stock pot. You ended up physically tired, sweaty, with aching hands, small cuts everywhere, and slime to your elbows. You felt good, accomplished, weary. But it was hard to avoid the idea that you had cut up an animal, or five.

Or take a *matanza*, a pig killing, in Magdalena. After shooting the pig in the head (if you do it right, the other pigs watch but nobody, even the hero of the feast, gets upset), it's work, work that will give you an appetite. The pig is carried out on a door, wrapped with burlap sacks boiled in one half of a fifty gallon drum, scraped, hung up. It is eviscerated, and the viscera are washed and saved. The bulk of the "real" meat, all that will not be eaten that day, goes to the freezer. The chicharonnes are cut up and heaped into the other half of the drum, to sizzle themselves crispy in their own fat. Everything steams in the cold air—the fires and vats, your breath, the pig's innards. Those innards are quickly fried with green chiles and wrapped in fresh flour tortillas so hot they'll burn your tongue, to give you energy to rock that carcass around, to stir the chicharonne vat with a two-by-four. The blood is taken in and fried with raisins ("sweet blood") or chiles ("hot blood") and brought out to where you are working. By afternoon you are as hungry as you have ever been. You eat like a wolf. You also can't avoid the idea that you have taken a life. Afterward, you all lie around like lions in the sun.

I once mentioned a matanza in a piece I wrote for the *Albuquerque Journal*. An indignant letter writer (from Massachusetts!) called me "refuse" for my "Hemingwayesque" love of blood, "hot and sweet," which he assumed was a grim metaphor rather than a rural delicacy. He hurt my feelings. But maybe he was right, in a way he hadn't intended.

So, okay, death. And cruelty.

Deliberate cruelty is inexcusable; I won't say much about it here. As I get older I actually use bigger calibers and gauges than when I was young; I can't stand wounding anything.

But death? We all cause it, every day. We can't not. Tom McGuane once said, "The blood is on your hands. It's inescapable." Vegetarians kill too. Do they seriously think that farming kills nothing? Or maybe they're like the Buddhist Sherpas that Libby used to guide with, who would ask her to kill their chickens and goats so the karma would be on her hands.

An acceptance of all this is not always easy, even for the hunter and small farmer, who usually know animals far better than the vegetarian or consumer. I find that as I get older, I am more and more reluctant to kill anything, though I still love to hunt for animals, to shoot, and to eat.

Still, I am determined to affirm my being a part of the whole mystery, to take personal responsibility, to remind myself that death exists, that animals and plants die for me, that one day I'll die and become part of them. "Protestant" "objectifying" "Northern" culture—in quotes because none of those concepts is totally fair or accurate, though they do mean something—seems to be constantly in the act of distancing itself from the real, which does exist—birth, eating, juicy sex, aging, dirt, smells, animality, and death. Such distancing ends in the philosophical idiocies of the ornithologist Robert Skutch, who believes sincerely that God and/or evolution got the universe wrong by allowing predation and that he, a Connecticut Yankee, would have done better.

I, on the other hand, don't feel I know enough about anything to dictate to the consciences of others. I certainly don't think that anyone should kill, so long as they realize they are no more moral than those who do; I can find it hard enough myself. While I suspect the culture would be saner if we all lived a bit more like peasants, grew some veggies out of the dirt, killed our own pigeons and rabbits, ate "all of it" like bushmen or Provencal hunters or the Chinese, I have no illusions that this is going to happen tomorrow. I can only, in the deepest sense, cultivate my garden, sing my songs of praise, and perfect my skills. I'll try to have what Ferenc Máté calls "a reasonable life," strive to be aware and compassionate and only intermittently greedy, to eat as well as my ancestors, to cook well and eat well as a discipline and a joy. The French say of a man who has lived well that "*Il bouffe bien, il boit bien, il baise bien*": he eats well, he drinks well, he (in this context) fucks well. Sounds like a life to me.

And in living my good and reasonable life, I suspect I should sometimes kill some beautiful animal and eat it, to remind myself what I am: a fragile animal, on a fierce fragile magnificent planet, who eats and thinks and feels and will someday die: an animal, made of meat.

Dear Bowl

⚜ SUSAN A. COHEN

Dear Bowl,

I write to you with so little sense of how to address you. So little sense of what I want to say. What is the polite way to begin our relationship? It seems rash for me to launch so directly into my feelings for you; after all, we've only just met. But when I lifted you from the Sterling College bookstore table, separating you from the other hand-turned wooden bowls and plates and the two side-by-side rolling pins, I was astonishingly forward, tipping you toward my body and pressing you against my heart before any sort of formal introduction. Please forgive me as I learn what is proper.

Rim to rim, when I hold you, you rest just below my collar bone, touch both sides of my torso, and reach down to my seventh rib. Smooth and warm against my body, you circle my heart. You are just the weight of the dead fledgling hawk I once carried before burying her. You are the color of the pup I rescued ten years ago. You are the size of my second child moments after his birth, in his curled-up state when placed in my arms. I don't ask your permission, I don't know how you feel about being up for sale or sold or how you will feel about leaving these Vermont woods, I just tip you backwards on your base, place you on the counter, pay my money and take you.

And then we sit. You in my lap, me on the floor with my back against the wall for balance. We sit in the quiet for what feels like a long time to me, and then, I recognize that you do not feel time the way I do. What are minutes or hours or class sessions or birthdays or watches to you? Once, perhaps, you kept time in snow time and leaf time and rain time and wind time. This was when you were a rooted tree. A cherry tree. In the quiet, I try hard to listen for your story. It seems the only way to hear your story is through my hands. I press them, overlapped, into your shallow curved center. Hand on hand on warm wood. I rub my fingers along your rim, slowly, until the tips of my fingers feel tickled.

But my fingers stiffen and pull away from your skin with something they recall. Bowl, you don't know this about me, but I played piano through most of my childhood, my fingertips trained to intimacy with wood and ivory keys. My fingers have memories of their own. So thirty years later, I can still sit down at a piano to play a bit of a Chopin etude, even though my conscious mind no longer remembers the notes. When my fingers jerk away from your body, it is because my piano-trained, wood-sensitive fingers recognize the absence of your tree bark, the loss of leaves and roots. I am afraid of discovering some violence beneath your surface. So I play a few notes along your rim, trying to understand your story. I wonder what happened to you. Were you ill or caught in a storm and uprooted? Where are your scars from being cut and lathed and trimmed and shaped? My fingers tremble, but Bowl, you show no signs at all of a troubled past. How well you hide those scars beneath your new curves and oiled surfaces, how easily you accept change. I cradle you, sorrowing for only a moment when I touch the loss in your story. But you, Bowl, you are calm.

I look more carefully at your surface. If I hold you at arms length, in your belly I see a pale yellow half moon slipping into a butterscotch sky. A partial lunar eclipse. The word eclipse, my father used to say, means, "I cease to exist." Is this true of you? No, not really. You may have ceased to exist in your treeness, but, ah, now you have reached bowlness. How good to meet you now, you of curve and practical roundedness.

I hope it's not presumptuous to ask, but when we go home, would you mind being the keeper of my daughter's letters, or of the keys I tend to misplace, or the ripening peaches from the Saturday morning farmer's market? You are certainly shaped to the task. And I promise to place you by a curtainless south-facing window where some mornings we can sit together, just you and me, Bowl, warming to the day.

Bowl, the better I know you, the more I look forward to our future together.

Sincerely,

Susan

Demeter, Fond of Cycles

🐝 JANICE DUKES

Thursday is bread day
when I make the trek to market
where loaves prop their golden heels
on wooden shelves. I study their round
and oblong shapes, so like
the seeds that made them.

As I draw knife through crust
seeds leap and scatter
counter to floor as if
to sow themselves. I lick
my fingertip and press it down
to gather one small harvest, just
a taste of all the mysteries
compressed within.

I'm content to leave
your mysteries be, humble in
my weekly rounds
so distant from your fields,
yet still I feel your pulse
beneath the street
and see how in the smallest crack
your finger pokes up, green.

Bean by Bean

❧ Terra Brockman

The haricots verts are masters of disguise. Unlike the yellow wax or royal burgundy beans, they are nearly indistinguishable from the stems of the bean plant. They also tend to hide down low near the base of the bush, hugging the stem and the earth, resisting the searching hand and the easy pluck from plant to basket.

Which is just as well, because after the wet week, some near the soil are starting to soften. Every once in a while you see the white-cotton fuzz of mold beginning. Those beans you toss aside, along with any that have more than a touch of rust, or more than one or two nibbles by a bean beetle. Those not-quite-perfect beans get tossed into the neighboring bed of spent plants, recently tilled under and seeded with cover crops.

Only the most perfect beans go into the half bushel basket that moves with you, half-foot by lurching half-foot, down the row. These are the organic green beans that our farmer's market customers will grab by the easy handful tomorrow morning—a time that seems impossibly far away as you realize there are four hundred half-feet in a two hundred-foot row, and that you are spending maybe five minutes picking the beans from every six inches of row. You do the math, and feel the chill air slip in from the hillside.

Not wanting to still be picking beans at midnight, you start plucking faster. You concentrate on the way the beans arrange themselves, and the way your fingers can grab the greatest number in one motion from bush to basket. You play games with yourself, saying you're not going to look up to see if Matt, the farmhand who started at the other end of the row, has gotten any nearer. You simply reach and pluck and toss. Bend the plant to the other side. Reach and pluck and toss. Move the basket to the next plant. Reach and toss. Reach and toss.

Somehow the Zen of repetition takes over, the efficient pathways establishing themselves in your brain and down your arm to your fingertips. You listen to the evening calls of the birds, the beginning of the insect chorus muted by the coolness. You gradually notice the first goosebumps on your arms.

And then, suddenly, you almost knock heads with Matt. You slowly unbend your body—ankles, knees, vertebrae, neck, head. Bipedal and erect once again, you notice the perfect half moon halfway up the deepening sky. The evening softens, deepens, brings perspective. You are a dot on the horizon, a small part of something much bigger, much longer than one human life. Standing on the earth, you know that you are a part of the same something that everything came from, and to which you and everything will return, and from which you can never be separated.

You scoop up a handful of soil and hold a miracle—the product of death, the promise of life. You balance the bushel basket of beans on your head and walk—half weary, half triumphant—to the end of the row where the pickup is waiting. A job well done. Bean by bean.

Rolling the Turf

🍀 MEGHAN MCCARTHY MCPHAUL

When Breege and I arrived at the bog, the men had already been working for an hour or more. The day was fine, as the locals said, usually tacking on a "Thanks be to God," although they said that whether it was pissing rain or pouring sunshine. Today was cool and bright, and Breege wanted to escape from her work in the Diamonds' dank pub.

Breege was my boss and one of the few people I knew in Renvyle. She and her husband Liam owned a fish wholesale business, an unpopular pub, and a horse-trekking center. I was there to tend to the seven horses and lead tourists on treks to the beach and along the narrow roads of the country, but there were few visitors so far west that early in the spring. And so I was happy to go to the bog rather than sit and wonder what I was supposed to be doing for this family, who diverged from the persona of most Irish people I've known by saying little and smiling even less.

Breege drove her new Peugot sedan as far up the bog road as she thought it could go, and we walked the rest of the way, over hills of grass and heather to where the men were working. As a Yank I hadn't spent much time in bogs, where the Irish harvest turf for burning like we chop wood in New England. I hadn't spent all that much time chopping and stacking wood, either. When my brothers and I were kids, I always sensed firewood work coming and would sneak up the road to my friend Lisa's house, an event so common in the autumns of my childhood that my brothers still chastise me for it.

As we approached the section of bog cut into long rows of turf, about four inches wide and ready for rolling, I watched the half dozen men bend and stand, bend and stand. Each had a tool of choice, a pitchfork or shovel, to help loosen the turf from the anchoring grass before bending to expose the dense, black underside for drying.

Breege and I joined the row at the end of the rectangular plot, and I quickly got into the repetition of digging and rolling. The muscles of my neck and shoulders tightened with the rhythmic strain, and my flannel over-shirt soon joined the frayed tweed coats discarded at the side of the turf patch. The work went quickly at first and I was pleased with myself, a novice turf roller, for keeping up with the practiced men. My energy quickly waned, however, and I started to pace myself for the long day.

Now and then I looked up and around me and smiled at my good luck. Sure, the work was hard, and my hamstrings and back were already beginning to ache, but to a girl who so wanted to be more closely connected to Ireland, a day in the bog was a dream. Here was the fabled land of my ancestors, the bogs of Seamus Heaney's poems, the lovely melancholy of W. B. Yeats.

I was surrounded by an unwavering landscape of cut turf and heather, which hadn't yet started to bloom and blended in its starkness with the dull yellow-brown of the bogs. Before us was the narrow Clifden road, a main route traveled by few cars. All around there were small, square houses with whitewashed walls and slate roofs nestled into hedges and fields. Beyond the bog lay green pastures scattered with new lambs, and beyond the fields was the sea, whose mysterious gravity pulled at me for the six months I was there, pulls at me still.

When we stopped for lunch, the men settled behind a knoll that blocked the wind and pulled out sandwiches and containers of cold tea. Some were regular employees of the Diamonds, van drivers relegated to bog work for the day. Others were frequent patrons of the pub, lifelong bachelors who spent their days half drunk or more and had been lured to the bog by the promise of a bit of pay and a few free pints.

I settled into a bank of grassy peat and kept quiet, content to rest for a moment, to watch the grass and heather sway in the wind and listen to the lilt of the Irish voices, interrupted now and again by John's strange Welsh accent and David's Scottish one. The breeze carried the faint salty

scent of the sea, but mostly the bog smelled of the sweet, organic mustiness of settled peat.

All too soon we returned to our turf rows, minus Petey, one of the
regular pub patrons, who stayed behind for a smoke and a nap. About
an hour after lunch, Liam arrived in the bog with a fellow fish vendor, a
man originally from Iran but living now in Dublin.

A tour bus, a common sighting in Ireland, stopped along the road,
about one hundred yards away from where we worked. As the tourists
filed out to take pictures, I imagined them returning to their homes in
England or America or Germany and proudly displaying photos of the
Irish folk working in the bog. I bent to roll another length of turf, thinking how disappointed the tourists would be to know our group con-
sisted of only a few Paddys, along with a Yank, a Scot, an Iranian, and a
Welshman.

Lured by the promise of a few free pints, the boys gave a push at the
end, their enthusiasm carrying me along, and we finished the whole lot.
I went home tired, but content with a day of hard work, wondering if my
brothers would agree that I had redeemed myself for the years of leaving
the splitting and stacking to them.

For the Love of a Good Tomato

CHARLOTTE PYLE

Shortly after we first moved to Conrad Hollow, my husband David and I sat on the porch with our friend, JoAnn, watching a beat-up Chevy Nova creep along to where the road dead-ended at the next house. JoAnn, an east Tennessee native, took one look at the car's occupants. "Your neighbors are *real*," she pronounced with surprise.

A few days later, as newcomers ready to explore, we walked up the road to introduce ourselves. Several small dogs announced our presence, loudly and well before we reached the house.

"Hush!" a clean-shaven man admonished as he came out of the house. The dogs quieted. We explained who we were and found out his name was Ernest. We asked permission to walk in the woods beyond the house, saying that we liked to look at wild plants and birds. Ern's face, well tanned with deep wrinkles around the mouth and eyes, showed a bit of bewilderment. However, he smiled at us when his wife, Mary, came out to be introduced. I mentioned I originally was from California.

"You tawk lack 'em people on TV," Mary noted. Ern told Mary that we wanted to walk up in the woods past their house.

"They's an ol' house way on up in yan holler," Mary informed us. A rangy, big-boned woman with flat, blue eyes and red, work-hardened hands, she stood nearly as tall as her husband. She knew the hollow well, having grown up within walking distance of where she lived now. It was an aunt and uncle who had once lived in the little, abandoned house we later came upon. A few years after we had moved in, Mary's cousin and his wife, in dire need of a place to live, stayed up there for a while.

At home in Conrad Hollow, away from our jobs and typical activities with friends of our own age, we lived as though on a rural retreat, relaxing around the house and making frequent forays up in the wild part of the hollow. We worked the land a bit, too. We soon cleared a small section of brambles from the sunny, steep hillside on our side of the barbed wire fence that separated the two properties. There we made a terraced version of two French bio-intensive, raised garden beds. We began building up the heavily eroded soil with leaf mulch and sawdust seasoned with urine and lime. The urine was something I had learned about when I participated in a tomato-growing experiment as a university student in California.

When summer's heat began to fill the hollow, we spent weekend mornings sipping coffee on the front porch, eyes surveying the "holler" before it got too warm to enjoy the sun. Behind the house, in our small garden, the tomatoes were mulched and did not need too much attention. At the same time, it was worth a trip up the hillside to adjust the ties to ensure all the fruit would be out of reach of that pesky box turtle with the chipped shell, who liked to sample low-growing tomatoes just as they ripened. Mostly, though, on weekends, we were lazy in the heat, knowing that the tomatoes would take care of themselves.

As the summer developed, the overwhelming August heat brought the intense sound of katydids at night. The sound was nothing like what we hear now, in Connecticut, where katydids sing in a finite number of voices, most merely saying *Katy did*. (Some just creak out *Kay Tee* as August rainstorms cool the air.) Back in Conrad Hollow, the din of katydids dominated the hot August nights. Out of the incessant hum, a multitude of dry voices emerged: *Katy did. Katy didn't, DIDN'T, didn't. Kadee diddle, Katy did't. Katy didn't diddle. Katydid.* Along with the songs of katydids, we learned that the incessant August heat produced sweet, rich tomatoes unlike anything we had ever eaten.

The jazz of katydids connected everything in the hollow. A chorus from beyond Mary and Ern's house: *Kadee didn't. Did. Didn't.* Outside the bedroom window, another chorus: *Katy did't. KATY did diddle.*

Didn't. Both choruses sang simultaneously and independently, yet there was a give and take in the rhythm of the sound from the head of the hollow down to our house and back.

"Come on in," Ern had invited one day that first summer. We looked over from the road to see him leaning out the kitchen door alerted to our presence by the canine cacophony. That day, Mary was canning peaches. Ern removed the quart jars one by one from the hot oven where they had been sterilized. He steadied the wide-mouth funnel while Mary ladled in peaches. Ray, their son, whom we most often saw working on his car, capped the jars with lids taken from water boiling on the stove. The kitchen was stifling.

"'Ar, 'at's done," Mary said, filling the last jar and stepping back to wipe her dripping brow. Her eyes sparkled as she added, "Ah've done fifty-six jar this year."

Ern smiled with pride as he pulled back the yellow-printed fabric tacked to a tall, wide bookshelf shelf and displayed a selection of quart jars for me to admire. There were early tomatoes, green beans, more peaches, and half pints of strawberry and blackberry jam along with a dusty jar of pickled hot peppers from last year.

Early in our second summer, while reading by the open window, my eye was caught by the sight of a riderless horse walking across the steep hillside on the other side of the fence. Upon closer inspection, I saw that it was Mary's brother, Orville, plowing behind a thin, gray mule. The next time I saw Ern, I asked what they grew up there. "Backuh," he said. It was not until harvest time that I figured out what he had said.

Tobacco takes considerable tending. More than once, we saw Ern and his four grown sons up on the steep slope. Sometimes they waved to us as we worked in our garden on the other side of the wire fence.

In the fall, with the help of the extended family, the plants on the hillside were cut down. Each stem was speared over the end of a long, sharp-pointed stick. Each stick, with multiple leafy stems hanging from it, was loaded onto a trailer behind the tractor of Mary's brother Bob and transported to her cousin Jerry's barn where the tobacco "poles" were hung until the leaves were cured.

Another day, later in that second summer, Ern called out from near the washing machine on his front porch as we walked by. "Hot enough for you'ns?" As David laughed softly, Ern added, "I seen you'ns a-workin' out back t'house. Got you'ns a garden up 'ar?"

"Lots of tomato plants, and basil and peppers," David told him. He did not elaborate on our organic nitrogen source; nevertheless, I was hugely pleased to know it had proved itself in the produce we grew.

Though exploring the hollow and sitting back in lazy enjoyment of tomatoes were major highlights of our life in Conrad Hollow, we also enjoyed transforming the front yard from a wasteland. One April we embarked on a digging project. After we had dug with pickaxe and shovel for a few hours every weekend over an entire month, Arlen, Mary and Ern's oldest boy, stopped his lawn mower for a rest and came toward us from the orchard. Looking through the fence, he asked, "What you'ns a-diggin'?"

"We want to see the creek," I explained from where I stood on top of the now-exposed end of the culvert.

"Old Harold McMahon, he put that culvert in," Arlen replied. "Hit used to flood. House was rat 'ar down by the branch, too, afore he move' 't up where you'ns live now." Arlen was warm-hearted, but shy, his speech more strongly clipped than Mary's and Ern's. It was a way of speaking very different from that of my mother's Deep South relatives, but occasionally the voices in the hollow recalled my grandparents to me.

Not many days later, Harold McMahon just happened to drive up the road. It was the first time we had seen him since he sold us the house.

"You'ns can't take that culvert out!" he said, appalled at us and then at himself as he hastily added, "Well, yes, 'course you can." He paused. "But why?"

I explained that we wanted to be able to see the stream on our land. He told us how the culvert that crossed a fifty-foot wide section of our property was actually three culverts pieced together.

"How long do you think this first section is?"

"Mebbe 18 foot." Eighteen very long feet it was.

Mary and Ern's son-in-law, Carl, walked out from the orchard with Ern and Arlen on a tour of the city folks' latest insanity. The culvert was now completely exposed to its first joint. We were filling buckets with dirt and gravel pulled up from its sides.

"You'ns might could jack it on up outta 'ar," Carl suggested. Excellent idea that was.

We dug more. Finally, at the end of July, we jacked the culvert out. It sat in the front yard, both a symbol of our triumph in freeing a bit of nature and a rather large eyesore.

"What you'ns plan to do with that culvert?" Ern asked. He had taken a small detour coming down from tending the tobacco and now stood peering down at us through the fence while we placed rocks on the stream bank to protect the remaining section of buried culvert.

"Nothing," said David.

"Like to get it out of here," I added.

The next weekend, Bob's truck stopped in front of our house as we worked in the stream. "What you'ns plan to do with that culvert?"

"Nothing," David said.

"Could you use it?" I added.

Bob came back, this time driving his tractor. Arlen showed up to help. Soon, for different reasons, we and they were both highly gratified by the sight and sound of the rusty culvert bouncing down the road behind the big, slowly turning tractor tires.

Early in the fall after the summer we had "day-lighted" the stream, I was out working in the yard by the road. Ern stopped the car on the way out. "You'ns want some green?" Mary asked.

"What kind?"

"Turn'p."

"You kin come pick with us," Judy (Mary and Ern's married daughter) offered from the back seat. I got in the car with Judy and we drove a few miles to Ern's cousin Jolene's house. On the driveway, Jolene was carrying two heavy grocery bags.

"Kin you hep me with these sacks, Ern?" she asked.

"I don't care," Ern replied. I was amazed at the coldness of Ern's words until he took a bag out of her hand and I realized he meant that he did not *mind* helping.

Mary, Judy, and I filled large plastic bags with succulent turnip greens that turned out to be the sweetest and most tender I had ever eaten. It was only after my bag was gone that I (the die-hard, organic gardener) found out the greens had been grown on a heavily fertilized and pesticided bed in which the previous spring's tobacco plants had been grown to a transplantable size.

The years went by. In Conrad Hollow, we and Mary's family lived our different lives. In the hot, hot days of August, while they canned quart after quart of tomatoes, green beans, and other garden produce for the winter, we gloried in the season by devouring the fresh, sun-ripened tomatoes with no thought beyond the next meal. Tomato and basil omelets. Tomato, basil, and cheese sandwiches. Quick stir-fries with tomato, green pepper, and onion, sometimes with okra (courtesy of Mary and Ern) complemented by chilled tomato and basil salads.

One year, combined vacation and job-related travel took us away just as our tomatoes were beginning to ripen. We had a wonderful time in Colorado. Then, in the Knoxville airport we saw a newspaper headline, "Drought Continues for Third Week." After an hour's drive, we turned up the dirt road heading toward Conrad Hollow. In the headlights, we noticed with foreboding that the roadside plants were ghostly with a thick covering of dust.

In the driveway, David and I got out of the car, greeted by a huge chorus of *Katy did. Didn't, didn't, didn't* coming from up the hollow, followed by a distinct voice in the chorus from the woods next to the driveway: *Katy DID!* Back and forth, back and forth, the rhythm of summer in the hollow. Hot, yes. But it was so good to be back home. And it was home, even as we remained perpetual newcomers to the closely knit mountain family next door.

The night was still hot after we unloaded the car. We took flashlights up to the garden. The tomatoes seemed all right except for some nibbled ones that lay rotting.

The next morning at first light, we went out. The tomatoes were, indeed, just fine. In fact, the plants were greener than anything else on the hillside. "That mulch you put down really did its job," I said, relieved, as I picked a small basketful of red, perfect, sun-ripened tomatoes. Biting into one, I found it as sweet and luscious as only a good, hot summer could make it.

Coming back to the house, I noticed a cardboard matchstick in the grass. I looked around carefully, but couldn't find any signs of mischief or attempted break-in.

The next time we went up the hollow, I saw Ern at the henhouse and asked if he had noticed anyone poking around the house while we were gone. When Ern asked why, I explained about the matchstick in our front yard.

"Well, we saw your 'maties was awful wilted, so we come over to water 'em." He looked a little self-conscious as he added, "I hope you don't care."

PART IV

On Perceiving
and Knowing

*"Look deep into nature, and then
you will understand everything better."*

—Albert Einstein

Earth's Eye

ॐ EDWARD HOAGLAND

Water is our birthplace. We need and love it. In a bathtub, or by a lake or at the sea, we go to it for rest, refreshment, and solace. "I'm going to the water," people say when August comes and they crave a break. The sea is a democracy, so big it's free of access, often a bus or subway ride away, a meritocracy, sink or swim, and yet a swallower of grief because of its boundless scale—beyond the horizon, the home of icebergs, islands, whales. Tears alone are a mysterious, magisterial solvent that bring a smile, a softening of hard thoughts, lend us a merciful and inexpensive respite, almost like half an hour at the beach. In any landscape, in fact, a pond or creek catches and centers our attention as magnetically as if it were, in Thoreau's phrase, "Earth's eye."

Lying on your back in deep meadow grass facing a bottomless sky is less focusing, but worth a drive of many hours, as weekend traffic will attest. Yet the very dimensions of the sky, which are unfathomable after the early surge of pleasure that they carry, cause many of us to mitigate their power with preoccupations such as golf or sunbathing as soon as we get outdoors. That sense of first principles can be unnerving, whereas the ground against our backs—if we lie gazing up into the starry night or a piebald day—is seething with roots and sprouting seeds, and feels like home, as the friendly dappled clouds can't be. Beyond the prettiest azure blue is black, as nightfall will remind us, and when the day ends, cold is the temperature of black.

A pond, though, is a gentle spot (unless you are Ophelia). Amber or pewter-colored, it's a drinking fountain for scurrying raccoons and mincing deer, a water bugs' and minnows' arena for hunting insect larvae, a holding pen for rain that may coalesce into ocean waves next year.

Mine flows into the St. Lawrence River. I live in Vermont. I spent a hundred dollars once to bulldoze a tadpole pond next to my little stretch of stream. A silent great blue heron, as tall as a Christmas tree, and a castanet-rattling kingfisher, a faster flier and brighter blue, showed up to forage for amphibians the next year.

Garter snakes also benefited from the occasional meal of a frog, and a red-tailed hawk, cruising by, might grab a snake or frog. More exciting, a bull moose began using it as a hot-weather wallow, soaking for half an hour, mouthing algae, munching sedges, and browsing on the willows that lean from the bank. A beaver cut down some poplar saplings to gnaw and stitch into a dam for creating a proper flow, but the depth remained insufficient to withstand a New England winter, so he retreated downstream to a wetland in my woods.

I bought this land for eighty-five dollars an acre in 1969, and today a comparable hideaway would probably still cost no more than about the price of a good car. We're not talking luxury: As with so much of life, your priorities are what count, and what you wish to protect and pay attention to. I've been a sinner in other ways, but not in this respect.

Remoteness bestows the amenity of uninterrupted sleep. No telephone or electric line runs by, and the hikers and pickups are gone by sunset. When the season of extravagant daylight shortens so I can't simply sleep from dusk to dawn, I light candles or kerosene, but in balmy weather I can nap with equal ease at any hour in the meadow, too, or watch the swallows and dragonflies hawk after midges, as the breezes finger me and a yellowthroat hops in the bushes to eat a daddy longlegs.

At dark the bats hawk for bugs instead, or an owl hunts, all wings, slow and mothlike, till it sees a rodent. The trees hang over a swimming hole nearby, with a dovish or a moonlit sky showing beyond the leaves like a kind of vastly enlarged swimming hole, until I feel I was born floating in both the water and the air. It's a hammock all the more beguiling because if you relax too much while swimming and let yourself sink, you might conceivably drown. Similarly, in the meadow, if you lazed too late into the fall, woolgathering, snow could fill your mouth.

Nature is not sentimental. The scenery that recruits our spirits in temperate weather may turn unforgiving in the winter. It doesn't care whether we love it and pay the property taxes to save it from development, having walked over it yard by yard in clement conditions. When the birds flee south and other creatures, from bears to beetles, have crawled underground to wait out the cold, we who remain have either got to fish or cut bait: burn some energy in those summer-lazy muscles cutting wood, or take some money out of the bank.

A mountain can be like that all at once. Summer at the bottom, winter at the top; and you climb through all the climates of the year as you scramble up. In the past half century I've climbed Mt. Jefferson in Oregon (a cousin died there in a fall soon afterward) and Mt. Washington in New Hampshire; Mt. Katahdin in Maine and Mt. Etna in Sicily. I've clambered a bit in Wyoming's Wind Rivers and in the Absaroka Range; also in British Columbia and North Yemen; in the Western Ghats in southern India and the Alpes-Maritimes in the south of France; and have scrambled modestly in the High Sierra, Alaska's Brooks Range, and on the lower slopes of Mt. Kinyeti in the Imatong Massif in the southern Sudan. Here at home, I climbed all of Vermont's fire-tower mountains, back when Vermont still used towers to locate fires, instead of planes.

This feast of variety is part of a writer's life, the coin of the realm you inhabit if you sacrifice the security Americans used to think they'd have if they weren't freelance in their working lives. In reality everybody winds up being freelance, but mountains telescope the experience. During a weekend you climb from flowery summer glades to the tundra above tree line, slipping on patches of ice, trudging through snowdrifts; the rain turns to sleet. The view is rarefied until a bellying, bruise-colored sky turns formidable, not pretty. Like climbing combers in a strong surf, there's no indemnity if you come to grief. You labor upward not for money but for joy, or to have been somewhere, closer to the mysteries, during your life. Finding a hidden alpine col, a bowl of fragile grassy beauty, you aren't just gleeful; you are linked differently.

Leaving aside specific dangers like riptides, vertigo, or terrific cold, I found I was comfortable on mountainsides or in seawater or in caves or wilderness swatches. In other words, I was fearful of danger but not of nature. I didn't harbor notions of any special dispensation, only that I too was part of it.

I fought forest fires in the Santa Ana Mountains of southern California when I was twenty and had discovered that moderate hardship energized yet tempered me, as it does many people, just like the natural sorties for which one puts on hiking shoes and ventures where barefoot peoples used to go. In central Africa I've walked a little with tribesmen like the Acholi and the Didinga, who still tend to be comfortable when nearly naked, and have seen that the gap between us seems not of temperament or of intuitions, but only acculturation.

As virtual reality captures our time and obsessive attention, some of the pressures that are killing nature may begin to relent. Not the primary one of overpopulation, which is strangling the tropics; but as people peer more and more into computer screens and at television, the outdoors, in affluent countries, may be left in relative peace. This won't stop the wholesale extinction of species, the mauling of the ocean, or other tragedies, but close to home may give a respite to what's left of nature. Where I live alone each summer, four families lived year round eighty years ago. The other new landowners don't choose to occupy their holdings even in warm weather because of the absence of electricity. An unusual case, yet I think indicative, and supported by the recent return of numbers of adaptive sorts of wildlife, like moose and fisher, to New England—though, in contrast, along the lake a few miles downhill, cottages perch atop one another, motorboats and water-skiers buzz around, and trollers use radar fish-finders to trace the final sanctuaries of the schools that the lake still holds.

Just as habitat is the central factor in whether birds and animals can survive, what *we* are able to do in the woods will be determined by land regulation or taxing policy and public purchases. Maine's private timberlands have remained unpopulated because of America's lavish need for toilet paper—as Vermont's trees, too, make paper, cottonmill bobbins, cedar fencing, and yellow-birch or maple dowels that become furniture legs.

Any day, I watch truckloads of pulpwood go by. And in the California Sierras above Lake Tahoe, or on the pristine sea island of Ossabaw, off Savannah, Georgia, I've devoted lovely, utterly timeless hours to exploring refuges that seem quite empty of people, but are actually allotted in careful fashion by state or federal agencies for intensive recreational use. The animals hide while the sun is up and feed when it's down. This is the way it will have to work. Levels of life on the same acreage. Or else it won't work at all.

I can be as jubilant indoors, listening to Schubert or Scott Joplin, as when sauntering underneath a mackerel sky on a day striped yellow, red, and green. Indeed, the density of sensations in which we live is such that one can do both—enjoy a virtuoso pianist through a headset outside. We live two lives or more in one nowadays, with our scads of travel, absurd excesses of unread informational material, the barrage of Internet and TV screens, wallpaper music, the serializing of polygamy and the elongation of youth blurring old age. A sort of mental gridlock sometimes blocks out the amber pond, the mackerel sky, the seething leaves in a fresh breeze up in a canopy of trees, and the Walkman's lavish outpouring of genius, too. Even when we just go for a walk, the data jam.

Verisimilitude, on computer screens or in pictorial simulation, is carrying us we don't entirely know where. I need my months each year without electricity and a telephone, living by the sun and looking down the hill a hundred times a day at the little pond. The toads sing passionately when breeding, observing a hiatus only at midmorning when the moose descends from the woods for his therapeutic wallow, or when a heron sails in for a meal.

I see these things so clearly I think our ears have possibly changed more than our eyes under the impact of civilization—both the level of noise and subtleties of sound are so different from hunter-gatherer whisperings. I'm a worrier, if not a Luddite. The gluttonies that are devouring nature are remorseless, and the imbalances within the human family give me vertigo. The lovely old idea that human life is sacred, each soul immortal, is in the throes of a grand mal seizure; overpopulation is doing it in. I didn't believe that, anyway, but did adhere to the transcendental idea that heaven is right here on Earth, if we perceive and insist on it. And this faith is also becoming harder to sustain.

"Religion is what the individual does with his own solitariness," as A. N. Whitehead said. ("Thus religion is solitariness; and if you are never solitary, you are never religious," he added.) I fall back on elemental pleasures like my love of ponds, or how my first sight of any river invariably leaves me grinning. And the sheen of rain water on a bare, black field in March. The thump of surf, combed in the wind and foaming, glistening, yet humping up again like a dinosaur. Yet fish don't touch me as much as animals, perhaps because they never leave the water. Frogs *do*; and I seem to like frog songs even more than bird songs, maybe because they're two-legged like us but can't fly either and were the first vertebrate singers. But I especially respond to them because they live a good deal more than we do in the water.

Frogs are disappearing worldwide in a drastic fashion, perhaps because of ultraviolet rays or acid rain; and I may finally cease to believe that heaven is on Earth, if they do. Water without dolphins, frogs, pelicans, cormorants will not mean much to me. But in the meantime I like to search out springs in the high woods where brooks begin—a shallow sink in the ground, perpetually filling. If you carefully lift away the bottom covering of waterlogged leaves, you'll see the penny-sized or pencil-point sources of the groundwater welling up, where it all originates—the brook, the pond, the stream, the lake, the river, and the ocean, till rain brings it back again.

La Joie du Criquet

The Joy of Grasshoppers

🦗 JEFFREY A. LOCKWOOD

G rasshoppers have taken me to the Tibetan Plateau, the Mongo-
lian steppe, the deserts of Kazakhstan, the Australian outback, the
grasslands of Siberia, and the Brazilian cerrado. Of course these creatures
haven't literally underwritten or guided my travels, but they've provided
a compelling reason for governments, agencies, and corporations to fund
my entomological excursions. The scientific opportunities and economic
problems that grasshoppers represent opened doors to a world of experiences. In the course of variously catching, protecting, monitoring, and—
most often—suppressing these insects, I've dined on strips of sautéed
pig's ear accompanied by barely clotted blood-sausage, toasted my hosts
with vodka made from fermented mare's milk, weathered forty mile-per-
hour winds in one hundred and twenty-degree heat, and been stranded
because the Ethiopians were bombing the Eritrean airport. My only re-
gret is that such adventures—none of which have been truly dangerous,
although sometimes a bit uncomfortable—have been without my human loved ones.

So I was delighted when grasshoppers took me to France. My family
joined in the odyssey, from the giant hamster tubes of Charles de Gaulle
airport (the network of Lucite tunnels need only an exercise wheel and
some cedar shavings on the floor to complete the impression) to the top-
less beaches of the Mediterranean (leaving no doubt that we were not
in Wyoming anymore). The city of Montpellier hosted an international
meeting of the Orthopterists Society, a bonafide scientific association
comprised of about three hundred people from nearly fifty nations. And
all of these folks, incredible as it may seem, devote their professional lives

to the study of grasshoppers, crickets, and katydids. The conference was fine, even spectacular in terms of the program and facilities. Montpellier is a sun-drenched coastal city that combines a neoclassical grandeur with an abundance of lively cafés and exquisite restaurants to please the bon vivant. But my most treasured memories—now nearly a decade old—are rooted in small places and fleeting moments encountered on the way to the big event. Sometimes the journey, rather than the destination, is what matters most. Our ambling route from Paris to the sea took us through the heart of the French countryside. For a romantic entomologist, the Loire Valley offered much more than the finest scientific presentations in the most exquisite of meeting halls.

France is, above all, sensual—sometimes in erotic terms (there is a reason why we have the expressions *French kisses* and *French letters*) and certainly with respect to one's senses. During a week of bicycling, we discovered that the Loire Valley can taste as pure as the simple farms that blanket the hills and as rich as the cuisine of the kings who dotted the landscape with their chateaux. The air is redolent with an earthy-floral infusion, as if burying one's nose in a handful of freshly uprooted lavender with soil still clinging to the roots. The valley feels as hard as the stone walls of the countryside and as soft as the tilled soil of the fields. A vista of rolling hills covered by a quilt of emerald green and golden brown under an azure sky is a feast for the eyes. But it was the sounds of this enchanting land—the soothing hum of life—that became indelibly linked with my memories of the fields, glades, and villages.

Being an entomologist in France is like being an entrepreneur in America. The inclinations and dispositions of entomologists are valued by French culture. I am used to people not taking me seriously— how can a man who never outgrew chasing bugs be a threat? But France embraces the unconventional, the quirky, and the daft. After all, the country produced Jean Henri Fabre, a man who devoted his life to meticulously studying the insects around his small farmstead near the village of Sérignan in the early 1900s. Too poor to travel, he spent the last thirty-odd years of his life recording his painstaking observations, simple experiments, and gentle insights. What emerged from the pen of this eccentric is a set of the most lyrical and gracious essays on the natural world that have ever been crafted. So it was that a humble hamlet, not a celebrated city, produced this national treasure. A century later, we found that Paris still bustles with the vibrant sounds of people and Blois murmurs like the Loire River flowing past the city's winding streets. But the Loire Valley—nestling the serene village of Chitenay, where we found a cozy refuge on the second floor of the Auberge du Centre—was infused with natural romance: the love songs of insects.

Sunrise in the Loire Valley belongs to the birds. The insects and I wake more slowly. My idea of a vacation accords with the dictionary definition: an interval of rest or relief. Not so for my family. By 7:00 a.m. Nan and the kids (Erin, age 12; Ethan, age 10) are ready for a basket overflowing with *pain au chocolat* and buttery croissants—a gastronomic indulgence that we rationalize by our daily fifteen to forty mile bicycle expeditions. Pedaling along the country lanes drenches us in the land as surely as swimming in the Loire would bathe us in the river. Without the drone of traffic (it is possible to ride for half an hour without encountering a car), the peal of church bells in a village and the drone of a tractor in the field are carried along with chirps and twitters on the whispering breeze. By midmorning, the grasshoppers begin to climb to the swaying seed heads of meadow grasses and move onto the gravelly roadsides, as if in search of the strong, black coffee that animated my daybreak. They are seeking heat, the thermal caffeine of the insect morning. Basking in the warmth of the sun and tuning their fiddles for the day's concert, the grasshoppers are as lazy as the children's fable suggests (but how much pleasure do the ants enjoy?). The first tentative buzzing and strumming come from the dew-sparkled grasses by ten thirty. In fact, we learn that if the insectan orchestra begins tuning up before ten o'clock, then we'd better check our water bottles, because the day is sure to be hot.

By noon, the grasshoppers are in full song—usually. When the day starts out cloudy and the sun doesn't break through until midday, the insects sleep in. They may be drowsy into the lunch hour, but once the sun melts through the clouds and its rays toast the fields, the songsters are frantic to make up for lost time. In the refulgence following a light morning sprinkle, the rain-washed air transmits colors, fragrances, and sounds in high fidelity. The grasshoppers' chirps, hums, and rattles take on a splendid—and sometimes bewildering—clarity.

There's one species that does a perfect imitation of the clicking free-wheel on a coasting bicycle. I overlook the presence of this remarkable mimic until I am bringing up the rear and find it odd—and upon further consideration, mechanically impossible—that this machinelike ticking persists even while we are all pedaling. I should admit, much to my chagrin, that I once spent half an hour searching my basement for a cricket until I realized that our smoke detector does a wonderful imitation of a chirping insect as a warning that the battery needs changing. Nan seems to find this story much funnier than it really is—elaborating on my hands-and-knees stalking along baseboards and under couches while, overhead, the inanimate device issued its chirps with the cautious irregularity of a living creature.

The day after my first suspicions of a mechanical mimic in our midst, I confirm the origin of this clicking during a water-and-baguette break. We are all dismounted when the little scamp launches into its version of "The Coasting Cycle Roundelay." Crawling on all fours, I manage to sneak up on the source—which this time is nestled in the grass, rather than affixed to a ceiling—drop my cupped hand into the thatch and gently capture a tiny katydid with elegantly elongated hind legs and chocolate-brown stripes on her mint-green body. Ethan is rather more impressed with my tracking skills and Erin with the shapeliness of my captive than Nan is with either.

The other grasshoppers are equally evocative, if not quite so deceptive, in their songs. Some fields reverberate with the sounds of Lilliputian jackhammers. And on the way to Château de Chambord, our picnic of cheese and fresh fruit is disrupted by my compulsion to hunt down what sounds like an elfin man, scolding us with a clucking tongue for intruding on his meadow. With persistence I discover that the pasture is not magical; rather, a grasshopper (in the genus *Chorthippus* based on my fleeting glimpse) is responsible for the chiding *tch-tch-tch*. After lunch, the grasshoppers maintain the fairytale ambience—a most apropos accompaniment for a trip to one of France's most flamboyant castles. Their back-and-forth songs from the roadsides give the impression that dozens of gnomes are hiding in the wildflowers, rubbing their fingers along an assortment of combs, sending messages in secret code. Other stretches of road greet us with the rattling of tiny maracas or the less whimsical clattering of stuck electrical relays.

To hear my favorite grasshopper of the Loire Valley—a marvelous little tettigoniid—say "visit" as fast as you can three or four times. When the vowel sounds compress to nothingness and the word is pure consonants you have it. To imitate being there, take life as slowly as possible and luxuriate in your senses, attending to the present moment and to the deep memories evoked by these pleasures. "You are a sentimentalist," my scientific critics will contend, as if romance was a false path to understanding or truth was the exclusive purview of reason. Can spending long, pointless hours absorbing an insectan rhapsody in the tranquil countryside be a rational experience? For an entomologist with a heart, could a six-legged serenade in a meadow evocative of a Monet painting be anything other than romantic?

In the afternoon, the Loire Valley becomes a symphony with distinct movements. There is the pianissimo of the forest glades that dot the landscape. As the road enters the serenity of the woods, a hush prevails. But not all quiet is the same. While the silence of an empty house can be unnerving, this quietness is profoundly soothing. Invariably our pace slows, as we try to absorb and store the coolness. The stillness is broken by the hum of our tires and the erratic, metallic chirps from the overhanging canopy of branches—perhaps the call of a lonely katydid or a lustful tree frog.

Emerging into the brilliant sunlight, the earned sweat of the fields replaces the complimentary dampness of the forest. With the heat comes the insistent *chk-chk* alongside the hayfields, the lazy *bzzzzt...bzzzzt... bzzzzt* among the poppies, and the sporadic ticking arguments between the rows of wheat. The vineyards are the rests in the musical score. It seems that the grasshoppers don't find much to their liking among the vineyards, which is one element of their lives that I simply can't understand.

Resting in the shade of a tree-lined avenue that bisects a listless village, we become immersed in the throb of cicadas—a pulsation that captivated Fabre more than a century ago (he once arranged for the firing of artillery to see if such a concussion would disrupt the seemingly imperturbable thrum of the insects, who did not miss beat). When we arrived, the initially uncoordinated efforts of a few spirited individuals were reminiscent of a symphony's discordant warm-up. But it seems that an insectan conductor amidst the branches (or, more scientifically speaking, the players themselves) cannot stand the cacophony. And so, the individual fits and starts soon synchronize into the heartbeat of the Loire Valley—an ebb and flow that washes over the parched village.

Evening brings a softness to the French countryside. Back at our hotel, we luxuriate on the patio, savoring each course of dinner and listening to the insectan love songs in the garden. On these warm nights, their trills are a perfect accompaniment to the elegant clink of silver on china and the ripples of French conversation. It is as if the humans and the insects of France have reached a graceful and refined linguistic compromise—the people speak in vowel-suffused murmurs and the crickets chirp in consonant-spattered staccato. The tranquility is punctuated by the cheerful popping of a cork, announcing the arrival of an exquisite wine that was nurtured and bottled by one of the vintners through whose land we rode today.

I look at my son, who is attempting to scoop the last molecule of strawberry sorbet from his bowl. My gaze drifts to my daughter, who is trying to overhear a child's conversation at the next table to test her budding French. Then I watch my wife penning a postcard of Château de Cheverny to friends back home. I close my eyes and I find myself making a sound that has become all too rare—a sigh of pure contentment. The conference is yet to come, a new semester months away, and my children's leaving home in the future; this moment is all that exists, the only sure thing. As the lilac flush of dusk darkens to a deep plum, we too begin to wane and head up to our snug room, serenaded by the crickets still in search of lovers.

When morning comes, stiff thighs and sore rears are again set in motion, and I look forward to a day of being intrigued, incurrent, inspired, incarnate, incomputable: In love. Jean Henri Fabre captured the essence of France for romantic entomologists. In *Life of a Grasshopper*, he wrote,

> I see in the Grasshopper's fiddle, the Tree-frog's bagpipes and the cymbals of the Cacan [Cicada] but so many methods of expressing the joy of living, the universal joy which every animal species celebrates after its own kind.

Simple creatures manifesting a "joy of living"—can this be the interpretation of a scientist? Perhaps. After all, Charles Darwin proposed that in evolution, "the vigorous, the healthy, and the happy survive and multiply." The "happy?" Indeed.

Fabre's writings leave no doubt that he had a keen mind and the ability to deduce scientific insights from interminable hours of observations. But reason could take him only so far, and he was unwilling to limit himself to this single way of knowing the world. Fabre was drawn to the elements of nature that stretched beyond what objectivity could reveal. This French naturalist found that grasshoppers transcended the Laws of Science:

> What purpose is served by the Grasshopper's musical instrument? I will not go so far as to refuse it a part in the pairing, or to deny it a persuasive murmur, sweet to her who hears it; it would be flying in the face of evidence. But this is not the principal function. Before anything else, the insect uses it to express its joy

in living, to sing the delights of existence with a belly well filled and a back warmed by the sun, as witnessed by the big Decticus and the male Grasshopper, who, after the wedding, exhausted for good and all and taking no further interest in pairing, continue to strum merrily so long as their strength holds out.

And so as we head off for another ride, my daughter and I strike up a silly ditty, an absurd sequence of lyrics that we learned from a pair of storytelling minstrels one summer night, well past her bedtime, a year ago, in a musty barn converted to a roughhewn theater, with floorboards spaced just right to provide refuge for crickets. This song serves no purpose—other than to manifest our uncontainable joy of living. Fabre would understand.

Divination

❧ SYDNEY LEA

Under the hornbeam you always lean on in summer for ease from
    whatever hike
the day has chosen for you, there's a sun-paled wishbone, small almost to
    infinite.

Birdbone.

Warbler? Creeper? Wren? No matter, except that the bone may move a
    mind,
if, that is, it wants to be moved, wants for instance to identify

the killer.

Predator? Sickness? Weather? And yet such questions are no matter
    either. Somewhere
you've read of a tribe or nation—which tribe, which nation appears
    likewise to be

unimportant—

who used the sterna of birds for divination. So you pinch the pin-thin
    arms
of the bone and aim it outward over a valley so huge just now there can
    be

no way

to read it, but what on earth would that signify, *to read it?* You gave away
any claim to science so many years back that now the sortings of schist
    from granite

in the vista,

of conifer from hardwood timber, of this cloud from that, will serve no
    purpose.
And what could ever be meant by *purpose?* For you there's nothing
    higher encoded

in Nature.

Still you wear the human wound: your urge for significance throbs like a
    bruise.
And for whatever reason the bone, the physical bright-white bone itself,
    appears

a wonder,

even though you know it's nothing against the continents and seas, afire
with murder and rapine. *Put down the wishbone,* you say to yourself. *Lie
    back against*

your hornbeam.

You know you forge your construals from idle dreams. Yet you persist:
    you lean
forward, tense, gripping those near-invisible calcified tines in front of

your heart,

and in the bone's knuckle you feel a shiver—you *do!*—then a
microscopic bucking,
as if you reined a horse so tiny that its only capacity was a stirring

of air,

its own mere speck of it. You choose to think something's out there. You
   name it hope.
You choose that name. And whatever superstition prompts the
   conviction, you're sure

—you insist

on being sure—it's there, beneath the selfsame hornbeam which you're
   pleased
to lean on in summer, in whatever ramble occurs to you on whatever day,

for ease.

Degrees of Damage in Blue River

ALISON HAWTHORNE DEMING

Sometimes a giant tree
will crack vertically
opening like a clothespin
from the torque
of a slow landslide
that splits it
clean as cordwood:

runnel-barked fir,
striated red cedar,
drapery of hemlock,
others unrecognizable
as trees so disguised
in veils and sleeves
of lichen and moss—

trees travel, their speed
not perceivable except
after five or six centuries
they stand several feet from
the spot where they sprouted.
How gradual is the tension,
the grain holding fast against

the strain of slipping ground
until one day some ligature

pops, then the trunk splinters,
tears, and cracks, the tree
thunders to ground,
beginning its long death—
two centuries of devil's club
(*Oplopanax horridus*)

caning over the deadwood,
fungi lacing sugary threads
through the rot, moss
carpeting the living room
where beetles build galleries,
voles tunnel nests and decay
grows so boisterous the tree
forgets its own name.

The Web

ALISON HAWTHORNE DEMING

Is it possible there is a certain
kind of beauty as large as the trees
that survive the five-hundred-year fire
the fifty-year flood, trees we can't
comprehend even standing
beside them with outstretched arms
to gauge their span,
a certain kind of beauty
so strong, so deeply concealed
in relationship—black truffle
to red-backed vole to spotted owl
to Douglas fir, bats and gnats,
beetles and moss, flying squirrel
and the high-rise of a snag,
each needing and feeding the other—
a conversation so quiet
the human world can vanish into it.
A beauty moves in such a place
like snowmelt sieving through
the fungal mats that underlie and
interlace the giant firs, tunneling
under streams where cutthroat fry
live a meter deep in gravel, a beauty
fluming downstream over rocks
that have a hold on place
lasting longer than most nations,
sluicing under deadfall spanners
that rise and float to let floodwaters pass,

a beauty that fills the space of the forest
with music that can erupt as
varied thrush or warbler, calypso
orchid or stream violet, forest
a conversation not an argument,
a beauty gathering such clarity and force
it breaks the mind's fearful hold on its
little moment steeping it *in a more dense
intelligibility, within which centuries
and distances answer each other
and speak at last with one and the same voice.*

—lines from Claude Levi-Strauss

Cow of the Virgin

ROBERT J. ROMANO JR.

From the window of my den I watch a cold, steady drizzle melting away whatever patches of snow remain under the trees and in the lee of the woodshed. The morning would be gloomy but for the fact that the rain is good for plants and fish, those wild brook trout with blood red dots on their flanks, trout that I'll be stalking later this afternoon if the temperature will only go up a few more degrees.

Meanwhile, I'm seated at my desk, writing a story about early spring. Well, it's really about Magalloway, a black Labrador named after a favorite river in Maine, an old friend who is about as old as a dog his size can expect to live. More to the point, it's an essay about the cycle of life. You can see why writers hate to explain their work.

For me writing is a great adventure. More times than not, I'm looking down at the laptop, intending to write about one subject when something completely different unravels on the screen. Here I am, trying to complete this early-spring essay, homage to an old canine friend, parable of life and death, when along comes a ladybug from behind the computer, wobbling upon the maroon mat in the center of my desk.

The beetle's orange shell is dotted with tiny black spots. Its six legs are also orange, although it is difficult to tell because the gaily colored little beast is making good speed, crossing between two small note cards folded like pup tents to allow them to stand freely on the desk—one of a brook trout, reproduced from a James Prosek print, the other of a cabin in the Maine woods, originally painted in oil by Michael Hillmann, an artist confined to a wheelchair as a result of spina bifida.

I close out of the spring essay and open a new page on the laptop while watching the tiny bug chug toward a framed photograph set back about six inches from the smaller postcard-size prints. Trish and I are smiling out from the black-and-white photo, sitting in white sand, a clump of seaweed to our left, the Atlantic Ocean at our backs. Our feet are bare with sand between the toes, a braided cord around my ankle.

We are both quite young and not yet married, in our twenties, healthy and tan. Looking through glasses rather than the contacts she now prefers, Trish's hand is holding my arm, her long blonde hair blown back toward the sea. She is wearing jeans and a long sleeve shirt, all in white. I am wearing flared jeans, back then we called them bell-bottoms, and a dark sweatshirt, today the kids call them hoodies, the sleeves rolled up to my elbows. My hair is thick, black curls sticking out from the sides of a baseball cap.

I can remember that summer afternoon, Trish resting her thirty-five-millimeter Nikon camera on a piece of driftwood, the anticipation as the timer whirled, the sound when the shutter opened, then clicked closed. The ladybug, climbing along the edge of the cheap wood that frames this lovely memory, reels upward, wings twirling, ricochets off a wall, and lands once more between the two note cards. The whirling dervish appears to pause, its wings folded backward, sticking outward behind its compact shell, tiny antennae probing, resuming its journey once more.

Each October, clouds of these seemingly gregarious creatures hatch by the side of the stream where I fish, a few invariably hitching a ride on my sleeve or cap to overwinter in our house. Reaching for my reference books, I'm surprised to learn that the British refer to ladybugs as ladybird beetles, the French calling them *les vaches de la Vierge*, which roughly translated means "cow of the Virgin."

A power cord stretches from a port in the side of my computer, along the maroon mat and down a crack between the back of the desk and the wall. I lift the cord, easing her ladyship's labor.

Like a tank rolling into a trench, the intrepid traveler creeps down one side of a bevel, rising up out of the other, now no more than a quarter of an inch from the edge of the desk. I continue to type, one eye on the insect, the other on the computer screen. Outside, the rain has turned to snow. A white-throated sparrow is perched in a cedar tree, breast feathers puffed out against the cold, a bead of moisture running down its beak.

My attention is drawn back to the ladybug, which has hurled itself through the crack between the desk and wall, diving into the abyss without the slightest hesitation. Rising from my chair, I stare down, but find only darkness. I envy the beetle's ability to leap off ledges, a trait required of lovers, writers, and other daredevils.

The snow has turned to hail. It pelts against the window, the sound like kindling crackling in the woodstove. The sparrow huddles silently in the branches of the cedar. I suppose my trip to the stream must wait until tomorrow.

Wondering how I'm going to complete this essay, I watch the tangerine insect emerge from the void, buzzing past my head like some hallucinogenic helicopter. For a moment, I imagine Neal Cassady at the wheel, steering this psychedelic flying machine across the computer screen. Careening past the words "hallucinogenic" and "helicopter," the Cow of the Virgin gains altitude, disappearing behind the printer, but not before Ken Kesey pokes his head up, his best McMurphy grin spread wide across a face with as many wrinkles as my old canvas shirt, the one I like to wear when out fishing.

Least Terns, St. Catherine's Island, Georgia

David Haskell

This bar reeks of spilled life.
A gathering place
for hard-diving, sleek-sliding sea swallows.

Only the ocean is deep enough
to slake our pale longing
for foam
and salty flesh.

But offshore,
the wind has too much fetch, too much time
to build swell that snags, tumbles, and drowns
light-winged lovers.

So, we flutter,
turn and dive
in the shallows

and wing home
hollow
as washed-up sandspit bottles.

A Day at Agua Dulce

G. Davies Jandrey

Early Morning

This is my first day in the Cabeza Prieta Wildlife Refuge as a volunteer bighorn sheep watcher for the U.S. Fish and Wildlife. They call it the annual water hole count, though in June many of the *tinajas*, or natural tanks, cloistered in the craggy mountains of the Cabeza Prieta are dry or nearly so.

The canyon is predawn blue-gray. I shine my flashlight on the slim margin of rock, more act of faith than trail, that skirts the wall of the canyon. Keeping a close eye on my feet, I wobble along, bending my knees away from the cholla cactus that is everywhere. For the most part I am successful, but occasionally I stop and take the tweezers from my pocket to remove the tiny spines that attack without provocation.

In the middle of the trail, my light shines upon the darkly glistening and beaded scat of a coyote that has been feeding on the fruit of the saguaro. The coyote is unable to digest the seeds, which later will provide a second-hand meal for some bird or rodent.

The canyon lightens. All about me is a rugged vista dominated by enormous saguaro and organ pipe cacti. There is also palo verde, creosote, sage, brittlebush, and an occasional diminished mesquite. All take root in the barest fissures in the granite, defying gravity, intense heat, and drought.

I think I spooked a desert bighorn sheep on the hillside. I hear rocks clacking, but in the dim light can see nothing when I scan the canyon walls. Nose back to the trail, I see the faint outlines of running shoes and realize someone else has recently been in this canyon.

There is all manner of chirping, twittering, and trilling, but I can't lift my eyes from my feet to see who's making the racket. The only thing I see on my way to the blind is a stink bug, a Pinacate beetle actually, and not a true bug at all. But a stink bug is not such an uninteresting find. He's performing one of his two tricks, a head stand. His glossy rear reaches for the sky. If I'm not suitably impressed by trick number one, he will show me trick number two, which is to exude a liquid from his abdomen. This liquid is a smelly, caustic deterrent to predators. It can cause irritation to humans if you rub the beetle on your mucus membranes. No danger there.

I pick the beetle up. The little abdomen flexes and a drop of amber liquid appears. I touch the drop, give it a tentative whiff, and make a mental note not to pick my nose. I put the beetle down and it resumes its headstand.

At last I arrive at the blind, a five-by-five-by-five-foot saguaro rib cell, the ceiling a patchwork of recycled Fish and Game signs: "try by Permit Onl," "arms Prohi," "Littering." The floor is sprinkled with sheep droppings the size and shape of olive pits. There is a strong, musky odor about the place and just enough room for the battered Walmart camp chair I hauled in with me.

I am perched in this blind in the Agua Dulce Mountains, a rocky spine rising fifteen hundred feet above the desert pan, located just north of the Mexican boarder in southwest Arizona. My job is to observe sheep over a four day period and record their numbers and general health.

This is a "land of many uses." Adjacent to the refuge is the Barry M. Goldwater Range, a miltary training area. Before going into the Cabeza Prieta, a person must sign a release form that warns of the dangers from unexploded bombs and errant missiles. If you don't sign the form, you don't go in. It's a unique concept: game refuge/bombing range. In addition, the notorious *Camino del Diablo,* or Devil's Highway, passes right though the heart of the refuge, and hundreds of trails have been etched across its surface by illegal pilgrims trudging toward an elusive better future in *El Norte*.

A real desert-lover's desert, the Cabeza Prieta is hot—upwards of 110 degrees is usual for June—and dry. It may rain three inches a year here, but you can't count on it. But right now it's a cool seventy-four degrees as I sit down and inventory the contents of my pack: three liters of water, flashlight, bird book, Gale Monson's *The Desert Bighorn*—the sheep watcher's bible—notebook, lifesavers, a baggie of toilet paper, camera, brasero scarf, a baggie of Wheat Thins, two navel oranges, assorted pens, drawing tablet, a baggie of gorp, tweezers, Chapstick, hat, extra emergency baggies, and finally a sheaf of important papers, including illustrations that will help me determine the age and health of the sheep, and the forms to be filled out for each and every sighting. I stack these next to the chair and I am ready for the bighorn sheep to begin their crepuscular activities. Sounds sinister, doesn't it?

I am still waiting, straining to hear the sounds of unhinged rocks and the click of hooves.

Silence, I understand, is necessary if I am to observe bighorn sheep.

The sun's a fist-width above the canyon rim when the bees arrive. The spring I'm watching is nearly dry, although enough moisture wicks up to the surface to suit the bees, which spend a good deal of time sucking it out of the sand. They make too much noise. I can't hear the sheep.

In fact, this whole canyon is a noise factory. Lots of whistles and ratchets out there in the brush. Lots of *tew, tew, tew*. A canyon wren's derisive laughter echoes off the rocks. It probably knows something I don't.

There are no clouds. There is no wind. I glass the spring. Nothing, not even a white-winged dove, though I hear them cooing.

That Agua Dulce Spring is almost dry does not matter, I am told. The sheep are creatures of habit. They will come simply to socialize. That bighorn sheep will come to a dry spring to socialize in the blazing heat of June seems strange to me, but I am not a sheep expert. Not yet.

I have read that sheep can go days, weeks, months even, without drinking free-standing water, getting all the moisture they need from what they eat. I look down at the sere landscape with its rock, cactus, and sparce, brittle grasses. Hmmm.

I think of that footprint I saw on the trail. Wonder if someone looking for water had come to the spring, found it dry, and continued on without. Every summer, hundreds of illegal aliens die in the intense heat of sourthern Arizona. Reflexively, I take a long tug of water. It's warm and tastes like plastic, but it's wet.

A big black bumblebee comes in, creating his own little breeze. He fans my face. I am nose-to-nose with whatever passes for a nose on a bumblebee.

Later

A couple of screaming jets from the bombing range jolt me out of a sound sleep. The bighorn sheep watcher's bible falls off my chest. Until sleep overwhelmed me, I had muscled through three chapters. I look down at the spring where a few more doves have gathered.

A spiny lizard with a bright turquoise belly circumnavigates the blind, humping his way along the saguaro ribs. I'm not sure who his humpity dance is for. He's the only one of the lizard persuasion in the blind.

The world's tallest saguaro rises out of the rock by the spring. It must be fifty feet tall and its crown and arms are capped with bright red fruit. There are two large, black gouges on its side. Called "boots," these are actually scabbed-over wounds caused by the persistent attacks of Gila woodpeckers that use the holes for nesting. This giant has been thoroughly chewed on from its base to a level of about four feet. It's a marvel that it still stands. When it finally comes down, I hope no one is sitting in this blind. It sways gently in the breeze.

Things are slowing down as the desert heats up. An anthill that was the site of great activity an hour ago is quiet, except for the few who are cleaning up debris that could only have meaning to an ant.

Noon and After

News is not good. The sheep count at Agua Dulce is still zero.

Ants have discovered my Wheat Thins. They are the big black kind, the kind that bite to the soul. They can have the crackers.

The blue-bellied lizard joins me. Hope he goes to work on the ants.

It's 111 degrees. The wind, now a constant ten to fifteen miles per hour, rasps across my salt-crusted skin like a cat's tongue. I wet the bracero scarf and slap it against my back. The effect is startling. Instant goose bumps. The humidity is perhaps 4 percent and evaporation is nearly instantaneous.

A velvet ant just walked in. She realizes her error and changes course. I say she because she is wingless. Only male velvet ants have wings. Seems unfair, but nature is not big on equality among the sexes. An attractive, fuzzy creature, she's not an ant at all but a wasp who has the unattractive habit of laying her egg in the stunned but living body of her prey, chiefly other wasps. When the larval young hatches, it eats the "living nest." If she comes back, I could introduce her to the big wolf spider cloistered in the corner.

A red-tailed hawk flies into the canyon and out again. Rocks pitch down the sides of the canyon. I'm alert, glasses poised. My eyes scan the crags and crannies trying to pick out a sheep shape. Nothing. Perhaps the rocks pitch themselves down the canyon.

Again I think of the footprints on the trail and wonder if someone is watching me watch the spring. I push the thought aside.

Suddenly, my rear's all pins and needles. I can't stand to sit another moment. I put my hat on, wrap the damp scarf around my neck and step out into the sun to stretch my legs. Not ten feet from the blind is a gutted barrel cactus. There are sheep prints all around and fresh droppings.

A neighboring saguaro is bleeding from an injury. The butt of a ram? So they are here, and when the spring is dry they will eat the pulp of a barrel cactus.

I come across a saguaro with arms twisted down instead of up. It affords me an excellent view of the fruit. When the fruit is ripe it splits open and the fleshy, green skin peels back, exposing magenta insides. Looking like a large, tropical flower, its lushness seems out of place. The dark, inner core is a cluster of black, shiny seeds held together in a matrix of sticky fruit. This ruby, phallic fruit seems far removed from the white and waxy flowers that recently crowned the saguaros. In May, they look like prim bridesmaids. By June they've become wanton.

I pick a fruit and blow off what ants I can see. I take a bite. The fruit tastes like a fig, but crunchier, seedier. Now, like the coyote, fox, squirrel, and wren, I will become a disseminator of saguaro seeds. A fine thought, but such are the thoughts of a baked brain. The glare of the sun off the rocks reduces everything to monochrome. I head back for the blind.

The spiny lizard humps me a splendid welcome, all pumped up and glowing bluely.

Later Still

Solstice. The sun sets early behind the canyon rim. So much for the longest day of the year.

Whoa! A giant desert centipede has just walked in on his multifeet. He's a beauty, maybe six inches long. Unfortunately, he sees me too and disappears, apparently unwilling to share the premises with such an unattractive and dangerous creature.

The sun's down and the temperature has plummeted to 106 degrees. Surely that's cool enough for a sheep to want to take a stroll down a canyon wall. I wedge my squat camp chair between a rock and a hard place, taking care not to poke my feet through the rickety saguaro ribs. I grab my binoculars. I am alert. I am ready. I am desperate to empty my bladder.

I step outside and add another scent to the environment. Hope it's inviting.

I rewedge myself into place and rearrange the all-important forms. There is space to record each sheep's age, sex, and state of health. There's a place to note evidence of sinusitis. An infection caused by the bot fly larvae, it is terminal.

The centipede is back, scruffling about the saguaro ribs. He's large and honey colored, with three black segments at the head and awesome "feelers" on both ends. He's longer than my pen and has a wriggly sort of appeal.

Once I coaxed a tarantula onto my hand and was delighted to find she was uninterested in any part of me as prey. A centipede may be poisonous to a degree, but no more than a tarantula. I lean over and put my hand in the centipede's path. He pats my finger with one feeler, pats it with the other, then takes an enormous bite. We both withdraw.

That was an interesting experience. Now I know how it feels to be bitten by a centipede. It hurts! As for the poison, we'll just wait and see. There are two small incisions, a few millimeters apart, on the tip of the middle finger of my left hand. That was good thinking, using my left hand. My finger aches, it bleeds a bit when I squeeze it. Perhaps I feel a little tingle in my wrist. Perhaps not. The area around the site does not appear to be swollen or red. Good sign.

I'm obviously a victim of a classic "Sheena, Queen of the Desert Delusion" brought on by hours of heat, sun, wind, and solitude. I mean, what am I doing here sitting amid a pile of sheep turds, trying to commune with a centipede? You can't commune with a centipede. Usually I know that.

A cactus wren is squawking at an antelope ground squirrel, who has just had the good fortune of finding an intact saguaro fruit. He must have been standing under the saguaro at the moment the wren knocked it to the ground. Lucky guy. He knows it and is stuffing the seedy pulp into his mouth with both paws. These little chipmunk-like guys are perfectly adapted for the desert heat and scurry about even in the hottest part of the day. Their body temperature is high—around 107 degrees—and they're equipped with a fluffy tail, which they flip over their backs like a parasol to provide shade.

I turn my attention back to the spring, vowing not to move for the next hour.

I am immobile. I am hungry. Slowly I reach for the Wheat Thins. Quietly I extricate one from the baggie. I don't bite down, but wait until it becomes soggy. Silently I chew and watch, chew and watch. The Wheat Thins make me thirsty. My water bottle is leaning against the wall, just beyond my reach.

Still Later

The centipede wriggles from behind a post. Apparently he wasn't poisoned either. That's a relief.

A half-dozen white-winged doves are perched on the saguaro. One zips down to the spring, body whistling though the air like a billiard ball in a dead fall. Another is on a junket from the saguaro to the top of a barrel cactus. The friction of wind through feathers causes its wings to squeak as if they are attached by rusty hinges.

The velvet ant makes another appearance. Her sting is said to be pretty painful, but she's so small and has this fuzzy sort of appeal. I wonder if I were to simply hold out my hand....

Evening

The canyon walls have faded from peach to plum and no longer shimmer with heat. I start to load up my gear.

This blind is a small ecosystem. It is a place where sheep come to lounge. Their droppings attract insects, which in turn attract the insect eaters: the wren, the centipede, the spider, the velvet ant, and the spiny lizard. When the musky odor of human occupancy dissipates, the sheep will return to the shade of the blind and things will get back to normal.

My shirt is stiff and unlovely. I keep my flashlight handy, but if I hurry I'll reach camp before dark. I would like to avoid scrambling over that last, rugged quarter mile in a mere polka dot of light.

I ease myself down the steep canyon wall, gripping boulders with fingers and toes. I try to make a noiseless decent, but the rocks cascade before me, warning all the sheep within a mile's radius that some large intruder is in their midst. Finally, I sit on my bottom and allow gravity to have its way.

The light is swiftly draining from the desert floor as I reach camp. It's that time of night when stars can still be counted. I get the peculiar feeling I'm not alone. Perhaps at last a bighorn sheep. Slowly I turn in the direction from which the feeling of occupied space emanates. Nothing. Nothing that I can see.

Small things

🍀 JOHN BATES

In late April, I find trailing arbutus in flower
under the ridged old white pines.

In early May, I discover the first hermit thrush
singing within the hemlocks
its spiraling opera.

Every day, new things arrive,
or bloom, or are born, or die.
I try to find as many of them as I can.

I don't collect them in plastic bags,
or put them in vases,
or pin them on cardboard,
or exile them to my freezer,

or eat them.

I just try to find them.

Sometimes I find them with my ears,
sometimes by nearly stepping on them,
sometimes they just come to me.

If I were to put them all in a container,
they would look like nothing more than where I am now

which is lying under a white pine
that is leaning over the river
a river flowing so softly I can only hear it
now and again
amidst the birds that sing
among the needles that fall when the wind rises.

The Wisdom of Turtles

🦑 Michael J. Caduto

Many years ago, soon after I moved to the north country, I was told by friends of Abenaki and Mohawk descent that all turtles have thirteen scales on their backs, and that each scale represents one of the moons we see throughout the year. My training as a scientist prompted me to search for proof among the shells of turtles from around the world. To my amazement, everything from giant leatherback sea turtles—which can weigh 1,500 pounds—to our familiar painted turtles, have thirteen scales, or *scutes*, on their backs.

Some indigenous cultures in North America correlate each moon on a turtle's back with a natural event or with something people do outdoors at that time of year. September's moon is the Cornmaker (Abenaki), Wild Rice Gathering Moon (Santee Dakota), and Moon of the Black Buffalo Calf (Oglala Lakota). Since there are twelve lunar cycles plus an extra eleven or so days in each solar year, a thirteenth moon comes around about every three years as reckoned by the sun. This is the Big Moon to the Abenaki, *Kchi Kisos*. The Maliseet of northern Maine and the Maritime Provinces know the moon as *Paguas*, "he who borrows or begs light from the sun." Scientific knowledge and indigenous wisdom seem to converge on a terrapin's carapace.

The elegant symmetry of scutes and moons, however, was not adopted by early immigrants to this land. Ever since the dawn of the enlightenment in the early seventeenth century, western society has increasingly paid obeisance to science. To demonstrate something with facts born of solid research means it is true. The word *science* is itself rooted in the Latin *scientia*, meaning "knowledge." Today's world is an empirical realm. But it was not always so.

. Ask someone from among the six nations of the Haudenosaunee (Iroquois), and they will tell you that Earth rests on the back of a giant turtle. Long ago, they say, in the heart of Sky Land, in a world above the clouds, grew a magnificent tree. Its branches were covered with blossoms of every color and many kinds of nuts and fruit. One day, Sky Woman fell asleep leaning against the trunk of the great tree. She dreamt that someone pulled the tree up by its roots. When Sky Woman had this vision two more times, she told it to the elders. As was their tradition, the elders decided any dream that appeared three times must be honored.

So the tree was uprooted, and this left a hole so deep that the Sky People could see water far beneath them. Sky Woman leaned so far over that her hand slipped off the branch of Sky Tree and she fell through the hole in Sky Land. There was nothing but ocean down below. Seeing that Sky Woman would drown, some swans flew up and caught her on their backs while the other animals tried to bring some earth up from the bottom of the sea for her to stand on. Beaver, loon, and diving duck tried, and failed. Only the strong-willed little muskrat succeeded. She placed the earth on the back of a giant sea turtle, where it grew to become all the land we now see. The swans flew down and Sky Woman stepped off their backs, saying "Thank you for saving my life." In her hands, Sky Woman still held seeds of many kinds from the branch of Sky Tree, which she sowed, bringing all good plants to Earth.

Each turtle is a sage in a shell, a beneficent Buddha in the beliefs of traditional peoples around the world. There seems to be an ancient wisdom in the eyes of turtles that is born of their antiquity. For 200 million years turtles have inhabited the land and water. During half of that time they shared their world with dinosaurs, including the swift-moving prosauropod *Otozoum*, "giant animal," and the twenty-foot theropod, *Eubrontes giganteus*, "large true thunder," two giants that once walked the land we now know as New England. Turtles have ducked inside their shells when packs of the turkey-sized, carnivorous *Grallator* swarmed across the Connecticut Valley on two feet and mounted rapacious attacks, each appearing like a miniature *Tyrannosaurus rex*. One hundred million years ago, young sea turtles fell prey to fifty-foot long, fish-shaped reptiles called mesosaurs, or the thirty-five-foot plesiosaurs that would one day inspire those who believe they have spotted the Loch Ness Monster. Turtles somehow survived the mass extinction of 65 million years ago that put an end to the dinosaurs' reign. And turtles swam the seas fifty-five million years ago when the ancestor of today's loons sliced the water with powerful webbed feet, snapping at prey with their deadly rows of dentition. Mastodons, dire wolves, giant beavers as big as black bears, and even mountains themselves rose and fell, but turtles lumbered on through time. When human beings appeared in recent geologic history, it is little wonder that these ancient creatures crept into the folklore of cultures from around the world.

Stories from Asia associate turtles with the creation of Earth. In China a divine turtle spent 20,000 years making the moon and the stars and Earth, and in popular culture evolved into a symbol of longevity— not surprising since some tortoises can live for 150 to 200 years. Turtles bring good fortune and are a symbol of peace in Japan. They are even associated with the fertility of the sea in the waters around New Guinea, where it was once forbidden to disturb mating turtles for fear of diminishing the fecundity of other marine life. There is a Hawaiian legend of a green sea turtle who could change herself into a girl and protect children playing on the beach. And from the mountains of Tibet to the open skies of the North American plains—land of the Dakota peoples—tales are told about how birds helped turtles to fly.

Turtles play a central role in indigenous North American cultures. In stories of creation and moral tales—like those of Toleba, the Abenaki trickster—turtles inhabit the fabled worlds of land, air, and water. Sacred turtles were used in Zuni fertility rites in the American Southwest. The Anishinabe of the Great Lakes region tell of how Turtle enlists the other animals in a great battle to stop people from hunting. In a classic trickster tale that plays on the infamous torpidity of terrapins, a Seneca story recalls how Turtle takes to the air and outwits Beaver in a race across their pond.

People are arguably the greatest tricksters of them all, but as Turtle often does in the traditional tales, we frequently outwit even ourselves. We have amassed an impressive body of scientific knowledge, yet this intellectual storehouse is no match for the pace and appetites of humankind. As an evolutionary strategy, going slow and steady has served turtles well through the ages. Fortunately, we can still read the stories in a turtle's scales—tales that show us how to wisely wield what we know.

Crow Speaks His Mind

H. C. PALMER

After you have learned all their secrets
And think the way they do... they will
fly away and take you with them.

—Richard Brautigan, from "Crow Maiden"

Crow ascends from the corner hedge
as if Southwind will lift him above
all creation, then, in his usual way, suspends

himself over this gap-gate, crossing the two-track
to summer pasture. He's made a habit of hanging
around, watching me open this gate.

I consider Crow from my pickup,
windows down, radio full blast. He hovers
through the weather forecast and a seed

corn commercial, but, at the top
of the hour, with news of the casualty count,
he turns his back, his black robes caught

by the wind, and with a clamor of caws, sails over
the rimrock to the bluestem below—where long ago,
he considered my blood soaking prairie incursion,

and where now, he will pretend I never walked.

The Work of Turkey Vultures

🍂 H. C. PALMER

Under the tough old stars—
In the shadow of bluffs…

—Gary Snyder, from "I Went Into the Maverick Bar"

Prairie artisans sail from their roost,
muted flights to ride the morning thermal—
that long-winged ritual of tilting, wheeling,
searching for the dead and dying.

There will be no sacrament of last rites.
Dissection and digestion is their craft—
transforming a carcass to vapor and dust.
The real work, what is to be done.

A Pure Color

✿ SIMMONS B. BUNTIN

> *Hue: The property of light by which the color of an object is classified as red, blue, green, or yellow in reference to the spectrum.*

I.

From the first morning, I see red. I feel it even more: fine claret dust on my teeth, beneath my fingernails, on my skin like the smooth scales of a coral snake. Sleeping in the teepee has something to do with it: wrapped in a tight turquoise bag on a cot along the banks of Professor Creek, twenty miles from Moab, Utah, I wake and shake off the particulates that hang in the air and in my dreams like the icy residue of fog.

The red of southern Utah is visible eyes open or closed. With camera in hand, that scarlet hue is what I'm after. Yet there's a broader pursuit, a central question: In the spectrum of place, what can I learn from the hues of the land? Though I write, it is often my camera that leads me, that captures and channels the light and holds it. The digital lens is my regular guide to beauty, but on what paths: passion, serenity, vibrancy? And how does the experience of beauty—the seeking and obtaining—inform the landscape and our place in it?

Here, where it seems that only the Colorado River isn't red (it's milky brown or, in the evening, green tinged with indigo) the color seems inescapable. And yet it eludes me, for the light moves like a phantom across this high desert landscape: cliffs shift from vermilion to charcoal, arroyos wash from carmine to coffee. The changing light is a constant, and my desire is to hold it for the moment it takes to strike an image. In that respect I am a thief. I seek to steal the light, and in stealing so save it. Who can still such desires?

Red has long been the color of desire in Western cultures, and despite the autumn chill and thick cottonwoods along the creek, the color transports me to my house in Tucson. Our bungalow is not red but purple, the home's exterior decorated in paints labeled Putnam Plum, Concord Jam, and Ode to Purple. Contrasted against these tints, a prickly pear grows at the front of the house. Once only a trio of pale green pads, the cactus has sprawled into a spiny structure the size of a sedan. Barbed pads jut from shin-thick trunks that were themselves once only pads. Not long ago, my daughters pointed out something odd on the plant, something white and waxy. From a distance, the growth looked like tufts of cotton caught in small patches along the cactus's spines, or like the remnants of "a spit-wad war zone," suggests entomologist Carl Olsen. It's a sure sign of cochineal, a small insect that uses its beak to spear the cactus pad and then slowly suck it dry. Cochineal means *scarlet-colored*, and stripping away the wax reveals the female: bright red, baglike, a quarter-inch long.

Their history is also one of desire. According to Olsen, who studies the group of insects called scales, the cochineal was the basis for a thriving Aztec textile industry known for its bright red garments. The Aztecs called it *nochezli*, and it lived on the cactus *nopal*. After the conquest of the Aztecs, the Spaniards shipped bags of dried cochineal back to Spain; from there it became popular throughout Europe. Cochineal dye is found in Michelangelo's paintings, in the first U.S. flags, and in the red coats of British soldiers and Canadian mounted police. Harvested today in Mexico, Algeria, and the Canary Islands, it is also used in cosmetics and food color, a natural alternative to artificial dyes.

From the frosty look of the prickly pear beneath the plum windowsill, cochineal could be harvested from our front yard, as well. My daughters urge me to spray the wax from the pads. Get rid of it before it kills the cactus, they say. But I'm reluctant. Prickly pears are hardy, and though a pad or two has already fallen, I can't help but think these small beads of desire deserve a chance. While they are mostly sessile, the morning light that brings me back to Utah reminds me that desire shifts often, shimmering like the iridescent scales of a fish. The color of desire may be red, but I suspect the spectrum is not so easily divided, nor passion so clearly defined. Is it better, then, to focus less on color and more on landscape, those open spaces that likewise shift in the spectrum of memory and mood?

"Where I live," says author and naturalist Terry Tempest Williams, "the open space of desire is red." She lives one valley over. I live one state down, but have traveled north less to contemplate color than to participate in a convergence of environmental writers and activists, red-faced denizens who—like Terry, like any of us concerned with the vanishing of natural landscape and our place in it—wring their hands and then their minds in a collective desire for what we might call harmony. Or holism. Or healing. How, we ask and sometimes succeed in answering, can we counter the industry of progress with its singular conclusion of loss? Desire may be the answer, but that too may be lost in the valley's frigid morning. Or perhaps desire is exactly what I've found.

The sun has not yet risen over the vast rock formations that bulge like the silhouettes of ancient, unlit cities. I walk toward them, my feet sweeping sand, my boots heavy with the stuff, as if the velvet ribbon of this arroyo could hold me as easily as I hope to hold it. Of course it could. Of course it has. We are never beyond the landscape, never fully able to claim it—though with camera in hand I am certain to try. A pack of coyotes calls from a distant ledge, the yipping a premature burst before sunrise. Then silence. How long can they hold it? How long can any of us hold the perfect moment before the break of day?

The sun rises and I stop. A cottontail scrambles. The sun's radiance lights the clouds in the east, though the orb has not yet breached the horizon. I raise my camera and turn to the west: a panorama of red. Sculpted, the arroyo flows and the easy metaphor is blood. But the riverbed is dry, dyed and bloodless. I think back to the cochineal, which digs in, covers itself with wax, and stays. That is a strong desire, even if humble, innate. The streambed's banks blaze with rabbitbrush and sage, foreground to tipping scarps and mesas. Burgundy then magenta then scarlet. In the distance: cliffs and spires of vermilion, rose, salmon, garnet—too many reds to count, more than my camera can claim or decipher. The rabbit rushes across the wash and I turn, lens whirring into focus, but miss the shot. It slows then and transforms to juniper, to hill, to ruddy bluff, to the mesas and the sky beyond, red and—like an old desire made new—redder still.

2.

If red is desire, then psychologists like Morton Walker, author of *The Power of Color*, tell us that blue is serenity, cool both in temperature (based on the frequencies and literal temperature of its light wavelength) and identity, finding its way onto a majority of business logos, business suits. I admit less interest in blue as the corporate color of choice than as the color of landscape. And here I'm initially drawn to the discrete blue, like A. R. Ammons in his poem "Corsons Inlet," in which he compares the tiny blue flower of a weed to a "carapace of crab," to a "snail shell," all as "pulsations of order."

I think of pulsations not so much of order as of connectedness, transcendence. A deep link to the unconscious and the Earth—to aggregate grace and spirit that is the color blue. Yet it was a recent experience that bridged the color between landscape and self, a kind of passage embodied in the salty thrash of seawater, the struggle with flippers and mask and snorkel. I had never before snorkeled, and I struggled to relax, to float in a state of what I call *amniosis*. If such a word existed, it might mean, "You get my drift" or "I am adrift."

Still, the hook of the tube and the tasteless layer of rubber between teeth and cheek were alien. Head down, nose pinched in the mask, my breathing felt unnatural—frantic and forced. "Force yourself to be steady," I remember saying. Imagine scuba diving, I thought, the whole body submerged, the full atmosphere of comfort strapped in a canister on your back, weights on your belt. The sinking in nautical light to darkness. This was nothing, relatively; this was only snorkeling in a protected cove off Isla Coronado in the Sea of Cortés.

Only inches below the water, maybe ten feet above the brilliant ocean floor, panic was nonetheless my first reaction. I strained to keep my head down, to force the taste of saltwater from my snorkel so I could breathe unhindered. Though I saw blue I could not absorb it. But slowly the tension subsided, lost to the bay's mild currents and the weightlessness of my surroundings. Above, the azure sky was cloudless, only a moderate breeze from mainland Baja California Sur and the town of Loreto, flanked by the Sierra de la Giganta, blue and brown-blue as they faded into afternoon. Below, white sand tinted the water aquamarine, nearly green. Green, like blue, is an abundance in this garden of the desert's sea—the great inverted peninsula, rich in rare sealife. Yet in the vast blue, I also saw red. Like tranquility responding to desire, the ocean is a blue that relies on red. "Water owes its intrinsic blueness to selective absorption in the red part of its visible spectrum," say chemists Charles Braun and Sergei Smirnov. "Because the absorption which gives water its color is in the red end of the visible spectrum, one sees blue, the complementary color of red." Serenity as the complement of desire? Had my tranquility arrived because of the struggle, the hard desire, that came from forcing myself to relax? Perhaps any transformation to a higher state—a landscape internal or external—requires a challenge? Here at least, there is no equilibrium without change, no blue without red.

But here, too, my words vanished, and when the words run their length, what is left is image. And at the core of image: color. At Loreto Bay, I swam among a hundred dolphins, spied moray eels in the tidepools, and found myself voiceless in the synchronized fin sweeps of stingrays. Floating in the water of the turquoise sea, I could have been drifting anywhere: in the amniotic fluids of the womb, perhaps, or above the pearl of the Earth. "At a few hundred kilometers altitude, the Earth fills half your sky," says astronomer and author Carl Sagan, "and the band of blue that stretches from Mindanao to Bombay, which your eye encompasses in a single glance, can break your heart with its beauty…that relentless and exquisite blue."

Under that relentless, exquisite blue, the rhythm of the waves, draw of the current, and click-thrumming of the reef worked like a drug. I had felt this way only once before, under the influence of Valium. Then I was certain I was a jellyfish, buoyed without a care on the peaceful sea. Here, I was attuned to the trio of angelfish beneath me, the curious triggerfish, those colorful wrasses weaving in and out of the coral. If only my wife and daughters were with me to experience this equilibrium. If only I had my camera, protected in a clear plastic case. But I am not certain that the lens would have captured the full spectrum of the scene, the light refracted and reflected, returning the image I thought I'd seen. And I am not certain I would have tried in such an absorbed state of mind.

3.

The absorption of light by the landscape, and all physical matter, is deceiving. "The color of an object is not actually within the object itself," says chemist Tom Henderson. "Rather, the color is in the light which shines upon it and is ultimately reflected or transmitted to our eyes." The red rocks of Utah and piercing blues of the Sea of Cortés are not fundamentally red and blue, though their atomic structure may absorb light of certain wavelengths—certain colors—so that the frequencies of other colors are not revealed. It is a dance at the atomic level I struggle to comprehend, just as I strained to breathe mask down in the sea. Yet the significance does not escape me: color is neither inherent nor absolute. If beauty is in the eye of the beholder, then color is an algorithm among the eye, the object, and the energy between. It may be as appropriate to define color as emotion or character or spirit, then, as to label it by the frequency of its wavelength—the physical hue and intensity of light that is the perception of color. Indeed, it may be more appropriate.

Take green: the color of healing, of freshness and nature, says Walker in *The Power of Color*. The origin of the word itself, *groeni* from the Old English, is related to the verb *growan*, meaning "to grow." Green as in verdure, from the Old Norse *visir*, for "bud, sprout," and in more recent etymology, as in vibrancy, "vigorous, full of life." Green not as physical representation of color—only a perception, after all—but as embodiment of a state of being. And of distinct landscapes: the idea of landscapes?

In the Sonoran highlands of southern Arizona—where last summer I climbed the dry snake of a trail into the shadows of Sabino Canyon—green is also the color of the desert. From spreading fleabane to waxy creosote, from airy brittlebush to palo verde, and from pineapple cactus to saguaro, here, in the foothills of the Santa Catalina Mountains that rim Tucson's northern edge, the desert is green: green thorns and branches and knotted trunks. Green shadows. Green flesh.

"If your knees aren't green by the end of the day, you ought to seriously re-examine your life," says Bill Watterson, author and illustrator of *Calvin & Hobbes*, the popular comic strip that subtly critiqued American culture and commerce. So beside the path, after scanning for rattlesnakes, I kneeled and pressed my knees into the desert soil, atop the minimal plants whose swollen buds were wrapped in leaves as dark as jade or, just as often, the light silver-green of chromis, the flash-finned tropical fish.

We also flash. One summer afternoon, seven inches of rain fell in the blue fir and pine forests of the Catalinas' highest peaks, collecting, rushing through the canyon, and blowing out the road.

Flash flood: flash forward to a U.S. Forest Service public meeting, following two months of input from neighbors and activists, convened to determine whether the canyon's road should be rebuilt. And if so, whether the tram that accommodates passengers of all ages, at six dollars per ticket, should continue to run. The concerns, on one hand, were tram noise, pollution, the unsightly string of red and white cars against brilliant desert peaks, and on the other access, comfort, knowledge (perhaps) in the guide's amplified voice.

I wanted to lend my own words, if not my images, to the lush and spiny mix. So I voted no tram, but supported the road. That's access and a bit more comfort. Knowledge? Bring a guide—human or field—and learn about the cactus wren and coyote, javelina and desert hare the old-fashioned way. Observation. Patience. The silent conversation with the land that is not possible in or from any machine. Seek there the color that is within oneself—the landscape, the vibrant spirit, may in turn absorb or else reflect. In either case, the light and its viewer have changed.

On my knees, I was tempted to slide my hands over the ground, to grasp the rocky soil and succulent plants. But in the Sonoran desert, you're a fool if you try. The cholla, vibrant green with yellow, inch-long spines, is deceptive. Backlit and from a distance, the branching cactus looks soft. But the spines are barbed. They won't release without pliers and, generally, no small amount of pain. And then more anguish, for they carry an inflammatory, a mild poison that stiffens the wounds and slows the healing.

A risky landscape, then, in the deceptive green. And usually an arid landscape despite the verdure. Yet what I now fear is not the deception, nor the absence of water. What I fear is encroachment, one subdivision after another leaching into the canyon, so that green becomes something else altogether: the red of tile roofs, tan of stucco, black of asphalt. What representations, like the blue of trust and duty, does green confer in the salvation of the canyon? Not commerce, I hope, as in greenback, nor the green-eyed monster of envy found in *Othello*. Choose instead resilience, vibrancy.

Despite my better judgment, I touched the ground that day, my fingertips finding a saguaro seedling beneath mesquite. It may have been a week old or a year, but no older. In time—in one hundred fifty or two hundred years—it will grow to be nearly fifty feet tall and weigh six tons, thick arms sprawling. White flowers will bloom in May and then drop, followed by the fruit of June, glistening. The sweet flesh is red, like blood, like desire. Sharp contrast against green.

4.

If there is a contrast between color and landscape, and in that contrast a thread of connection between people and place, I may not be able to hold it. Words and photographs can fail, for they too are only perception. Perhaps, then, a new vision is needed? Perhaps we should trust the eyes of another form of art—the ability to transform color and in fact create it anew? "Some painters transform the sun into a yellow spot," says Pablo Picasso. "Others transform a yellow spot into the sun." And still others—those seeking the landscape's most saturated hues—are themselves transformed: one season barren and wind-blown, the next aflame in saffron and gold.

It is early March on the dunes of Sonora's Pinacate desert, six miles south of the Arizona border. Early March following a glorious winter of rain, when forgotten rivers raced in eddies of ochre and bronze. An early morning march through the waist-high sunflowers, black eyes and yellow petals; through the tangled evening primrose now closing for dawn; through the violent blooms of verbena. Through and above it all, the horizon bends to white. All frequencies of light, all wavelengths are scattered, and the landscape can absorb no more. Among the flowering dunes that seem endless this morning, I too feel white. But not colorless, technically *achromatic* because white has no hue. Rather, white as the combination of all colors of the visible light spectrum.

Moving among the flowers, my camera captures image after image of the dewy scene, a rarity here in Mexico's largest desert, where the dunes bloom on average every decade or less. Though I am filled with the full spectrum of colors, delighted to the brim, there is a hue brighter than all others, and it calls to me in its Spanish name: *amarillo*. Yellow.

After a photograph taken on my knees, my head dowsed in the petals, I realize I cannot go on. I cannot go on for all the yellow. I don't need a book of color psychology to understand that it is the color of praise and promise and hope. In a word, beauty. It consumes me: the wide field of sunflowers, the burning disc of the sun, the golden tint of my own skin. Everything brilliant and blazing and yellow. Yet everything ephemeral, for in two weeks the temperature will arc into the nineties or higher, and the flowers will fade and fall, the dunes regaining the wind-carved cleft of the landscape.

Everything ephemeral. That's not what we're taught, but what we learn in studying the land. Or stopping to watch, camera to eye or otherwise. Who can think in terms of geologic time? The mauve Sierra Pinta across Mexico Highway 2 were not even hills a hundred million years ago. Who can question the arid wisdom of Pinacate's *maar* craters, those mile-wide calderas formed between five million and two hundred thousand years ago, when rising magma collided with groundwater in atomic-force blasts that created a moonscape of black pumice and red-walled cliffs? And who among us can lend an Earth-old voice to the great and terrible changes of our own age?

"The people who live in a golden age usually go around complaining how yellow everything looks," says the poet Randall Jarrell. Yellow not as praise but tarnish. Yet all I see over these miles of sloping dunes is yellow, blooming even if short-lived. The poet contends that people cannot appreciate the colors in the landscapes, and therefore the landscapes themselves, if we can even see them at all. Yet all around us is beauty. It is easier to see, perhaps, in the red canyons of Utah, the blue shoals of the sea, the green scarps of the Sonoran Desert, or among the flaring yellow wildflowers of Pinacate. But it takes neither a photographer's eye nor a dramatic vista to realize that beauty shines across all our landscapes. To see the beauty, to focus the light to a brilliant white, can be a considerable task, at times more frustrating than the crafting of a poem that seeks its own certain beauty. So perhaps we begin just by stopping. Maybe none of us can go on until we resign, refocus, and reconsider. Or maybe in stopping we need only absorb, find our complement in the landscape, and accept that we too may complement the landscape rather than oppose it?

Only yesterday I came across a throng of blister beetles—black crossed by copper—on the wind-worn edge of Pinacate's largest crater. The insects crawled and swarmed. They transformed the landscape, moving in fervor to find a mate, to take their brief transparency of time and push on. Push forth without pulling away. The beetles reminded me of the cochineal, whose waxy threads litter the prickly pears of my yard in search of mates. Science tells us of this drive for progeny, and that much is clear. Still, it seems there is a deeper drive in each of us, something along the lines of the color yellow, if I had to name it by hue.

The blister beetles couldn't stop in all their focused frenzy, but I could. Looking up, I saw that the edge of the caldera was bronze in the afternoon light. Here and there, chollas glowed amber against the volcanic soil. Green-leafed ocotillos wore caps of scarlet blooms, yellow-centered, and the bees were delirious in their own frenzied work among these eclectic desert plants. Looking down and into the crater, iridescent buzzards circled five hundred feet above the poppy-covered floor that emanated in rings of yellow and orange. It was a strange scene, full of odd colors and odder shapes; but whoever said beauty meant popularity, conformity? Each landscape is unique. Each color can be newly revealed—humans can see up to ten million of them—and beauty strikes at every opportunity.

There is a strange property of light, too, in the Pinacate, leaving me silent along the edge of this caldera, or in the morning's intoxicating dunes, or among the yellow-green senita cacti that glow like candles from a black desert floor. It is a light that feels exact, like the definition of hue itself, "a pure color, one without tint or shade." If I could paint that light, striving for the dabs and strokes of Picasso, I might find the canvas is inside me as surely as out. There, the landscape begins with red and blue, green and yellow. Here, it concludes in desire, serenity, vibrancy: a certain beauty, ephemeral but pure.

Standing Still

❦ ALERIA JENSEN

Flat ground is a hard thing to come by in southeast Alaska. Life is wedged between sea and mountains. The town of Juneau climbs the flanks of ridges and peaks until the landscape becomes too vertical for building, or the threat of avalanche becomes too great. What flat we have is generally the result of mining tailings, upon which downtown sits, or it is muskeg, the terrain of scattered bogs left over by glacial depressions, areas of high acidity and little drainage.

All this is to say that we have very few meadows. And I love meadows—wind-danced blades of grass, sky, open space to be swallowed by. Of the scant few meadows accessible near town, my favorite is found by driving north thirty-five miles to the end of the road and hiking an hour along the Point Bridget Trail. The trail takes you first along a boardwalk through a muskeg sprinkled with stunted jackpine, bog rosemary, and Labrador tea. Then into the woods, over roots and narrow wooden bridges, past blueberry bushes and the yellow torches of skunk cabbage. Along the trail, sometimes a tuft of deer hair, some porcupine quills, an eagle feather. And then you emerge into the meadow.

If you go in the third week of June, the open space is filled with color. Shades of purple sweep away before you to meet a dark border of spruce and hemlock in the distance. If you are lucky, you will hit the peak—the wild iris in full bloom, sprinkled with lupine, wild geranium, shooting star, chocolate lily. The lily is a brown bell-shaped flower, stinking like an outhouse, but nonetheless a beloved inhabitant of summer as part of our familiar blooming wild. The trail takes you into the heart of this great sea.

Usually, I pause here. I bend down to sniff things. I take pictures. I try to take the place inside me in whatever way I can. But inevitably, I am in the company of faster-paced hikers, and we move on.

But today is different. This day, with a different companion, we stop and we stay. A strong breeze is blowing, eliminating the mosquitoes and no-see-ums that usually inhabit these grasslands. We step off the trail and gravitate to the respective spots that suit us. My friend, a painter, takes out her sketchbook.

I lie down in the field. The wind blows over my body, irises lean in around me. I feel as though I may be in a painting myself, Van Gogh's *Les Irises* a good choice. From this perspective, it is easy to lose one's sense of self, to merge with the simple sensations of color and moving air. The meadow's dampness soaks into my back. I finger the fluted edges of an iris's violet arms, the texture of its body. Why have I never done this before, I ask myself. Why have I not *stopped*?

Over the rush of air moving across the field, I become aware of a humming. A bee has landed on the lupine next to me. We've all watched bees buzz among flowers, but how many times at ground level, immobile, with full attention? The lupine, a member of the pea family, has numerous two-parted blossoms shaped like little boats, ringing a spire. Landing on one blossom, the bee begins to pump the purple and white flower parts open with its back legs. The flower parts spring back, the bee moves to the next blossom and does the same thing. *Bzzz*, bounce, bounce, bounce. Its tiny body reminds me of a baby in a Johnny Jump-Up swing, pumping away on a suspended seat with growing legs. The bee works a systematic pattern around the lupine, climbing its tower in orbits, stretching each single blossom open for a brief visit.

Then it's off to the shooting star near my foot, nodding toward the ground with a long yellow collection of stamens extending out beyond its magenta petals. For this, the bee uses an entirely different approach. It flies underneath the flower, clings to the tip and curls its body around to capture the pollen the plant has to give. The flower bows in response.

I am reminded of a friend's daughter, now two and half, who has entered a stage where she asks for confirmation, as though she's checking to see whether grown-ups are really paying attention. "See it?" she says as she places her finger in her paint and makes orange spots on paper. "See it?" she says, holding out her green sandals to me. And the same for every object she holds up. Yes, yes, I say, I see it.

But do I? I realize I should take her mantra seriously. I've had thirty-six years to do it, but I don't remember laying my body down inches away to *see* pollination taking place. Lupine is one of my favorite wildflowers, but I've never carefully considered the purpose of its shape and structure. Nor realized how multitalented a bee must be to move from flower to flower, recognizing different shapes and instantly choosing the right adaptation to access, like a musician effortlessly switching keys.

Here in the meadow, poet Mary Oliver's words come to mind. In her poem "Messenger" she talks about keeping her mind on what matters—her work—"which is mostly standing still and learning to be / astonished." That's my lesson today, coming at me across the tops of indigo petals, carried in the buzzing, whirring, winged air. Be still, attend to detail.

Even though I am trained in biology and work in a scientific field, another part of me is still the child, the two-year-old, delighted to simply have a sensory experience. The child-mind can roam here and there, untethered. So it is in this spirit that I unloose my imagination, let go my rational brain, and trade places with the bee. I imagine myself diving headlong into this field on busy, glassy wings. Collecting pollen on my legs, on my back, carrying it as protein back for developing larvae in the nest. I imagine tremendous joy in this harvest, in this smorgasbord of sweetness, despite the fact that death waits at the onset of the cold while only the queen overwinters in the soil.

Stretched out, I trade places again. I lose the wings, and look up out of the meadow as the lupine does. My body becomes purple, I grow palmate leaves. I grow patient. For how long has the lupine been waiting?

I think I would cry out to the buzzing overhead, "Choose *me!*" Then shudder with relief, somewhere deep in my cells, at the first touch of the bee's legs.

It's all here, the seeking and the waiting. A moment when what is meant to happen, does. When the evolution of one creature matches another in perfect alliance. When an unspoken agreement, signed into being millions of years ago, is still honored: you will feed me, and I will be the agent of your procreation.

Perhaps the relationship is even more complete when there is the human perception of its beauty. When we choose to do the work of what matters and let ourselves be astonished.

Beauty and the Birds

❧ TED CABLE

"A mouse is miracle."

—Walt Whitman

Starlings, house sparrows, and pigeons are the house mice of the bird world. Jaded bird watchers and stuffy naturalists call these ubiquitous species "junk birds" or "trash birds."

Biologists call these species "exotics," but not in the good sense of the word. These birds came from another place and multiplied like avian weeds. Legislatively categorized as vermin, federal wildlife laws afford no protection. And, you won't find Save the Starling Clubs or letter-writing campaigns on behalf of beleaguered house sparrows or pigeons.

Yet, in the eyes and hearts of some observers, starlings, house sparrows, and pigeons are not junk birds, but amazing survivors whose ancestors were trapped and transported to a new world to serve human desires. Their use of our trashed landscapes has created the perception that these are *trash* birds. If, as Whitman noted, a mouse is a miracle, then starlings, house sparrows, and pigeons qualify as avian miracles, albeit much maligned miracles.

Flying Stars

European Starling (*Sturnus vulgarus*). Even its scientific name casts aspersions on starlings. Although *vulgarus* carries the meaning "common," the modern connotation of vulgar better communicates how many birders feel about this species.

This bird fared better with Old English. "Starling" comes from the Anglo-Saxon word meaning "little star." According to naturalist-author Laura Erickson, sterling silver probably takes its name from starlinglike birds on the silver coins of Edward the Confessor.

The starling's story in America is a story of a misidentification, a love of birds, and a passion for literature that exceeded an understanding of natural processes. If you are like most Americans you will encounter a starling as you go about your business today—under the eaves of an office building, sitting on a roadside telephone wire, or stealing suet from your backyard birdfeeder. Each North American starling's story begins in the year 1597 when William Shakespeare wrote *Henry IV, Part 1*. In that play, the character Hotspur says, "I'll have a starling shall be taught to speak nothing but 'Mortimer.'" Ancient Romans reportedly taught starlings to mimic human speech. (Pliny the Elder reported that when Nero was a child, tutors taught his pet starling (and nightingales) to speak complete sentences in both Latin and Greek.) Although Shakespeare may have been aware of this astounding claim, many believe that he confused the starling with the mynah, a closely related and more accomplished mimic.

In the late nineteenth century, Eugene Schieffelin of The American Acclimatization Society desired to import every bird species mentioned in Shakespeare's writings. That one mistaken reference by Shakespeare to the starling put it on Schieffelen's most-wanted list. Schieffelin, a New York drug manufacturer, was not easily discouraged by the previous failure of European species to survive in the New World. Twice starlings had been released unsuccessfully. On March 16, 1890, the persistent and passionate Eugene Schieffelin conducted a third release. This time he released sixty starlings into Central Park. Starlings were soon nesting under the eaves at the American Museum of Natural History. Forty more were released in the spring of 1891 to supplement the original sixty. The population grew and spread.

Twenty-five years later, in 1916, ornithologist Frank Chapman, in his classic book *Handbook of Birds of Eastern North America*, writes of "thousands of starlings now occupying the country for one hundred miles or more from New York City." He noted records from as far as Springfield, Massachusetts, and Philadelphia. He speculated, "within two decades the starling will occupy the greater part of the eastern States."

Chapman's prediction was correct. Starlings made it to Chicago by December 1925. They arrived in Kansas in 1926 and by 1933 they were common in Wichita. Covering the same ground as human European immigrants a few decades before, these avian European immigrants took only sixty years to make it to the Pacific Coast. Those one hundred starlings released in 1890 and 1891 have resulted in a North American population estimated now to be 200,000,000 birds. If the Bard were a better birder, starlings may never have become one of our most common birds.

The disdain for starlings is not because the bird is drab or dumb. Starlings exhibit qualities we admire in other species and ourselves—colorful, intelligent, skillful, adaptable, and assertive. In summer, starlings shine with a glossy iridescence of purple, bronze, and green. Their bill is a bright yellow and their legs a flesh pink. In winter, their appearance changes dramatically. The bill darkens from yellow to black. The glistening plumage of summer fades and becomes speckled with white or tan spots. The polka-dot, black-and-white, winter plumage befits gray winter days.

Starling flight is swift and straight. Sometimes enormous flocks form dark clouds constantly changing shape—twisting, expanding, and contracting like a psychedelic animation.

Their vocal repertoire includes not only their own vocalizations, but those of other birds. And they are not limited to the avian songbook. Starlings have been known to bark like a dog, meow like a cat, and give the human wolf whistle.

Unlike most birds, the starling's jaw muscles work in reverse. Instead of strongly clamping the bill shut, these muscles allow starlings to forcefully open their bill. This allows them to not only hold objects in their bill, but they can use their bill to open holes in fruits or turf. As the bill spreads apart, the eyes move forward to provide binocular vision and depth perception, thereby allowing starlings to home in accurately on their prey. This muscle arrangement gives them the key to a subterranean food pantry and a can opener once inside.

Most humans would consider the starling's housekeeping methods laudable, if not outright amazing—at least in the beginning. According to The Birders Handbook, unlike most cavity nesters who merely lay eggs on a bed of wood chips or feathers, starlings build complete nests inside the cavity. Besides lining the nest with dry grass, they add certain green leaves that contain chemicals that act as fumigants against parasites and pathogens. Starlings remove the fecal sacs of the young to keep the nest dry and clean. Once feathers protect the young, these sanitation activities become unnecessary and they cease. Soon the nest is infested with pests, fecal wastes, and rotting vegetation. This too may be strategic, in that starlings have a higher tolerance for such harsh conditions and therefore they reduce the energy devoted to housekeeping, while making the nest site less desirable for competing species.

If there is beauty in being beneficial, then starlings qualify by their diet. More than 50 percent of their diet is insects. They are the most effective predators against the clover weevil in the United States. Starlings also eat Japanese beetles and cutworms, other creatures that negatively impact agricultural and horticultural crops. In contrast to North America, where we put out bluebird houses to help bluebirds survive the starling invasion, farmers in New Zealand, believing starlings control outbreaks of insects in pastures, build houses to *attract* starlings. People have found other uses for starlings, including using their feathers for fishing flies and, at least in Europe, sometimes serving starling meat in the form of a pâté.

Starlings can inspire those who look with an eye unencumbered with ecological prejudices. Mozart is said to have been inspired by the sound of starlings. Terry Tempest Williams, while counting birds at the Salt Lake City landfill, was inspired by starling movements. In her book *Refuge* she writes,

"The symmetry of starling flocks takes my breath away, I lose track of time and space. They reel and turn, twist and glide, with no apparent leader. They are the collective. A flight of frenzy. They are black stars against a blue sky. I watch them above the dump, expanding, and contracting along the meridian of a winged universe."

So what's the problem between people and starlings? The affront that these immigrants commit is successfully competing with our native cavity-nesting species for nest sites. This ecological crime is perpetrated mainly against our beloved bluebirds, although woodpeckers, flycatchers, and other birds have lost their homes to these aggressive interlopers. Starlings also have been charged with damaging human food crops, defecating on our buildings and walkways, and possibly transmitting to humans a fungal disease called histoplasmosis.

Amazing adaptability allows starlings to occasionally move into remote wilderness areas, although they appear more out of place the farther they get from civilization. And in doing so, they attract even more negative attention. Starlings poking their heads out of a golden cottonwood in a red-rock Southwestern canyon or flying confidently against a picture postcard backdrop of snow-capped mountain peaks, particularly perturb those who like their nature natural.

Typically, enormous numbers of starlings coexist with enormous numbers of humans. Starlings thrive in human-dominated landscapes of cities and farms. With few exceptions the starlings and humans coexist oblivious to each other. Starlings seem comfortably at home as they warm themselves around the avian hearths of rooftop chimneys or methodically graze on the smorgasbord spread throughout a cattle feedlot.

If this is bothersome, and if blame is to be assigned, it should not be directed at the starlings nor Mr. Schieffelen. "The man who wanted Shakespeare's birds flying in Central Park and altruistically brought starlings to America from England is not to blame," writes Terry Tempest Williams. "We are—for creating more and more habitat for a bird we despise...."

Household Weavers

House Sparrow (*Passer domesticus*). The Latin name of this species carries the meaning of "belonging to a household." Before being brought to North America, house sparrows belonged to households throughout Europe, Asia, the Middle East, and parts of Africa. Now they belong to our households as well.

In the spring of 1851, Nicolas Pike, director of the Brooklyn Institute, released eight pairs of house sparrows into Brooklyn's Green-Wood Cemetery. This group did not become established, so he returned to England and shipped more sparrows to Brooklyn for release in the cemetery. After this second release the house sparrows began multiplying and spreading. These European immigrants took only forty years to inhabit the entire United States. The population growth and widespread distribution were accelerated by many other releases, including releases by human immigrants who missed this familiar member of their Old World households.

In the late 1800s, a dispute known as the Sparrow War raged among ornithologists regarding the economic and aesthetic merits of the house sparrow. Those responsible for introductions thought house sparrows would eat insect pests. Others thought they were attractive, particularly the dapper males with their black throats, gray crown, and chestnut nape. Skeptics saw them as dingy birds destined to become pests.

House sparrows reached their peak abundance in the early 1900s. With the advent of the automobile their numbers declined, at least in urban areas. Urban sparrows fed on the grain used to feed horses and the undigested grain in horse manure. As cars replaced carriages, these food sources dwindled.

House sparrows are in the Weaver family, a group of birds famous for weaving blades of grass into intricate sphere-shaped nests. They probably originated in Africa, the continent most associated with these fascinating birds. In Europe they were originally migratory, leaving the cold European winters for warmer regions. They lost their migratory behavior as they adapted by finding warmth and year-round food supplies in cities and grainfields.

It seems that the more people know about birds, the less they tolerate the humble house sparrow, which sometimes eats grain set aside for farm animals and often fouls human edifices. Bird watchers begrudge house sparrows the birdseed provided at feeders for "better" birds. They shoo, or shoot, house sparrows to keep them from consuming the birdseed. But mostly, as with starlings, nature-lovers vilify them because they are not *natural*. They are ecological outsiders. They don't belong. Awareness of ecological "belonging" blinds some eyes to the beauty of house sparrows. Yet, what "belongs" in farmyard or factory? And what is natural about bird feeders or fields of wheat and corn grown by people whose ancestors, like house sparrows, were immigrants to this continent?

It's a matter of ornithological sophistication to dislike house sparrows, but for millions of people these are their only backyard birds. *Domesticus* lives among them. For thousands of city dwellers, watching and feeding house sparrows and pigeons (another European immigrant) provide a source of amusement and relaxation. These birds represent one of the few kinds of wildlife that these people will ever encounter: Mother Nature's missionaries to the unconverted. A glimpse of creation. Feathered animation. Life.

Because house sparrows would have been conspicuous to biblical writers, it may be the bird they had in mind when they wrote that God sees and notes when a sparrow falls to the ground. If, as the lyrics to the traditional spiritual say, "His eye is on the sparrow," does it not deserve a second glance from us?

Pigeons: Helpful and Heroic

Rock pigeons (*Columba livia*, formerly called rock dove), are just "pigeons" to most people. Except for a few remote islands in the Shetlands, Orkneys, and Hebrides, and a few spots along the Mediterranean coast and in the mountains of the Near East, rock pigeons have left their ancestral cliffs and precipices. They were brought to the Jamestown Colony in 1610 to serve as a food supply. Although they occasionally can be found on North American cliffs and rock formations, they more often grace shining skyscrapers, rusting steel mills, bright white grain elevators, and barn lofts. They perch on the Eiffel Tower and soar over Sydney's Opera House. Famous flocks define Central Park and Trafalgar Square, where as many as 30,000 pigeons gather daily.

On *Sesame Street* children are taught to enjoy pigeons—Burt's favorite birds. Away from *Sesame Street* and its congenial residents, pigeons do not get such favorable attention. Woody Allen called them "winged rats." Politicians work to eradicate the dirty bird of abandoned warehouses, steel mills, and ghetto rooftops. Cities spend thousands of dollars cleaning up pigeon messes. In rural areas, the pigeon is a barnyard bird, picking through fresh manure or spilled grain. They explode from barn lofts and swirl around silos, presenting a challenging target for farm boys with pellet guns.

However, there is much to like about pigeons. They are sources of amusement for city dwellers who feed them from park benches and flush them from sidewalks. As one of the few birds city folk notice, pigeons are avian ambassadors of what Roger Tory Peterson called "the most vivid expression of life."

Rock pigeon's blue-gray plumage is jazzed up with iridescent feathers on the neck reflecting green, bronze, and purple; two black bands on the wing; and a black band across the tail. The white rump is a field mark separating it from other species of pigeons.

If there is indeed beauty in utility, then rock pigeons qualify as a beautiful bird. They are one of the fastest birds, clocked at speeds up to ninety-four miles per hour. Ancient Romans used pigeons to carry news back to Rome of Caesar's conquest of Gaul. Centuries later news of Napoleon's defeat at Waterloo reached England by carrier pigeon four days ahead of the news carried by horse and ship.

Britain's National Pigeon Service included more than 500,000 birds during the two World Wars. The U.S. Army Signal Corps used 50,000 pigeons to carry correspondence during World War II. About 17,000 pigeons were parachuted to supporters of the Resistance in occupied Europe. Hitler ordered all pigeons flying toward Britain to be shot down. Many birds heroically delivered messages after having been shot or injured, some dying immediately after delivering their message. In Britain, twenty-six pigeons have earned the Dinkin Medal—the animal equivalent of the Victoria Cross. One bird named Cher Ami saved an entire U.S. battalion behind enemy lines, losing an eye and a leg in the process. Upon her return, medics fitted the pigeon with a wooden leg. To those soldiers, Cher Ami was anything but a trash bird.

Pigeons were domesticated as early as 4500 BC. Today, if you travel through Europe, particularly rural France, you will see towering "dovecots"—pigeon apartment buildings. Many dovecots are delightfully ornate, some dating back to the Middle Ages. In medieval times, pigeons were raised not only for food, but their guano was collected and used by peasants for fertilizer. Today pigeon as "breast of squab" still graces French menus.

Piegon racing is a thriving sport, particularly in Great Britain, where the Royal Pigeon Racing Association has 46,000 members and where even the Queen has a pigeon loft. Much like show dogs or stud horses, pigeons with a good pedigree fetch tens of thousands of dollars.

For thousands of years rock pigeons have provided humans with a means of critical communication, companionship, food, amusement, and sport. They have been couriers and letter carriers, providing the first airmail service. Pigeons have been both pets and pâté. Some pigeons have a pedigree and others have received military honors. Clearly, these colorful and courageous birds are much more than winged rats.

*   *   *

Trash or Treasures

> *Our ability to perceive quality in nature begins, as in art,*
> *with the pretty. It expands through successive stages of the*
> *beautiful to values as yet uncaptured by language.*

—Aldo Leopold, from *A Sound County Almanac*

Are starlings, sparrows, and pigeons pretty, and can we expand our perceptions to see beauty in these birds? If a shiny purplish-green bird with a yellow beak and red legs or a chestnut and gray weaver with black markings appeared to birders in a far off tropical forest, birders would jerk binoculars to their eyes amid whispered oohs and aahs uttered in recognition of the bird's beauty. It's a notorious fact that if we place a human in a gutter, or alongside a dumpster, we can make them look dangerous or derelict. The same is true for birds. Individual prettiness can be distorted by an ugly setting. If the landscape is perceived as trashed, the birds become trash birds.

Prettiness also can be dulled by familiarity. As the cliché says, "Familiarity breeds contempt." Many birders travel to the St. Louis area specifically to see the European tree sparrow. This species is another introduced species, closely related and similar in appearance to the house sparrow. Yet birders don't call this species a junk bird and, in fact, most birders are thrilled to see it. Contempt for starlings, house sparrows, and pigeons does indeed seem to be a result of familiarity. However, this familiar status may change. House sparrow and European starling populations are declining at an alarming rate in England. In 2002, the British Trust for Ornithology estimated that house sparrow numbers decreased from twelve million pairs to seven million pairs, and starlings have decreased from twenty million to eight-and-a-half million, declines that the Environment Minister has called "very worrying." Will they still be called junk birds if they become rare? Will they be missed?

As Aldo Leopold noted, beauty transcends prettiness. John Ruskin's view of beauty was that "fitness is the first element of beauty." European starlings, house sparrows and rock pigeons are eminently fit, thereby possessing this first element of beauty. Freeman Tilden, father of the National Park Service's environmental interpretation philosophy, presented the following dialogue to make this same point: "Can a dung basket, then," said Aristippus, "be a beautiful thing?" "Yes, by Jupiter," returned Socrates, "and a golden shield may be an ugly thing, if the one be beautifully formed for its particular uses, and the other ill formed." European starlings, house sparrows, and rock pigeons are well-formed.

Beyond prettiness, utility, and fitness exists another more personal notion of beauty. Antoine de Saint-Exupéry wrote, "The house, the stars…what gives them their beauty is something that is invisible!" The same is true for the *house* sparrow and the *star*-ling. Perceiving beauty requires certain sensitivities and perspectives on the part of the beholder, whether it be in a concert hall, art museum, or landfill. If we look deeply, we may see beauty in these creatures. And if we can't *see* it, maybe we can *feel* it. "It is only with the heart that one can see rightly: what is essential is invisible to the eye," wrote Saint-Exupéry, adding, "…the eyes are blind. One must look with the heart." Ultimately, that is how we see beauty in all beasts—native or alien—avian or human.

Then Come Crows

🐦 CHERIE STAPLES

Blue earth shadow creeping down the sky dropping to the horizon with its pink frosting to the blue plain blue sky why muted colors color our revolution evolution of the new sunlit day and moon begins to grow in the low swimming atmosphere of this sphere peering out my window at windrows of tree-covered hills and still the crows leave their night's haven in pine heavens gathered to by hundreds of gleaming bodies sheening black-feathered crows each evening arguing over where they spend the night raucous cawing diving soaring dashing from pine to pine this is fine no over there lodging shifts each night deciding flights in tight wheeling mobs 'til darkness falls and black feathers quiet for the night in morning's light cold muscles flex and slowly roily groups of crows ascend the sky out to work their day

The Ecologist

  Louise Fabiani

> *One of the penalties of an ecological education is that one lives*
> *alone in a world of wounds.*
>
> —Aldo Leopold, from *Essays on Conservation from Round River*

Going through the woods, I tread on scars.
The soil is compacted, dry, infertile, unable
to support anything but a sparse understory
consisting of many from-aways,
which crowd out the do-belongs
like guests overstaying their welcome.
The should- and shouldn't-be's
fight it out until the land
is crisscrossed with battle lines.

And where am I
in these bleakscapes,
prattling on, confusing
description with prescription,
is and ought?

I knew my place,
then I forgot.

What a fretful occupation this is,
studying lost paradises,
exulting in beauty

of the most ephemeral kind,
and warding off the influence
of intractable human tendencies.

Yet, sometimes, there are victories:
small zones of purity emerge,
lost landscapes reappear
like mirages, and hope continues
its long, fervent struggle with doubt.

We live our work,
and work on the edge of despair.

Knowing well that, all about,
living lights are going out:
terrestrial stars extinguished.

A Leaf is a Book is a River

𝕬 Mira Bartók

I once knew a boy who painted birds with turpentine
set them on fire with the swish of his hand
winged flames flew up then exploded
over a veil of trees. Is there a word for this
a word for this kind of fire

for how the body becomes an abyss on this planet
of old mountains, how we catch our paws in traps
become mute beasts tethered to poles? Is there a word
or something else past the horizon a dream of birds

wearing skirts of wild roses foxes and field mice
sharing a meal a place where boys can't set fire to dresses
or fluttering wings where the sun is everywhere at once
the moon is too and the wind writes poems in cattails

where a nest is an alphabet a leaf is a book is a river
a song and no one leads us to the pit of black thoughts.
Turn around five times and make a wish.
You could be a horse or a bird or the seven seas

or you could be me and I could be you both of us
besieged by music and the language of trees.
We can give names to things climb all the way up
a mountain, up a path of white stones

to where the oceans begin. Each stone is a word
each word a letter of fire a glittering sun a heron's
infinite eye. Inside the eye is a boat. In the boat
a drop of water falling from my oar.

PART V

For the Children/
For the Future

*From his cracked hands I watched brittle seed
Cast surely for the future, the unborn;
Those acts of affirmation his deep need*

—Robert Minhinnick, from "Grandfather in the Garden"

Peepers

✤ ALERIA JENSEN

On a dirt road full of darkness
comes the universe. Here is a night
smelling of horses and lilacs,
ferns and the bark of trees
whose names I do not know.

Near the pond I hear them.
My footsteps fall silent
and the chorus swallows me.
Calling, trilling, pulsing,
music arrives from all sides.
We are inside an organ
pumping out great gulping notes,
swallowing a spring night.
Frogs, in the darkened woods
hunch over bundles of eggs,
over their own silky bodies
as instruments of desire.

Then add the light of fireflies.
I thought it too early—June,
and still chilly—but yes, a blink
over my head, between the trees,
another, another. It's almost
too much, these trembling sparks
dancing to the amphibian choir,

animating blackness, enlarging
my heart.

I look up to eddies of stars,
Big Dipper overhead.
Within my belly,
you are the size of a fig.
You have grown fingerprints.
Tonight my wish is to lift you
from my body, to take your hand
in mine and trace this constellation
from star to star,
from cup to handle,
so that you will know
you are a child of the north
with something to reckon your life by.

A Letter to My Daughter

From the Bayley-Hazen Road, Greensboro, Vermont

✿ NED OLMSTED

Dear Wyeth,

This morning the road scraper made its first springtime swipe past the house, leveling remnants of frost heaves, filling in potholes, and scratching up a new berm of gravel in front of the driveway. Later, as I raked out the cobbles of quartz and schist kicked onto the grass by the scraper's blade, I realized that I'm looking forward to sitting with you on our granite doorstep and telling you what I know about this old road.

There are stories I want you to hear, some from my own childhood, some passed on to me by your grandfather, some I've probably misremembered from a generation of oldtimers long gone, others borrowed from various Vermont histories and folklore. I carry these tales with me in much the same manner as you carry your worn bunny rabbit from room to room reluctant to let it out of your sight. The rhythm of their retelling brings a centeredness to my life; it adds another heartbeat to the geography of this place.

As I trundle you in your stroller along this short stretch of the Bayley-Hazen Road, I wonder what it will look like when you're my age. Now it's smoothly graded and drained and has held up well under the mud-season traffic of school buses, farm trucks, and logging rigs. However, in another forty or fifty years it will surely be paved and something altogether different. By then you'll possess your own tales of changing landscapes, births and deaths, geese overhead in November, northern lights in February, black flies in May. But before you begin to accumulate those stories, I'd like to tell you a little bit about what passed down this road before you were born.

I'd like to tell you about the elms that bounded it, and how they died one by one; how I spent a teenage summer splitting the knotty stuff to sell as cordwood until my clothes and skin were saturated with its dank, pungent scent, and at night I dreamed of splitting wedges inextricably driven into the gnarled, cross-grained blocks. I'd like to tell you about your great uncle; how he helped me and your grandfather fell and buck the very last of those stately trees on the hottest day of the summer, and how, overtired and sweaty, he went alone for a swim in the lake and drowned.

Or about sitting on the porch watching the full moon rise in the east with the white pines and firs on the near horizon backlit and pointed like the teeth of a cross-cut saw, and about the dancing globes of yellow light from a thousand fireflies making the most of a rare warm June evening.

I'd like to tell you about the Holsteins that grazed in the sloping meadow in front of your great-grandparents' house; for you to picture that open space before it was subdivided and apportioned off to their progeny. I'd like to tell you about how I used to test the toughness of my callused bare feet on the late summer stubble of that meadow as I ran down to the lake for an end of the day swim.

I'd like you to know about the two Indian scouts, Constant Bliss and Moses Sleeper, caught in 1779 outside the walls of their blockhouse, a half mile down the road from here by a raiding party of Mohawks. About how they came to a gruesome end, and weeks later were buried where they fell.

Or about how your diminutive great-grandmother in her stout brown walking shoes, strolled slowly and quietly with her best friend up to the four corners and back every summer afternoon. Or about how on Christmas morning she'd man her kitchen wood stove like some stooped submarine captain deftly closing dampers and adjusting baffles, baking paper-thin ginger snaps that I'd stack like poker chips.

I'd like to tell you about the soft afternoon light on the August day we buried your grandfather's ashes in the cemetery a hundred yards up the road, about how I placed his favorite, beat-up old hat under the small headstone before we turned and walked home to the sound of a hay kicker fluffing up the windrows in the next field over.

Like most Vermont country lanes, the Bayley-Hazen Road is a good storyteller. It bends its way around the contours of the land, over bedrock and ledge, black loam and seeping springs; it speeds up and it slows down, and if you look closely enough you can find in between the washboards and the ruts clues to an authentic landscape. So, on summer evenings before you go up to bed, maybe we'll sit on the doorstep and watch and listen and see what goes by.

Jupiter Came Down on Tuesday

❧ Maureen Sullivan

I walk toward the garbage can with Saturn in my pocket; it's the third planet to fall this week. The tentative putty holding the plastic orbs to Olivia's ceiling gets cold at night, hardens, and discards the planets from their celestial paths, down to her hard floor or onto her sleeping body. Jupiter came down on Tuesday. The falling solar system wakes her, most often between two and four a.m. I've tried re-attaching the planets but they fall again. I am thankful that there are only Earth and Pluto to go.

A slight hesitation in my hand, I drop Saturn onto a pile of chicken bones and a nonrecyclable yogurt container and try to remember how this particular solar system came into her life. Was it a "just because" gift from Aunt Peggy, or a birthday present? It doesn't really matter. I've tried to hold back the tide of things that come into her world, but it is a Herculean effort.

Of all the pregnancy, mothering, and parenting books I read before her birth, only one remotely prepared me for this battle of the bulge. In the early nineties a photographer went to many countries around the world. He had one family from each culture place all of their belongings in front of their home. The Aborigines of Australia had the least stuff. The middle class family from Kansas had so much stuff that it was difficult to see the people in the midst of all their belongings.

My friends with young children had homes filled with gargantuan plastic pieces of furniture and Happy Meal toys. I decided that when I had my child, everything unnecessary to its survival from birth to age two would be saved and then photographed. In November of 1999 my daughter took her first breath. During her babyhood I was too tired to speak some days, let alone carry through on the photo project. A sparkle-loving, cowgirl-hat-wearing, singing-in-the-bathtub kind of child is my Olivia, and I love her with every cell of my body. I just wish her life was celebrated with visits and hugs rather then trinkets and tokens.

I feel like an ingrate when I think this way. Some of that mountain of stuff has been contributed by me: the tiny colorful caterpillar that made her baby face light up each time she rediscovered the rainbow insect, the mobile of smiling butterflies, the softest teddy bear on earth. The remainder of things were bestowed upon her by some of the kindest people I know, and all presented with only the best of the best intentions. No harm, no foul, right?

Rubber ducks, the ones that babies love to suck on, release dioxin into their toothless mouths. Dollar-store toys break after one use, or sometimes have a speedier demise and malfunction on the first try. Into the landfill they go. These *gifts* of dioxins, petroleum distillates, and recalled lead paint leech into the groundwater—her groundwater and her children's groundwater. We are a culture that puts mercury into vaccines designed to protect our children and poisons them with toys made for their intellectual stimulation. Land of plenty. "Plenty of what?" I wonder.

Saturn looks small and vulnerable on top of its pile of rubbish. I glance away and move toward the pile of clothes on the sofa. The laundry beckons. But then I turn back and pluck the planet from its littered resting place. Saturn now sits on my kitchen windowsill waiting for a chance to orbit in a new direction.

A step toward my laundry pile and another planet falls. I am certain that it is a planet because they make a distinctive *plink plink* sound when they bounce on her wood floor. Must be cold this November morning. The thermometer outside our kitchen window reads thirty-four degrees; the grass is twinkling and frosted. Low rays of sunlight, filtered through the bare elm branches, form shifting, shimmering patterns on the living room wall.

I hope it was Pluto that fell from her sky this morning and not Earth.

Blue Egg

PETER SHEPHERD

I didn't know.
I didn't know and I'm really sorry.
I am so sweetly sorry for your song.
I found you
The half of you open to the world
Shaped as a cup, like an ear, already.
Here's the story:
Once upon a time there was a baby Jesus
Whose mother was blue, with feathers,
    And her world was so light, so of light,
    And baby Jesus waited at the door,
        at the entrance, at the cave, at the
        heart of the womb, listening to the songs
        of joy of sky.
        Nest symphony.

So many colors
So many cathedrals of sky
Each tree, land here awhile, pass on the joy of air, we share…

    And the mother's despair,
    A song undone curling back
    And your song, unspooling,
        each sweetly reaching for the other

I am so sorry
I am so sweetly sorry for your song

All I can do is listen
(All I can do is hear)
The air remembers
And I have a piece of you
A drop of your blood's voice.

Hatch

✿ APRIL NEWLIN

It is Day 50. The southeasterlies stir early off the Gulf, sending grains of sand hopping like sand fleas, but the nest does not twitch. Sea turtle eggs hatch anytime between Day 50 and Day 70. I scan for a dip, a sunken center where life might be on the move, two feet below the surface. Nothing, a blank screen. Packed into the toe of a ten-foot dune, the nest sits on a lonely site, a motherless place, left to the whims of wind and water. The loggerhead laid and left as they always do. No patient waiting, no incubating, no bond to those she bore. The lady is off and gone. Nature can be so cut and dried.

During nesting season I walk for turtles, flagging tracks and false crawls, staking with posts and orange tape. Turtles nest at night. I wake at dawn to a barren beach cluttered with yesterday's bird tracks and flip flops, cockle shells and kayak drags, ghost crab dens and sandcastles. A crawl could get lost in the crowd. And yet, dawn stills the action, taking it down to a singular moment, a turn on the heel or a final push before flight. I sift and sort, looking for the pattern of flippers. The hot summer sea whispers a fishy turtle breath, a few gulls fidget at water's edge and a trio of nighthawks swoop and dive for bugs soon to recede with the tide. Sea oats shiver at the first hint of a sea breeze and light trickles across the dunes like morning glory vines, blooming a great blue heron silhouette by the coastal dune lake near the far end of my beat. Every tendril of sunlight raises the temperature on this steamy July morning. Least terns sit still on sandy nests, posing like the decoys placed there at season's start. A blue crab sprawls at the wrack line in a mess of splintered shell, shattered from the top, its insides picked clean. Heron tracks tiptoe away, pointing east. We are solo out here. Even the laughing gulls waddle off by themselves, watching and waiting.

The birds would like nothing more than to pluck a fine hatchling off the platter of beach detritus, but they have no idea when or where the hatchlings will arrive. Without the crawl as a guide, I too have no way of finding a nest. A fresh track leaves a conspicuous drag twenty to thirty yards from the tide line up and over the foreshore before it turns and trails out again. The imprint cuts and slices the sand into dainty scallops and swivels, the work of a two hundred-pound reptile with an eye for open spaces and a sloping rise to the dunes. The turtles like it here, so much so that they have become a subspecies of *Caretta caretta*, loggerheads of the northwest Florida coast. On the surface, these turtles look the same as any other *Caretta*, their crawls no different than the track left on a Mexican *playa* or a Cape Verde *praia*.

Turtling, as I have come to call it, means confining one's gaze to the ground, to the design that signals turtle amidst all of the competing scoops and peaks and ridges. It means parsing the track, making sense out of sand: parallel flippers for greens and alternating for loggerheads, a tail drag for greens but not loggerheads, a grand six-foot spread for a leatherback and a petite patrol for a Kemp's ridley. It means separating the false crawl from the true one, from the turtle that aborted a nesting attempt and the one that dug her pit and laid. It means digging up the nest buried too close to the high-tide line, shoveling a new hole and moving the clutch, egg by egg, until all are packed into a space that protects these facile swimmers from drowning. We dig in twos and threes.

Turtlers are volunteers. We work under the leadership of a turtle-tattooed woman named Sharon who paints her toenails green like scutes on her bared feet. She is driven, her no-nonsense devotion an armor over a soft and compassionate attentiveness to sea turtles. Spry and spunky with short, spiked hair, she laughs easily, jokes irreverently, and hardens her vowels with a distinctive Michigan nasality. Sharon directs a whole slew of local folks, a volunteer group devoted to the preservation and conservation of endangered sea turtles on the beaches of South Walton, Florida. She founded the Turtle Watch and serves as its director. We are eager, inspired, and committed. We walk every morning from May to October, culling for crawls and nests. We are a mixed bag—a young British lady who talks turtles with gleeful highs and lows, her speech a poetry of pitches; a retiree who covets his reflective time on the long solitary turtle walks, his pensive face haloed with a ring of grey hair; a couple who share dawn before work each morning; an environmental educator who simply does what he does; an athlete with a buff body and ankle bracelet; a displaced Yankee who has found a place he can attach to; a Vietnam vet who has discovered faith in turtles. We cover for one another, but we rarely meet. We act alone mostly, our work done before the world wakes.

Today is my birthday. I would like sixty-nine hatchlings, please. I know the exact number of eggs because I dug them up and held each one, coddled the dented white orbs in my hands and placed them, without so much as a tilt, into a new pit, a spot farther up the beach to lessen the odds of losing them in a tropical storm or hurricane. Three of us worked that morning, our hands cupped like hind flippers, scooping and lifting, throwing sand, and reaching down. We covered and patted, sprayed sand and pressed, mimicking a loggerhead labor. And then we left as she had done. My instincts said no. I have sons. I remember the hoarse gurgle of that first cry and the instant urge to respond. The hatchlings would emerge and run a gauntlet of ghost crabs and gulls; they would enter the water as easy prey, all two inches of them making haste for cover. One in a thousand would make it to maturity. Nature bets on odds. It strikes me as a heartless approach, a relinquishing of duty.

I check the nest each morning now, looking for hatchling tracks or signs of mischief around the site. Weather wears on the plat, rain and wind and sun tweaking the surface and playing havoc with my memory. By Day 60, I grow anxious. Perhaps, our human-made nest is flawed, our hands not as effective as flippers or our minds no match for the long evolutionary genius of loggerhead nesting behavior. I visit the nest mornings and nights. Turtles hatch after sunset, sensing the change in temperature as a green light for launch. At night, they use the light of the horizon as a beacon to find the sea. Artificial lights distract and confuse them. I sit with the nest for hours on this remote corner of beach, tucked up where no one notices, not even during the day. The nights here cool to a balmy eighty degrees. Wispy clouds wrap the stars like gifts in glittering tissue, and then moments later the thin sheets tear and fall away. An orange crescent of moon floats west and vanishes in folds of mist. Rollers slip in under the cover of darkness and break with a thud and hiss, remnants of Tropical Storm Edouard passing south. Voices drift in and out, a whiff of cologne, a giggle, a flash of light from a lantern. I am wary out here, the scrub woods behind the dunes as thick as fur, a coat matted with thorns and spines and burrs. Someone told me recently of coyotes that chased a woman as she jogged. A fellow turtler encountered a fox on her route one morning, the brazen canine drawn toward her rather than deterred by her frantic hand waving. Had it sensed her fear? Was it simply curious? Was it rabid as they sometimes are?

We don't always know what drives another creature, human or fox or turtle. I surprised a man one morning on my walk as he turned the corner with his dog. Before he saw me, I heard him admonish his companion who was bounding ahead out of reach, "What were you thinking?" Yes, that's the deal—how to know what goes on in the mind of another. You start by feeling your way in. You try them on, you become them for a moment if you can. But a turtle is tough. A loggerhead runs on instinct, her prehistoric processor spinning need, not nuance—or so it seems. She buries her eggs and then camouflages the nest, behaviors at once mechanical and maternal as if there is no discrepancy between the two. I glance up as Scorpio crawls across the sky, a few glimmers of its stinger flashing on and off. And then, a tip of orange hatches out of a gray shell of cloud and slowly takes form, curved and pendent, the moon a flipper swimming in starlight. It is 11:00 p.m. and I trudge home, hoping the nest will wait for me.

By morning, a fox track meanders around the nest site; could be it has a nose for eggs. A turtle volunteer calls to spread the news that a leatherback nested down the coast and I rush to get a look at the massive pit and the distinctive sinusoidal crawl. Word comes that another nest hatched, a green. We are having a good season. Numbers are up. I spend another night at the nest. The average incubation is fifty-nine days. They are late. On Day 62, I worry. A snake print trespasses the posts, slithers across the top of the nest, and disappears into the dunes. Reluctant to leave the nest at night, I grow weary with the loss of sleep and constant tending. I could abandon my watch, crawl off into the dunes, leave it for others to discern the scrape left behind, to tease out indifference from the burden of care. Lightning blinks in a darkening sky and clouds boil as the drum of thunder deepens. Cold downdrafts chill the air, but the nest does not budge. Rain does not waken them. I give up and go home. By morning, the tiny tracks of a cloudburst are everywhere. Another day passes. Day 64 dawns with a ghost crab hole smack in the center of the nest. All bets are off. Perhaps the crab pierced the chamber. They dine on hatchlings, taking their eyes first and returning later to eat them. Just days ago a school of pogeys, big-eyed minnows, stranded on the beach, chased into the shallows by ladyfish or hungry blues. They lay drying on the beach all night until I found them in the morning, their eyes gone, each and every one of them untouched but for the eyes.

I am not allowed to tamper, my maternal hands are tied, but I get permission to fill the hole, wondering if I have merely trapped the robber inside with the loot. Maybe a stethoscope would detect the sound of pipping as shells break. I grow impatient and take a long break. By 8:10 p.m., I arrive at the nest to find the opening enlarged and movement inside the canal. The crab must be eating. Several more checks turn up a black lump like soft tar, not a crab but a turtle. They are hatching.

Word spreads. Neighbors arrive and turtlers convene. A bright half moon illuminates a runway to the sea. We rake the sand, flattening out the furrows inflicted by the sheriff's nightly truck patrol, ruts that would impede a small head at ground level from seeing the light, ruts that take the eyes first. We are as ready as midwives, disposed to be attentive, eager for the earth to deliver her young. But the turtles take their time. A wee flipper sticks out of the sand, an elfin head pokes through the grains, sand stuck like sugar to the egg tooth. Minutes go by and another one boils up, settling just beneath the surface. More time and more sooty smudges; an hour ticks by; waves of movement and spans of stillness alternate. The sand quickens and then relaxes, the first hatchling now suspended in the air, its rear carapace buried, its front flippers askew, its head extended in space as if the birth halted midway. Again and again the cycle repeats, spasms of excited effort and then torpor as more babies cram onto the roof of their shifting home. "What are they waiting for?" someone whispers. They do not hatch and flee, but rise slowly to the top, their movements jostling the sand and building the scaffold that will lift the ones below them. They do not act alone. Each affects the other; one wiggles, then another, "pass it on." The turtles linger until all of the siblings are ready. Accumulating bodies pile on top of one another, barely visible beneath a thin veneer of sand, flecks and specks of turtle as if they are in pieces requiring assembly on arrival. And then, as though on cue, they bubble up, pouring out like lava from a venting hole atop a mountain. They keep coming, liquid turtles spreading black ooze over the white sand. They thin out and scatter into dozens of themselves. They zip and dash, one over another, flippers flapping, a charge to the surf, five yards, ten, fifteen yards, babies streaking toward people who jump aside at the speeding shadow. In ten minutes it is done, over, the last straggler lifted by an incoming wave and swoosh, the hatching complete. We counted sixty-seven hatchlings. Someone calls Sharon: "You're a momma!"

Sunrise on the following day erupts with the song of a mockingbird. I feel a vague post-partum emptiness. I miss the checking and anticipation, but the mockingbird intrudes with its renditions of towhees and wrens. The tunes do not mock as much as mimic. The bird is a keen listener, a master of imitation, and what is imitation but an archaic form of empathy? The hatching has left a track across my brain that will not give, an indelible impression that nature not only responds, but is responsive. Hatching is a concerted effort. The babies are attuned to one another in some primal way. Human newborns cry when they hear the cries of other infants, a hardwired perception that presages the beginning of empathy.

Perhaps turtles have it too, some elemental sensitivity to their own. Archie Carr, noted turtle researcher, describes the hatching as "aimless flailing that takes them steadily up to the surface of the ground," "a witless collaboration." Yet he acknowledges some sort of "unconscious cooperation." The turtles respond to each others' movements and they wait even as they risk being exposed. A fox would have a field day. Instinct becomes empathic perception when it is attuned to the other. These solitary creatures, for a time, act as a group, their synchronized birth enhancing their chances of survival. Nature is not as witless as it is inscrutable.

I'm turtling again this morning, looking for washed backs, hatchlings gone astray, swept by an incoming tide. We pick them up and release them at night, playing games with nature's numbers. We deem nature unfit to protect her own, but it is we who changed the rules, we who took the land from nesting mothers. Now, we work to build the scaffold that will lift a species from extinction, so many turtlers, scrambling, spreading out, passing it on. Miles out, my brood of sixty-seven is making a Phelpsian dash for the sargassum rafts, living off their remaining yolks, steering knowingly for a place they have never been. In three decades, having spent years in driftlines and ocean currents, one of them may be back. For all her random wanderings, she will seek and find her natal beach, this beach, the home that hatched her. She will scout for days at a time, heavy with eggs, craning her thick hard neck to see, looking goggle-eyed for her native ground. Her return at long last will reveal her bond, not an impulse but a devotion, a tie woven in strands of sea oats and sand.

The Drawer of Inhaled Objects

Mira Bartók

I remember reading about it once
how this man collected so many objects
into his nose breathing them in one by
one—If only I could remember there

must have been a thimble a cup of nails
a shiny beetle and a fly of course
there were things you'd expect like buttons and
pieces of food feathers lint and some chalk

how someone could take it all in like that
honeysuckles a peach anything full
of pollen and juice, like a Mexican
pear or a fig from Uruguay but what

about the hard things the ones too big to
believe? Let's start with the birds, all the
extinct ones, the great auk and the dodo how
someone could suck them up through that dark

passage of nose, two tiny slits like
fish gills or eyes, slide all those birds into
his head and then those other things inside
the drawer—the mammoth hide, the glyptodon

the rod of Moses for god sakes how did
they fit into that small tunnel of bone

or maybe it was a group a team—men
and women who liked to sniff things out and

take them in one by one up the limbic
path to the brain, a brave gang really
to shove all that stuff up there things could have
gotten stuck, blocked a vein or two but no

they kept at it kept at it as if there
was no tomorrow, but what if they were
right what if there is no day after the
next, what then, what would you take and would it

fit, and what if it came back spilled out on
the floor, all those things you stuck somewhere for
safekeeping in case you had to leave your
house in a hurry, in case there was no
one waiting at the door?

The Worst Trap in the World

Jules Older

So very many traps—danger lurks everywhere.

There's the rat trap and the Havahart trap. The velvet trap and the parent trap. The Wolf Trap and the Trapp Family Singers trap.

But the worst trap of all is the *Can't Do Anything Until You Do Everything* trap.

That's the trap with the biggest, baddest teeth. That's the trap that immobilizes you even before you take your first step. That's what makes it the worst trap in the world.

Say, for example, you're an outdoor type, say a skier or a snowshoer or a mountain hiker. And say you're getting a trifle concerned about the whole global warming thing. Overall, this has been a good snow year, but you remember last winter, and you can't help but wonder—which is the new norm and which is the aberration?

So you decide to take a first step. Something small. Like change the light bulbs. Or carpool to the mountain. Or buy a gas miser instead of guzzler. Whatever. It's your step.

You tell a "friend" your plan. The "friend" sets the Can't Do Anything Until You Do Everything trap. Goes like this:

"Change the bulbs? That's just pissing in the wind. You got, what, six bulbs? Ten? You think your puny little light bulbs are gonna have any effect whatsoever on the *planet*? Don't flatter yourself!"

Or like this: "Carpool? That saves *how* much gas? Do you know how much more a 747 uses just taxiing down the runway? Like one-zillion times more. Fuggedaboudit!"

Or this: "Why *not* buy a Hogger III? I'm tellin' you, and this is a fact—until capitalism is overthrown, until indigenous peoples are no longer marginalized, until sexism and militarism are brought to their knees, it all means nothing. NOTHING!"

Here's the truth. Our snow's at real risk. Our forests are at real risk. Our planet's at real risk. Your first step, when combined with my first step and his and her first steps may or may not be enough to turn the risk around.

Working together, can we save the snow, the woods, the Earth? Dunno. Too early to tell. Or maybe too late.

But what we do know, and know for sure, is this: If you and I and she and he *don't* take that step, if we let ourselves fall into the jaws of the Can't Do Anything Until You Do Everything trap, we're turning up the heat, not cooling our corner of the globe.

And if we let ourselves get talked out of taking that step and the next step and the next, we just may end up kissing our cool corner good-bye forever.

CALLOUT:

"Why *not* buy a Hogger III?"

Seeds

🎔 FLORENCE CAPLOW

·

It's late summer on a windswept, barren ridge above the Columbia River in eastern Washington State, and the hot wind is hard against my face. I can see for miles in the clear desert air: northwest up the Columbia to Sentinel Gap, where the river cuts through the Saddle Mountains, and south and east to the central part of the Hanford Nuclear Reservation, where the towers of eleven shuttered nuclear reactors rise up here and there above the vast sagebrush plain.

I'm here with three other botanists, and we've come to collect seed of Umtanum wild buckwheat, *Eriogonum codium*, which grows here and nowhere else in the world. Bright yellow clusters of buckwheat flowers wave gaily at our feet. Scattered around us are hundreds of plants, their small gray leaves and low spreading branches perfectly adapted to the drying winds, clinging to the bare pumice gravel of the ridge-top, just above talus slopes that plunge hundreds of feet down to the river.

My mother has a photo of these yellow flowers, tucked in her wallet among the photos of my siblings' children. I have no other children. More than a decade ago my field partner and I were hired by the Nature Conservancy to document the rare plants of Hanford. One day in the summer of 1995 we were walking on Umtanum Ridge and stumbled upon plants we'd never seen before, unidentifiable because no one had yet named them or described them. We found them and helped name them, and now we do what we can to help them survive.

Umtanum wild buckwheat is a candidate for listing under the Endangered Species Act, and so we closely monitor the population. Every year a few of the older plants die, but no new plants replace them. Although each plant produces thousands of seeds, and although every spring we find the tiny gray seedlings in the reddish pumice of the ridgetop, in all these years we've had only two seedlings survive the hot, dry summers. We don't know why the population is declining—global warming, the invasion of weeds, the end of an evolutionary road—but the graphs speak volumes: if this continues, one day there will be no more Umtanum wild buckwheat. My children, so lovely here in the afternoon sunlight, will be gone.

We're here to collect seed. Scattered among the flowers are little ghosts: wedding veil fabric tied around the flowering stems to catch the seeds as they fall, before they're blown far away. We were here a few weeks ago, kneeling in the pumice, carefully tying the fabric around each slender stem and its ball of flowers. Now we've come to harvest.

A few days later I take the seed to the Berry Botanic Garden in Portland, which maintains a seed bank of the wild plants of the Pacific Northwest. The seed bank doesn't look like much—a windowless drying room with metal racks, a few freezers much like the ones that sit on the back porches of farmhouses—but it's designed to keep seeds alive for hundreds of years, temperature and humidity carefully monitored and elaborately protected by backup electrical systems. This place holds, like an ark, the genetic diversity of the deserts and rainforests and high mountains of the Pacific Northwest.

Someday, perhaps in my lifetime, Umtanum wild buckwheat will be gone from the ridge where it has grown for longer than I can imagine. But if all goes well, its seeds will still be here, nestled in labeled packets in the dark freezer, waiting for a better time, for someone to bring them back into the light again.

I've been a botanist and conservation biologist for more than twenty years. My job, in various forms, has been to find and conserve some of the rarest plants on earth. I've spent most of my adult life wandering in wild places, all my senses open, feeling and looking and imagining where a rare plant might grow and what it might need to continue to thrive in a particular place. It's ancient work, I think, not unlike the work of the women and men who once knew how to find the hidden plants for food and healing. Sometimes it seems like the plant steps forward to be found, even invites itself to be found, like a dance or a conversation.

But being a conservation biologist requires an ongoing conversation and dialogue with despair. No one I know in this field is immune to it. It takes enormous effort, years of work, to protect even one population of a rare species, and so many others disappear every day. My friends who are ecologists have watched places they have studied and loved go under the bulldozer, or, if protected, fill up with virulent weeds. A friend who is a herpetologist goes out on rainy spring nights to throw frogs off country roads, knowing that hundreds of others will be run over before dawn.

I spent five years as a botanist for the State of Washington, working with other conservation biologists from all over the Pacific Northwest. It felt like the forces of destruction were everywhere, and a little handful of us were doing our best to stem the tide, like children with our fingers in holes in the dike, watching what we love disappear beneath the waters.

Now, as the scope and speed of climate change becomes clearer, I realize that those many rare plants that I've worked so hard to protect, that are known only from a single place or a handful of places—they're not likely to make it through this change. Unlike animals or more widespread plants, they have nowhere to go, and no way of moving north or up as the land dries and warms. They'll wink out, one by one, except for the little packets of seeds resting in their dark wombs in the seedbanks of the world, or a few carefully tended plants in some botanical garden, placeholders for once-wild species, like portraits on a wall.

I've spent half a lifetime dedicated to the protection of what may be gone by the time I die. I've found new species that may be gone in my lifetime. How do I go forward, knowing this?

I stand in the offices of the Berry Botanic Garden with my packets of precious seeds, the genetic legacy of Umtanum wild buckwheat in my hands. I'm talking with my friend Ed Guerrant, the conservation director, and listening to the birdsong in the graceful gardens out the window, when I notice a seed conservation newsletter on his desk. On the cover are a series of oval photographs, old brown portraits of nine men and women, each solemnly posed. When Ed is called out of the office for a moment, I pick up the newsletter.

The photographs are of nine caretakers of the great seedbank of Leningrad. Before the beginning of World War II, a place deep in the heart of Leningrad housed what was then the world's largest collection of plant seeds and tubers—more than 200,000 different species and varieties, including thousands of varieties of cultivated food plants. During the war, Hitler's army besieged the city for nearly nine hundred days. By the end of the siege, one and a half million people had died, almost all from exposure and starvation. The scientists who maintained the seedbank could have eaten what was stored there and survived. Instead, mindful of the heritage in their hands, knowing what it would mean to the world if these unique species and cultivars died out, they hid them and cared for them as the famine deepened. Nine scientists died of starvation before the siege ended, the nine faces that still looked out from their faded photographs. The collection survived, and is still one of the most important seed collections in the world.

This story has stayed with me as a talisman, a koan, a resonant mystery. It's easy to feel pessimistic about humanity, but what is this? Who were Alexander Stchukin, Liliya Rodina, and their colleagues, who died rather than consume their gifts for the future? There's something in this for me, some way of holding the despair. I turn it and turn it in my mind.

I heard Randy Hayes, founder of the Rainforest Action Network, say that it is time for each of us to adopt one species, one place, something we care about, and make a commitment, "I'll care for you. I'll carry you through the storm, as best I can."

I think each of us, when a crisis approaches, has to consider how we'll respond, and the deepest and most effective response is the one that is truest to who we are. All my life I've been drawn to the green world, where speech is in leaf and in flower and in seed. When I think about seeds, I begin to see a way through.

When those scientists in Leningrad kept the seeds safe, they protected both the past—the thousands of years of breeding and evolution that each seed represented—and the future—we who would need those seeds. And seeds come in many forms: seeds of plants, seeds of language, seeds of culture, seeds of all that is irreplaceable—the many gifts of the world.

My life is changing in front of me, as the world changes, and although I'm still a conservation biologist, I've become more than that too: my work has become larger. I gather the seeds of Umtanum wild buckwheat, but I also gather the seeds of what it means to go deep into silence, or how to listen with a willing heart, or how to spend a week in the wilderness. Some people have kept alive old music, or understand the mathematics of quantum mechanics, or know the deep language of poetry—all the beautiful ways of being human.

Whatever's ahead, I know that the world will always need people who are willing to carry what we know as a gift, holding our seeds close to our bodies, hiding them deep in the ground, offering them quietly from hand to hand, sharing them, guarding them as the storm rages over us, so that one day they may bloom again. That's what seeds know how to do: they know how to carry their message through every sort of disaster.

As I write this in late summer, the seeds of Umtanum wild buckwheat are ripening again on that high ridge above the Columbia River. Once, years ago, I held a few hundred seeds in the palm of my hand, and then, suddenly, the wind caught and scattered them. They flew away like sparks, like tiny prayer flags flung up against the sky, and then they tumbled to the waiting ground.

For the Children

🦎 SCOTT RUSSELL SANDERS

> *To climb these coming crests*
> *one word to you, to*
> *you and your children:*
>
> *stay together*
> *learn the flowers*
> *go light*

—Gary Snyder, from "For the Children"

You are still curled in the future, like seeds biding your time. Even though you are not yet born, I think of you often. I feel the promise of your coming the way I feel the surge of spring before it rises out of the frozen ground. What marvels await you on this wild Earth! When you do rise into the light of this world, you'll be glad of your fresh eyes and ears, your noses and tongues, your sensitive fingers, for they will bring you news of a planet more wonderful and mysterious than anything I can tell you about in mere words.

Mere words are all I have, though, to speak of what I've treasured during my days, and to say what I hope you'll find when you take your turn under the sun. So I write this letter. As I write, I'm leaning against the trunk of a fat old maple in the backyard of our house here in the southern Indiana hills. It's early one April morning, and the birds are loudly courting. I'm surrounded by the pink blossoms of wild geraniums, the yellow of celandine poppies, the blue of phlox. A thunderstorm is building in the western sky, and a brisk wind is rocking the just-opened leaves. My pleasure from wind and rain, from cloud drift and bird song, from the sound of creeks tossing in their stony beds, from the company of animals and the steady presence of trees—all of that immense delight is doubled when I think of you taking pleasure one day from these same glories.

Even here in a tame backyard, Earth's energy seems prodigious. The grasses and ferns are stiff with juice. The green pushing out of every twig and stem, the song pulsing out of every throat, the light gleaming on the needles of white pines and in the bright cups of flowers, the thunder clouds massing, the wind rising—all speak of an inexhaustible power. You will feel that power in your day, surely, for nothing we do could quench it. But everything we do may affect the way that power moves and the living shapes it takes on. Will there be whales for you to watch from a bluff on the Oregon coast, as I watched with my own children? Will there be ancient redwoods and cedars and white oaks and sycamores for you to press your cheeks against? In your day, will there be monarch butterflies sipping nectar in gardens, bluebirds nesting in meadows, crayfish scuttling in creeks, spring peepers calling from ponds?

Because of the way my generation and those that preceded us have acted, Earth has already suffered worrisome losses—forests cut down, swamps drained, topsoil washed away, animals and plants driven to extinction, clean rivers turned foul, the very atmosphere unsettled. I can't write you this letter without acknowledging these losses, for I wish to be honest with you about my fears as well as my hopes. But I must also tell you that I believe we can change our ways, we can choose to do less harm, we can take better care of the soils and waters and air, we can make more room for all the creatures who breathe. And we are far more likely to do so if we think about the many children who will come after us, as I think about you.

I think of you as lightning cracks the horizon and thunder comes rolling in like the distant rumble of trains. When I was little, thunderstorms frightened me, so when the rumbling began my father would wrap me in a blanket and carry me onto the porch and hold me close as the sky flashed and the air shook and the rain poured down. Safe in his arms, I soon came to love the boom and crash. So when my own two children were little, first Eva and then Jesse, I wrapped them in blankets and carried them onto the porch to watch the lightning and hear the thunder and feel the mist and smell the rain. Now I am doing the same with my grandchildren. Maybe one day a parent or grandparent will hold you during a storm and then you will not only read what I'm saying but will feel it in your bones.

The smell of rain reaches me now on a wind from the west, and my skin tingles. The stout maple thrums against my back, like a thick string plucked. This old tree is tougher than I am, more supple, more durable, for it stands here in all weathers, wrapped in bark against the heat and cold, deeply rooted, drawing all it needs from dirt and air and sun. Often, when I come home feeling frazzled from the demands of the day, before I go into the house I stop here in the yard and press my hands against this maple, and I grow calm.

I hope you will find companion trees of your own, where you can hear the birds hurling their lusty cries and watch the flowers tossing their bright blooms. May you climb into the branches to feel the huge body swaying beneath you and the wind brushing your face like the wings of angels.

I hope you'll be able to live in one place while you're growing up, so you'll know where home is, so you'll have a standard to measure other places by. If you live in a city or suburb, as chances are you will, I hope you'll visit parks, poke around in overgrown lots, keep an eye on the sky, and watch for the tough creatures that survive amidst the pavement and fumes. If you live where it never snows, I hope you'll be able to visit places where the snow lies deep in winter. I want you to see the world clarified by that coating of white, hear the stillness, bear the weight and cold of it, and then relish warmth all the more when you go indoors. Wherever you live, I hope you'll travel into country where the land obeys laws that people didn't make. May you visit deep forests, where you can walk all day and never hear a sound except the scurry and calls of animals and the rustle of leaves and the silken stroke of your own heart.

When I think of all the wild pleasures I wish for you, the list grows long. I want you to be able to chase fireflies as they glimmer in long grass, watch tadpoles turn into frogs in muddy pools, hear loons calling on clear lakes, glimpse deer grazing and foxes ambling, lay your fingers in the paw prints of grizzlies and wolves. I want there to be rivers you can raft without running into dams, the water pure and filled with the colors of sky. I want you to thrill in spring and fall to the ringing calls of geese and cranes as they fly overhead. I want you to see herds of caribou following the seasons to green pastures, turtles clambering onshore to lay their eggs, alewives and salmon fighting their way upstream to spawn. And I want you to feel in these movements Earth's great age and distances, and to sense how the whole planet is bound together by a web of breath.

As I sit here in this shaggy yard writing to you, I remember a favorite spot from the woods behind my childhood house in Ohio, a meadow encircled by trees and filled with long grass that turned the color of bright pennies in the fall. I loved to lie there and watch the clouds, as I'm watching the high, surly storm clouds rolling over me now. I want you to be able to lie in the grass without worrying that the kiss of the sun will poison your skin. I want you to be able to drink water from faucets and creeks, to eat fruits and vegetables straight from the soil. I want you to be safe from lightning and loneliness, from accidents and disease. I would spare you all harm if I could. But I also want you to know there are powers much older and grander than our own—earthquakes, volcanoes, tornados, thunderstorms, glaciers, floods. I pray that you will never be hurt by any of these powers, but I also pray that you will never forget them. And remember that nature is a lot bigger than our planet: it's the shaping energy that drives the whole universe, the wheeling galaxies as well as water striders, the shimmering pulsars as well as your beating heart.

Thoughts of you make me reflect soberly on how I lead my life. When I spend money, when I turn the key in my car, when I vote or refrain from voting, when I fill my head or belly with whatever's for sale, when I teach students or write books, ripples from my actions spread into the future, and sooner or later they will reach you. So I bear you in mind. I try to imagine what sort of world you will inherit. And when I forget, when I serve only my own appetite, more often than not I do something wasteful. By using up more than I need—of gas, food, wood, electricity, space—I add to the flames that are burning up the blessings I wish to preserve for you.

I worry that the choices all of us make today, in our homes and workplaces, in offices and legislatures, will leave fewer choices for you and your own children and grandchildren, fifty or a hundred years from now. By indulging our taste for luxuries, we may deprive you of necessities. Our laziness may cause you heavy labor. Our comfort may cause you pain. I worry that the world you find will be diminished from the one we enjoy.

If Earth remains a blessed place in the coming century, you'll hear crickets and locusts chirring away on summer nights. You'll hear owls hoot and whippoorwills lament. You'll smell wet rock, lilacs, new-mown hay, peppermint, lemon balm, split cedar, piles of autumn leaves. On damp mornings you'll find spider webs draped like handkerchiefs on the grass. You'll watch dragonflies zip and hover, then flash away, so fast, their wings thinner than whispers. You'll watch beavers nosing across the still waters of ponds, wild turkeys browsing in the stubble of cornfields, and snakes wriggling out of their old skins.

If we take good care in our lifetime, you'll be able to sit by the sea and watch the waves roll in, knowing that a seal or an otter may poke a sleek brown head out of the water and gaze back at you. The skies will be clear and dark enough for you to see the moon waxing and waning, the constellations gliding overhead, the Milky Way arching from horizon to horizon. The breeze will be sweet in your lungs and the rain will be innocent.

The rain has reached me now, rare drops at first, rattling the maple leaves over my head. There's scarcely a pause between lightning and thunder, and every loud crack makes me jump. It's time for me to get out from under this big old tree, and go inside to keep this paper dry. So a few more words, my darlings, and then goodbye for now.

Thinking about you draws my heart into the future. I want you to look back on those of us who lived at the beginning of the twenty-first century and know that we bore you in mind, we cared for you, and we cared for our fellow tribes—those cloaked in feathers or scales or chitin or fur, those covered in leaves and bark. One day it will be your turn to bear in mind the coming children, your turn to care for all the living tribes. The list of wild marvels I would save for you is endless. I want you to feel wonder and gratitude for the glories of Earth. I hope you'll come to feel, as I do, that we're already in paradise, right here and now.

Acknowledgments

The publisher gratefully acknowledges permission to reprint the following previously published material.

"Bean by Bean" by Terra Brockman was published in a slightly different form in *The Seasons on Henry's Farm* (Agate Publishing, Surrey Books, October 2009), copyright © 2009 by Terra Brockman. Reprinted by permission of the author.

"The Wisdom of Turtles" by Michael J. Caduto, copyright © 2010 by Michael J. Caduto. All Rights Reserved. Reprinted by permission of the author.

An adapted version of the essay by Jim Collins, "Fishing with George," previously appeared in the *Dartmouth Alumni Magazine*.

"Prairie Skin" by Susan Futrell was originally published in 2005 on the Iowa National Heritage Foundation website. Used by permission of the author.

"Degrees of Damage in Blue River," "This Ground Made of Trees," and "The Web," from *Rope* by Allison Hawthorne Deming, copyright © 2009 by Allison Hawthorne Deming. Used by permission of Penguin, a division of Penguin Group (USA) Inc.

"Earth's Eye" by Edward Hoagland was originally published by Lyons Press, copyright © 2003. Used by permission of the publisher and Edward Hoagland.

"Divination" by Sydney Lea, copyright © 2009 by Sydney Lea; first published in *Shenandoah* © 2009, reprinted by permission of the author.

"Dispute with Hardy" by Sydney Lea was originally posted on the Christian Century website in 2008, reprinted by permission of the author.

"La Joie du Criquet" by Jeffrey A. Lockwood was adapted from "Song of the Loire" published in a *Prairie Soul: Finding Grace in the Earth Beneath my Feet*(Skinner House, 2004). Copyright © 2004 by J. A. Lockwood; reprinted by permission of the author.

"The Worst Trap" by Jules Older, copyright © Jules Older 2008; first posted on the *Vermont Sports* website in 2008, reprinted by permission of the author.

"The Work of Turkey Vultures" and "Crow Speaks His Mind" copyright © H. C. Palmer. Reprinted by permission of the author.

"Cow of the Virgin" by Robert J. Romano Jr., copyright © 2008 by Robert J. Romano Jr.; first published in *Outdoors New England* in 2008, reprinted by permission of the author.

"For the Children" by Scott Russell Sanders, copyright © 2009 by Scott Russell Sanders; first published in *A Conservationist Manifesto* (Indiana University Press, 2009), reprinted by permission of the author.

"Leaving Dorland Mountain" by Alison Townsend, copyright © 2003 by Alison Townsend, first published in *The Blue Dress* (White Pines Press, 2003); "Between Green Flannel Sheets Splattered with Portuguese Roses" by Alison Townsend, copyright © 2009 by Alison Townsend, first published in *Persephone in America* (Southern Illinois University Press, 2009). Reprinted by permission of the author.

Wildbranch Faculty

(with years taught at Wildbranch)

David Abram	2008
Lionel Atwill	1988
Ian and Margo Baldwin	1991, 1992
John Barstow	2007
Tom Begner	1988
H. Emerson Blake	1996–2010
Steve Bodio	1988–1996
Richard Brown	1989
Michael J. Caduto	1991
Jim Collins	1988
Jack Cook	1990
Alison Hawthorne Deming	2007, 2009
John Elder	2002
Michael Frome	1988
David Gessner	2010
Jody Gladding	2004
Karl Grossman	1992
Ted Gup	1996–2006
Sue Halpern	1997
John Hay	1989
John Hewitt	1989
Edward Hoagland	1998, 1999
Peter Jennison	1993
Robert Jones	1990
Diana Kappel-Smith	1999–2005
Robert Kimber	1994
Gale Lawrence	1990–2002
Sydney Lea	2000

About the Authors

ELIZABETH WYNN "BETSY" BANKS lives in a 150-year-old Ohio farmhouse on 389 acres owned and managed by Case Western Reserve University for research, conservation, and education. She currently works at CWRU, coordinating academic and co-curricular service-learning programs that link campus and the Cleveland community. She also teaches a course in which students explore a sense of place and their local urban watershed. She attended Wildbranch in 2002 and studied with Diana Kappel-Smith.

MIRA BARTÓK is an artist and writer who lives in New Salem, Massachusetts. She is the author of over thirty children's books on world cultures, and her essays, book reviews, and poetry have appeared in *Another Chicago Magazine, Artful Dodge, Bellingham Review, Kenyon Review, Tikkun, Fourth Genre,* and *LINK Magazine* among others. Her work has been nominated for a Pushcart Prize and has been cited as a notable mention in *The Best American Essay* series. She attended Wildbranch in 2006 and studied with Ted Gup.

JENNIFER BARTON lives on the Chewonki Foundation's 400-acre saltwater peninsula in Wiscasset, Maine, which is home to the Chewonki Semester School. Jenn currently assists with the field component of the semester science course. As the project coordinator for Maine Woods Forever, Jenn collaborated in the establishment of the Thoreau-Wabanaki Trail. Her essay, "In Search of a Secret," was published in *Wildness Within, Wildness Without.* She attended Wildbranch in 2008 and studied with David Abram.

JOHN BATES lives on seven acres of land on the Manitowish River in Wisconsin, and has worked as a naturalist in Wisconsin's Northwoods for 20 years. He's written seven books, including *Graced by the Seasons;*

White Deer: Ghosts of the Forest; *River Life: The Natural and Cultural History of a Northern River*; *A Northwoods Companion*; *Seasonal Guide to the Natural Year for Minnesota, Michigan, and Wisconsin*; and *Trailside Botany*). He attended Wildbranch in 2007 and studied with Scott Russell Sanders.

STEPHEN BODIO is a writer on nature and travel who lives in rural New Mexico. His books include *Eagle Dreams*, about Mongolia, and *Querencia*, a memoir. He has traveled extensively in Europe, Africa, and especially Asia, and his articles, essays, and stories have appeared in publications as diverse as the *Atlantic Monthly*, *Smithsonian*, *Los Angeles Times Magazine*, *Northern Lights*, *Double Gun Journal*, and *Simple Cooking*, as well as in literary quarterlies. He was a founding faculty member of Wildbranch, and was on the faculty from 1988 through 1996.

TERRA BROCKMAN was raised and now lives in central Illinois, where four generations of her family have farmed. In 2001, she founded the Land Connection, a nonprofit working to save farmland, train new farmers, and connect consumers with fresh local foods. She is the author of *The Season's on Henry's Farm: A Year of Food and Life on a Sustainable Farm*. She attended Wildbranch in 2008 and studied with Scott Russell Sanders.

SIMMONS B. BUNTIN lives in southeast Tucson, Arizona. He is the founding editor of *Terrain.org: A Journal of the Built & Natural Environments*. His first book of poetry, *Riverfall*, was published in 2005 by Ireland's Salmon Poetry. His poetry and prose have appeared in *Isotope*, *Weber Studies*, *South Dakota Review*, *Mid-American Review*, and *Orion*. He is a recipient of a Colorado Artist's Fellowship for Poetry. He attended Wildbranch in 2008 and studied with Scott Russell Sanders.

TED CABLE is a professor of park management and conservation at Kansas State University. He is the author of nine books, including

Commitments of the Heart: Odysseys in West African Conservation: Interpretation for the Twenty-first Century; *Fifteen Guiding Principles for Interpreting Nature and Culture*; *Driving Across Kansas*; *Driving Across Missouri*; and I*nterpretive Perspectives: Essays on Interpreting Nature and History*. He attended Wildbranch in 1995 and studied with Steve Bodio.

MICHAEL J. CADUTO is an author, ecologist, educator and storyteller whose latest book is *Everyday Herbs in Spiritual Life: A Guide to Many Practices*. In 1984, he founded a service called P.E.A.C.E.°—Programs for Environmental Awareness and Cultural Exchange. He was a faculty member at Wildbranch in 1991.

FLORENCE CAPLOW is a wandering conservation botanist, essayist, and Zen priest, generally found somewhere west of the Rocky Mountains and east of the Pacific. Her essays have been published in *Tricycle*, *Nature Conservancy Magazine*, *Turning Wheel*, *Inquiring Mind*, and *Terrain*. She recently completed a book-length collection of essays about two years of pilgrimage, and is the co-editor of *Wildbranch: An Anthology of Nature, Environmental, and Place-based Writing*. She attended Wildbranch in 2008 and studied with Scott Russell Sanders.

SUSAN A. COHEN lives beside Rock Creek in the Chesapeake Bay region during the school year and spends her summers in Montauk Point, New York. She is professor of English at Anne Arundel Community College. Her essays have appeared in *Sea Stories; Women Writing Nature: A Feminist View* (ed. by Barbara Cook); *Early American Nature Writers* (ed. by Daniel Patterson); and *Gendered Landscapes*. Susan is the editor of *Shorewords: A Collection of Women's Coastal Writings* and she is the co-editor of *Wildbranch: An Anthology of Nature, Environmental, and Place-based Writing*. She attended Wildbranch in 2008 and studied with David Abram.

JIM COLLINS lives on the shoulder of Mount Cardigan in Orange, New Hampshire. His work has appeared in *Outside, LIFE, Reader's Digest, This Old House Magazine, Boston*, and *Yankee*. Two of his articles have been noted in the annual *Best American Sportswriting* anthology. His book *The Last Best League* won the 2005 New Hampshire Literary Award for Outstanding Work of Nonfiction. He attended Wildbranch in 1990 and studied with E. Annie Proulx.

GARRETT CONOVER has been a canoe and snowshoe guide for twenty-eight years as North Woods Ways. During that time he published *Beyond the Paddle*, and coauthored *The Snow Walker's Companion*. His story *Kristin's Wilderness* won four awards, Bronze medal from the Independent Publishers Association; Top honor of the Midwest Independent Publishers Award; Bronze medal from the MoonBeam Award; and the Lupin Award. He attended Wildbranch in 1997 and studied with Ted Gup.

GLENDA COTTER is a poet and essayist who lives in Salt Lake City, Utah. She is also an avid birdwatcher, photographer, and runner, and the mother of a wonderful teenage daughter, Elizabeth. She is the director and managing editor of the University of Utah Press. She attended Wildbranch in 2008 and studied with Janisse Ray.

TONY CROSS lives and works in San Francisco, and writes as often as possible. He studied writing briefly at Sarah Lawrence College and also studied music at the Oberlin Conservatory. He has attended Wildbranch twice, in 2007 and 2008, and had the privilege of studying with Alison Hawthorne Deming and Scott Russell Sanders.

DORINDA G. DALLMEYER is director of the Environmental Ethics Certificate Program at the University of Georgia. Since 2001 she has collaborated with a group of southern nature writers in creating the Southern Nature Project. In 2005 the Southern Environmental Law Center presented her with two Phillip Reed Memorial Awards for outstanding writing about the Southern environment. She attended Wildbranch in 2007 and studied with Alison Hawthorne Deming.

ANN B. DAY has lived in the Mad River Valley in Vermont for the last fifty-five years. She has published four books of nature poetry and has written weekly nature columns for the *Valley Reporter* and other publications for over forty years. Ann has attended every Wildbranch Writing Workshop since 1996 and was eighty when she returned in 2010.

ALISON HAWTHORNE DEMING is professor of creative writing at the University of Arizona. She lives near Aqua Caliente Hill in Tucson. She is the author of four books of poetry, *Science and Other Poems*; *The Monarchs: A Poem Sequence*; *Genius Loci*; and *Rope*. Deming has also published three nonfiction books, *Temporary Homelands*; *The Edges of the Civilized World*, which was a finalist for the PEN Center West Award; and *Writing the Sacred into the Real*. Her poems and essays have appeared in the *Georgia Review*; *Orion*; *Islands*; *Pushcart Prize XVIII: Best of the Small Presses*; *American Nature Writing*, *Writing it Down for James: Writers on Life and Craft*; *Verse*; *Universe: Poems on Science and Mathematics*; and the *Norton Book of Nature Writing*. She taught at Wildbranch in 2007 and 2009.

JANICE DUKES is a native of Indiana. For over twenty-five years she has worked at Saint Mary-of-the-Woods College in West Terre Haute, Indiana, where she is professor of communication and teaches creative writing and women's studies. Her interest in writing about the natural world grew through her work as literary editor for *Snowy Egret*. She attended Wildbranch in 2004 and studied with Diana Kappel-Smith.

LOUISE FABIANI is a science writer, naturalist, poet, and visual artist. She lives in Montreal, where she tends a nearby community garden plot, reviews books for several periodicals, and studies the ethical, physiological, and ecological aspects of food for an upcoming book. Her first volume of poetry, *The Green Alembic*, was published in 1999. She attended Wildbranch in 2008 and studied with Scott Russell Sanders.

HEATHER FITZGERALD lives in Burlington, Vermont, with her husband and son. She teaches field ecology and works as a freelance naturalist. Before moving to Burlington, she lived in Boston, Fairhaven, and Arlington, Massachusetts; Plano and Austin, Texas; Swarthmore, Pennsylvania; Seattle, Washington; and East Bethel, Lauderdale, and Minneapolis, Minnesota. She tries to be at home wherever she is. She has had varying levels of success, but she thinks she might be getting better at it. She attended Wildbranch in 2007 and studied with Sandra Steingraber.

SUSAN FUTRELL lives in Iowa, where she is a writer and consultant specializing in communications and marketing in the field of sustainable food, agriculture, and business. She is communications manager for Red Tomato, a nonprofit working with ecological produce farmers in the Northeast. She attended Wildbranch in 2007 and studied with Sandra Steingraber.

PAUL GRINDROD calls himself "an immutably right-brain being trapped in a left-brain world," and "a chronic academic underachiever until discovering a love of and affinity for words and language." He has worked in film/video production and environmental education, and recently completed an MS in environmental humanities at the University of Utah. He attended Wildbranch in 2007 and studied with Erik Reece.

DAVID HASKELL lives in Sewanee, Tennessee, where he studies and teaches biology at the University of the South. He has published scientific papers on the conservation and evolution of animals, with a special focus on the origin and future of bird diversity. He attended Wildbranch in 2007 and studied with Alison Hawthorne Deming.

EDWARD HOAGLAND lives in Bennington, Vermont. His first book, *Cat Man*, won the 1954 Houghton Mifflin Literary Fellowship. Since then he has written nearly twenty books, including *Walking the Dead Diamond River* (a 1974 National Book Award nominee), *African Calliope* (a 1980 American Book Award nominee), and *The Tugman's Passage* (a 1982 National Book Critics Circle Award nominee). In 1982 he was elected to the American Academy of Arts and Letters. Hoagland was the editor of *The Best American Essays* for 1999. He taught at Wildbranch in 1998 and 1999.

G. DAVIES JANDREY is a retired educator, poet, and writer of fiction who lives in Tucson, Arizona. She has worked as a fire lookout in Saguaro National Park and Chiricahua National Monument. Gayle's short fiction has appeared in *Calyx*, *Bilingual Review*, *Portland Review*, the *Berkeley Fiction Review*, and others. Her novel, *A Garden of Aloes*, was published in 2008. She attended Wildbranch in 1994 and studied with Gale Lawrence.

ALERIA JENSEN lives in Juneau, Alaska, where she works as a federal biologist coordinating marine mammal conservation programs. Her poems and essays have appeared in a variety of publications, including *Orion*, *Alaska Quarterly Review*, *Potomac Review*, *Camas*, *Terrain.org: A Journal of the Built and Natural Environments*, and *Sea Stories: An International Journal of Art and Writing*. She attended Wildbranch in 2001 and studied with Ted Gup, and again in 2008, studying with Scott Russell Sanders.

PHILIP JOHANSSON is a writer and editor for Marlboro College in Vermont. He has twenty years of experience writing articles and books on natural history, environmental science, travel, and health. For ten years, Philip worked as editor for Earthwatch, a nonprofit organization supporting field research around the world. He also wrote a series of award-winning books for young audiences on biomes of the world. He attended Wildbranch in 1988 and studied most closely with Ted Levin.

ANDREA M. JONES lives on a high ridge in central Colorado, from which she hikes, rides horses, and gardens during the short growing season. In addition to writing literary nonfiction, Andrea works as a freelance indexer. Her publication credits include essays in *Orion*, *Christian Science Monitor*, *Pilgrimage*, *Camas*, and *Snowy Egret*. She attended Wildbranch in 2001 and studied with Sandra Steingraber.

ROBERT KIMBER started exploring the Maine woods and paddling Maine waterways in 1955. He has written for *Audubon*, *Field and Stream*, *Harrowsmith*, *Horticulture*, *Minnesota Monthly*, *Northern Woodlands*, and *Yankee*, and been a columnist for *Country Journal* and *Down East* magazines. He has written four books, *Made for the Country*; *Upcountry: Reflections from a Rural Life*; *A Canoeist's Sketchbook*; and *Living Wild and Domestic: The Education of a Hunter-Gardener*. He was a guest faculty member at Wildbranch in 1994.

SYDNEY LEA lives in Newbury, Vermont. His books include *Ghost Pain*; *A Little Wildness: Some Notes On Rambling*; *Pursuit of a Wound*, which was one of three finalists for the 2001 Pulitzer Prize for Poetry; *To the Bone: New and Selected Poems*, a co-winner of the 1998 Poets' Prize; *A Place in Mind*; and *Hunting the Whole Way Home*. He founded the *New England Review* in 1977 and edited it until 1989. Lea has received fellowships from the Rockefeller, Fulbright, and Guggenheim Foundations, and has taught at Dartmouth, Yale, Wesleyan, Vermont, and Middlebury Colleges, as well as at Franklin College in Switzerland and the National Hungarian University in Budapest. His stories, poems, essays, and criticism have appeared in the *New Yorker*, *Atlantic*, *New Republic*, *New York Times*, and *Sports Illustrated*. He was a faculty member at Wildbranch in 2000.

JEFFREY A. LOCKWOOD was hired as an insect ecologist at the University of Wyoming, but over the course of twenty years he metamorphosed into a professor of natural sciences and humanities, with a joint appointment between the Department of Philosophy and the MFA program in creative writing. He is the author of five books, including *Grasshopper Dreaming: Reflections on Killing and Loving* and *Six-Legged Soldiers: Using Insects as Weapons of War*. His writings have been honored with a Pushcart Prize, a John Burroughs Award, and inclusion in *Best American Science and Nature Writing 2007*. He attended Wildbranch workshops in 2000 and 2001 and worked under the tutelage of Ted Gup and Diana Kappel-Smith.

LINDA MAREE is a freelance writer living in Sarasota, Florida. She has written regularly for a number of local Sarasota magazines, including a monthly column called "Living Green." She is the creator of Etain Creativity Workshops and the Sarasota Writers' Circle, and is on the continuing education faculty at the Ringling College of Art & Design. She attended Wildbranch in 2008 and studied with Sandra Steingraber.

BRENT MARTIN lives in the Cowee Community of western North Carolina where he currently works for the Wilderness Society. His poems and essays have appeared in the *Chattahoochee Review*, *New Southerner*, *Pisgah Review*, *Tiger's Eye*, *Rapid River*, *Wavelength*, and *Southern Hum*. A chapbook of his poetry, *Poems from Snow Hill Road*, was published by New Native Press in 2007. He attended Wildbranch in 2008 and studied with Janisse Ray.

MEGHAN MCCARTHY MCPHAUL lives in Franconia, New Hampshire. She is a freelance writer and former small-town newspaper reporter. Her work has appeared in Forest Notes, the conservation magazine of the Society for the Protection of New Hampshire Forests. She attended Wildbranch in 2004 and studied with Ted Gup.

April Newlin is a clinical psychologist who practiced for many years in New Orleans. She now lives in Florida on the edge of the Gulf of Mexico. She is a Master Naturalist in Coastal Systems and Wetlands. Her work has appeared in *Isle, Whole Terrain, Michigan Quarterly Review*, and *Audubon*. She is the author of *Horn of Plenty: Seasons in an Island Wilderness*. She attended Wildbranch in 1997 and studied with Ted Gup.

Jules Older lives in San Francisco, and he writes. He writes iPhone Apps, writes websites, writes ski articles, travel articles, food articles, and art articles. He writes children's books and outdoor books. He writes for medical journals and psychology journals, for newspapers and magazines, and...HE'S GOT A WRITING PROBLEM, OK? He was a faculty member at Wildbranch in 1997.

Ned Olmsted teaches writing and environmental literature at Landmark College in Putney, Vermont. He spends as much time as he can in the Northeast Kingdom where his family has put down roots for four generations. He was a participant at Wildbranch in 1997 and again in 2007, and is grateful for the support and guidance he received there from faculty members Gail Lawrence and Scott Russell Sanders.

H. C. Palmer is an internist who lives near the Flint Hills of Kansas. His fiction and essays have been published in *Gray's Sporting Journal, Big Sky Journal*, and *Fly Rod and Reel Magazine*. His book of poems, *The Flint Hills*, with accompanying woodcuts by Leon Loughridge, was honored by the *Kansas City Star* as one of the ten best books of poems in 2008. His poetry appears in the *Flint Hills Review, New Mexico Poetry Review*, and *Island Journal*. He is an assistant editor for *Narrative*. He attended Wildbranch in 1993 and again in 1994, studying with Gail Lawrence, Steve Bodio, and Joel Vance.

CHARLOTTE PYLE is a native of California and currently lives in southern New England. For ten years, she and her husband worked as biologists in Great Smoky Mountains National Park. Their son was born in East Tennessee. It is a place she looks back on with fond memories of people, places, music, dancing, and kayaking. Her previously published work is technical in nature. She attended Wildbranch in 2005 and studied with Diana Kappel-Smith.

EVE QUESNEL grew up in San Francisco and has worked in a variety of outdoor jobs in the West. She teaches composition and literature at Sierra College in Truckee, a small mountain town in California. Her essays and book reviews appear in her town's local independent newspaper. Eve attended Wildbranch in 2008 and she studied with Janisse Ray.

JANISSE RAY is a writer, naturalist, and environmental activist. Her books include *Ecology of a Cracker Childhood*, which won the American Book Award, the Southern Book Critics Circle Award, and the Southern Environmental Law Center Award for Outstanding Writing on the Southern environment; *Wild Card Quilt*; and *Pinhook*. She has also been a contributor to *Audubon*, *Orion*, and other magazines, as well as a commentator for NPR's Living on Earth. She teaches in the Chatham University Low-Residency Master of Fine Arts Program in Creative Writing. Janisse attended Wildbranch as a student in 2001 and returned as a faculty member from 2005 through 2008.

STEPHANIE JOELLE RENFROW grew up in Colorado as a third-generation native of the state and still lives in Boulder, Colorado. She has been a professional science writer for more than a decade, specializing in topics related to climate change and sustainability. She attended Wildbranch in 2008 and studied with Scott Russell Sanders.

ROBERT J. ROMANO JR. divides his time between his home in north-west New Jersey and his fishing camp in western Maine. He has authored three books, *Fishing with Faeries*; *Shadows in the Stream*; and his first novel, *North of Easie*. His stories and essays have appeared in numerous periodicals, including the *New Hampshire Outdoor Gazette, Fly Fishing New England, New Jersey Skylands Magazine,* and *New Jersey Sportsman's News.* He attended Wildbranch in 2004 and studied with Ted Gup.

SCOTT RUSSELL SANDERS lives in Bloomington, Indiana, in the hard-wood hill country of the White River Valley. From 1971 until his retire-ment in 2009, he taught at Indiana University, from 1995 onward as Distinguished Professor of English. Among his more than twenty books are novels, collections of stories, and works of personal nonfiction, in-cluding *Staying Put, Writing from the Center,* and *Hunting for Hope.* His latest books are *A Private History of Awe*, a coming-of-age memoir, love story, and spiritual testament, which was nominated for the Pulitzer Prize, and *A Conservationist Manifesto*, his vision of a shift from a culture of consumption to a culture of caretaking. He has received the Lannan Literary Award, the Associated Writing Programs Award in Creative Nonfiction, the Great Lakes Book Award, the Kenyon Review Literary Award, the John Burroughs Essay Award, and the Indiana Humanities Award, among other honors. He was a faculty member at Wildbranch in 2008 and 2010.

RACHEL SHAW is an off-again, on-again professor of environmental studies and the history of the American West, and a two-time Wild-branch Workshop participant. She is a contributor to *qarrtsiluni*, an on-line literary magazine. She attended Wildbranch in 2006 and studied with Chip Blake, then returned in 2007 to study with Alison Haw-thorne Deming.

PETER SHEPHERD lives in Cobargo in New South Wales, Australia. He runs workshops through the Heart & Place Writing Centre that focus on deep ecology, relationships, and activism. He has published essays in Tasmania's literary journal, *Island*, and in *ABC's Organic Gardener*, as well as in various local journals and newspapers and the Northern Rivers Writers' Centre's *Write Stuff* magazine. He was Writer-in-Residence at Byron College from 2007 to 2009. He attended Wildbranch in 2008 and studied with David Abram.

JULIA SHIPLEY is a former director of writing studies at Sterling College. She has been the recipient of the Grace Paley Poetry Fellowship at the Frost Place, the Ralph Nading Hill Award, and two artist grants from the Vermont Community Fund. Her work has appeared in *Vermont Life*, *Northern Woodlands*, and *Small Farmers Journal*. She attended Wildbranch in 2005 and studied with Diana Kappel-Smith, and she returned in 2007 and studied with Alison Hawthorne Deming.

CHERIE STAPLES is a Vermont photographer, painter, poet, and bookkeeper living on the edge of farm fields with two older sisters. To the west and north are sweeping views of chains of Green Mountains and from her bedroom windows she watches a quiet hedgerow of ash and butternut and cherry and an old apple tree. She attended Wildbranch in 2002 and studied with Ted Gup.

MAUREEN SULLIVAN lives in the Pacific Northwest. She is an active board member of the Friends of the Ridgefield National Wildlife Refuge. She attended Wildbranch in 2008 and studied with Sandra Steingraber.

ALISON TOWNSEND lives on four acres of restored prairie and oak savannah in the farm country outside Madison, Wisconsin, and teaches at the University of Wisconsin-Whitewater. Her second full-length collection, *Persephone in America*, won the 2008 Crab Orchard Open Poetry Competition. She has a book of poetry and prose poems, *The Blue Dress*, and two chapbooks, *And Still the Music* and *What the Body*

Knows. She has won a number of prizes, including the 2005 Lorine Niedecker Prize in Poetry from the Council of Wisconsin Writers, and the 2007 International Poetry Prize from *River Styx.* She attended Wildbranch in 2007 and studied with Alison Hawthorne Deming.